ML4

TELEVISION IN EUROPE

Jean K. Chalaby teaches Media History and Comparative Media Systems and International Communication at City University, London, where he is Director of the MA in Transnational Media and Globalization. He is the author of *The Invention of Journalism* (1998) and *The de Gaulle Presidency and the Media* (2002) and editor of *Transnational Television Worldwide* (I.B.Tauris, 2005).

TRANSNATIONAL TELEVISION IN EUROPE

RECONFIGURING GLOBAL COMMUNICATIONS NETWORKS

Jean K. Chalaby

I.B. TAURIS
LONDON · NEW YORK

Published in 2009 by I.B.Tauris & Co Ltd
6 Salem Road, London W2 4BU
175 Fifth Avenue, New York NY 10010
www.ibtauris.com

Distributed in the United States and Canada Exclusively by Palgrave Macmillan
175 Fifth Avenue, New York NY 10010

ISBN: 978 1 84511 953 9 (HB)
ISBN: 978 1 84511 954 6 (PB)

A full CIP record for this book is available from the British Library
A full CIP record is available from the Library of Congress

Library of Congress Catalog Card Number: available

Typeset in Monotype Fournier by Ellipsis Books Limited, Glasgow
Printed and bound in Great Britain by CPI Antony Rowe, Chippenham

Jean K. Chalaby is supported by

Arts & Humanities
Research Council

384-55094 CHA

080083404

FOR FELICITY, LUCY AND JEMIMA

CONTENTS

Part Three
Transnational Television in Europe

Part Four
Inside Globalization: The Transnational Shift

TABLES

ABBREVIATIONS

ABC	American Broadcasting Company
AETN	Arts & Entertainment Television Networks
AGICOA	Association de Gestion Internationale Collective des Œuvres Audiovisuelles
AJE	Al Ajazeera English
APTN	Associated Press Television News
ARD	Arbeitsgemeinschaft der öffentlich-rechtlichen Rundfunkanstalten der Bundesrepublik Deutschland
AVMS	Audiovisual Media Services (EU Directive)
BBC	British Broadcasting Corporation
BSB	British Satellite Broadcasting
BSkyB	British Sky Broadcasting
BT	British Telecom
CLT	Compagnie Luxembourgeoise de Télédiffusion
CNBC	Cable News and Business Channel
CNN	Cable News Network
DBS	Direct Broadcast by Satellite
DNI	Discovery Networks International
DTH	Direct-To-Home (satellite reception)
EBC	European Business Channel
EBU	European Broadcasting Union
ECS	European Communication Satellites
EMEA	Europe, Middle East and Africa
EMS	European Media and Marketing Survey
EOLS	Euopean Opinion Leaders Survey
EPG	Electronic Programming Guide
ESA	European Space Agency
ESPN	Entertainment and Sports Programming Network
ETN	European Television Networks

EVN   Eurovision News Exchange
FIC   Fox International Channels
FR3   France Régions 3
HBO   Home Box Office
IBA   Independent Broadcasting Authority
IPTV   Internet Protocol Television
ITN   Independent Television News
ITU   International Telecommunication Union
ITV   Independent Television
LNB   Low Noise Block downconverter
MAC   Multiplexed Analogue Components
MCM   Monte Carlo Musique
MGM   Metro-Goldwyn-Mayer
MTG   Modern Times Group
MTV   Music Television
MTVNE   MTV Networks Europe
NASN   North American Sports Network
NBC   National Broadcasting Company
NBC UGN   NBC Universal Global Networks
NHK   Nippon Hōsō Kyōkai
NOS   Nederlandse Omroep Stichting
ORF   Österreichischer Rundfunk
OTS   Orbital Test Satellite
PETAR   Pan-European Television Audience Research
PETV   Pan-European Television
PTT   Post, Telegraph and Telephone administration
RAI   Radiotelevisione Italiana
RCA   Radio Corporation of America
RTBF   Radio-télévision Belge de la Communauté française
RTE   Radio Telefis Eireann
RTL   Radio Télévision Luxembourg
RTP   Rádio e Televisão de Portugal
RTR   Russian Television and Radio Broadcasting Company
RTVE   Radio Televisión Española
SECEMIE   Société Editrice de la Chaîne Européene Multilingue
             d'Information EuroNews

SES	Société Européenne des Satellites
SMATV	Satellite to Master Antenna TV
SOCEMIE	Société Opératrice de la Chaîne Européene Multilingue d'Information EuroNews
SPTI	Sony Pictures Television International
SRG	Schweizerische Radio- und Fernsehgesellschaft
SSR	Société Suisse de Radiodiffusion et Télévision
SVT	Sveriges Television
TBS	Turner Broadcasting System
TCI	TeleCommunications Inc
TCM	Turner Classic Movies
TDF	Télédiffusion de France
TESN	The European Sports Network
TF1	Télévision Française 1
TMF	The Music Factory
TNS	Taylor Nelson Sofres
TNT	Turner Network Television
TVP	Telewizja Polska
TVWF	Television Without Frontiers (EU Directive)
UIP	United International Pictures
VH1	Video Hits One
WARC	World Administrative Radio Conference
WHSTV	WH Smith Television
ZDF	Zweites Deutsches Fernsehen

JOURNAL AND REPORT TITLES

C&SE	*Cable & Satellite Europe*
EAO Yearbook	*European Audiovisual Observatory Yearbook*
EMS Guide	*European Media and Marketing Survey Essential Guide*
M&M Europe	*Media and Marketing Europe*
M&M Guide	*Media and Marketing Europe Guide to Pan-European Television*
TBI	*Television Business International*
WSW	*World Screen Weekly*

ACKNOWLEDGEMENTS

This book is based on extensive research in the international television industry and would not have seen the light of day without the help of industry figures. I am greatly indebted to all those who took the time to share information with me and would like to express my deep gratitude to them all (see list below). In particular, I would like to acknowledge the special assistance I received from Andy Bird, Disney; Peter Flamman, Turner Broadcasting System Europe; Simon Guild, MTV Networks Europe; Sonia Marguin, EuroNews; Nick Mawditt, CNBC Europe; Jeremy Nye, BBC Global News; Malcolm Tallantire, formerly at Sky Channel; and Marian Williams, Discovery Networks Europe.

I am grateful to City University for providing me with a research fund, and to the Arts and Humanities Research Council (AHRC) who gave me a Research Leave Grant that enabled me to complete this project.

I am also indebted to Sheila Munton of City University library for her help in locating obscure sources, Jackie and Roy Shelton for transcribing many of the interviews, and my darling wife, Jane, for her invaluable help with the manuscript. I would like to extend my thanks to Philippa Brewster, senior commissioning editor at I.B.Tauris, who has always showed faith in this project, and Ian Brooke for project management.

LIST OF INTERVIEWEES

Job title and company name at time of interview. Title and company in brackets when the person was no longer in the position at time of interview.

Mike Aarons, satellite manager, CNBC Europe; Bjorn Andersson, chief executive officer, Broadcast Text International; Nicola Andrews, vice president (VP) – sales and marketing, BKN New Media; Lopes de Araújo, head of international broadcasting, RTP; Finn Arnesen, senior VP, original animation and acquisitions, TBS Europe; Gregory d'Assche, acquisition department, Eurosport; Rachel Attwell, deputy head of television news, BBC; Belinda Barker, managing director (MD), BSB Media; Anne Barnard, chief operating officer, BBC World; Adrian Barr-Smith, partner, Denton Wilde Sapte; Ian Bell, research manager, ZenithOptimedia; Géraud Benoit, client service director, Universal McCann; Andy Bird, president, Walt Disney International; Steve Birkill (technology consultant, *Cable & Satellite Europe*); Dirk Boehm, head of communication, Universal Studios Networks, Germany; Roger Bolton, business development director, Tandberg Television; Amanda Booker, programme and channel relations, Bloomberg Television; Johan Boserup, global director of trading and accountability, Omnicom Media Group; Sylvie Burger, directrice de publicité, Fashion TV; Shaney Burney, head of programming, Zee Network Europe; Jamie Caring, head of talent & artist relations, MTV Networks UK; Fredd Causevic, president & CEO, Otrum Asa; Walid Chamak, international research executive, EuroNews Sales; Peter Chase, relationship manager, Siemens Business Services Media; Ian Clarke, global account director, OMD; Julian Clover (editor, 1991–2, *Cable & Satellite Europe*); Steve Cole, VP, Zone Reality; Patrick Cox, (MD, Sky Channel and NBC Europe); Chris Cramer, president, CNN International; Jean-Luc Cronel, directeur du réseau commercial, TV5; Bronwyn Curtis, editor-in-chief, Bloomberg Television; Justin Davison, international sales director, EuroNews Sales; Philippe Deleplace, directeur général adjoint, Motors TV; Daniel Dodd, head of strategy for journalism, BBC; Wayne Dunsford, director of channels, BBC Worldwide; Daniel Fiedler, coordinator, 3Sat; Peter Flamman, VP, business development, TBS Europe; Tanja Flintoff, head of programming and production, MTV European; Christina Foley, director of distribution, EMEA, Hallmark; Francesca Ginocchi, communications director, NBC Universal Global Networks Italy; Richard Godfrey, senior VP, MTV Productions Europe; Chris Grave, MD, business development, Dow Jones; Simon Guild, chief operating officer, MTV Networks Europe; Nobuhiro Habuto, deputy MD, Japan Satellite TV (Europe); Ross Hair, senior VP of international networks, Sony Pictures Television International; John Hardie, MD, Walt Disney Television, EMEA; Brian Haynes (MD, Satellite Television, 1981–3); Jeff Hazell, director sales & distribution, BBC World; Georgina Hickey, international business director, Carat; Arjan Hoekstra, deputy MD, British Eurosport; Richard Hooper (MD, Super Channel, 1987–8); Matthew Hotten, Active Research, Jetix; Corinne In Albion, marketing manager, TNS Media Intelligence; Tan Ishikawa, deputy MD, Japan Satellite TV (Europe); Candace Johnson (board member, SES);

Huw Jones, account director, Mediaedge:cia; Phil Jones, MD, Europe, Extreme Sports channel; Marin Kariz, area sales manager, HBO Adria; Helmut Koszuszeck, legal and business manager, AGICOA; Jeff Kupsky, head of network development, TBS Europe; Phil Lawrie, VP, commercial distribution, TBS Europe; Charles Levison (MD, Music Box; joint MD, Super Channel); Kevin Livesey, head of product, BT Media & Broadcast; Ronan Lunven, président-directeur-général, Fox Kids France; Sylvie Macgraine, sales manager, Viaccess; Steve Maine (director, Visual & Broadcast Services, BT, 1990–4); Sangraam Marathe, executive producer, Zee Music; Sonia Marguin, head of research, EuroNews; Monica Mather, VP, international ad sales, Discovery Networks Europe; Nick Mawditt, head of research, CNBC Europe; Kevin McLellan, senior VP, international, E! International Network; Pierre Meyrat (chief operating officer, SES, 1986–94); Alexandre Michelin, senior VP, programs and services, Canal Plus; Ian Moir, VP operations & engineering, MTV Technology; Olivier de Monchenu, director, sales and distribution, EuroNews; Adrian Monck, head of journalism, City University; Ben Money, head of research, British Eurosport; Peter Monnery, director, Siemens Business Services Media; William Mould, head of travel distribution, BBC World; Angelika Newel, head of distribution, Deutsche Welle-TV; Jeremy Nye, head of research and planning, BBC Global News; Vanessa O'Connor, head of communication, Eutelsat; David Orman, sales director, UK, US & Scandinavia, Eurosport; Nigel Parsons, MD, Al Jazeera English; Markus Payer, VP media relations, SES Astra; Agnès Pierret, sport news producer, European Broadcasting Union; Jeremy Pink, VP of news and programming, CNBC Europe; Monica Pizzoli, area manager, Europe, RAI; Rick Plata, director of advertising sales, Fox Kids; Simon Pollock, VP and MD, Europe and Asia, AETN International; Dean Possenniskie, senior VP, Global Channels – EMEA, BBC Worldwide; Errol Pretorius, director of advertising sales, National Geographic; Stewart Purvis (CEO, ITN, and president, SOCEMIE, 1995–2003); Jacques Raynaud, general manager for advertising and affiliate sales, Eurosport; John Riley, head of Sky News; Gerry Ritchie, head of network development, BBC World; Tony Robinson, VP, Viacom Brand Solutions, Europe; Philippe Rouxel, VP, sales and marketing, Lagardère Networks International; Benoit Runel, senior VP for programming & acquisitions, Jetix; Lawrence Safir, VP for European affairs, Independent Film & Television Alliance; Richard Sambrook, director, BBC World Service and Global News; Dominique Sauvêtre, pan-European sponsorship manager, Motors TV; Reinier Schaper, director branding &

media, Interview-NSS; Dr Wengung Shao, chief operating officer, Phoenix Chinese News and Entertainment; Alan Simpson (chief technician, Worldnet); Adrian Smith, account director, MediaCom; Melanie Smith, account director, Carat International; James Smyllie, international media planner, Starcom; Nick Snow (editor, *Cable & Satellite Europe*); Tony Stimpson, director of programming, Europe, ESPN Classic; Gilles Storme, head of research, National Geographic and Sky News; Toby Syfret (head of new media research, J. Walter Thompson and Ogilvy & Mather); Malcolm Tallantire (network director, Sky Channel); Paul Taylor, chief executive officer, Jetix; Phil Teeman, account director, Mindshare; François Thiellet, président-directeur général, Thema; Stuart Thomson, editor, *Cable & Satellite Europe*; Jason Thorp, head of programming, Universal Television Networks; Luc Tomasino, MD, SDI Media; Stella Tooth, senior publicist, Sky News; Sir John Tusa (MD, BBC World Service, 1986–1992); Anne-Laure Vandamme, permanent services market manager, EMEA, GlobeCast; Donna Vergier, director of international, Mute International; Marian Williams, VP programming, EMEA, Discovery Networks Europe; Dan Winter, head of press, NBC Universal Global Networks Europe; Monika Wirth-Schreiber, junior regional marketing manager, HBO Central Europe; Richard Wolfe, chief executive officer, The Travel Channel (MD, The Children's Channel, 1984–93); Chris Wronski, chairman, Zonevision; Marc Young, MD, BBC Prime; Alessandra Zane, chargée de mission, Multithématiques; Martin Ziegele, editor assigned to the editor-in-chief, Deutsche Welle-TV.

INTRODUCTION

TELEVISION'S TRANSNATIONAL PARADIGM SHIFT

This book tells the story of transnational television in Europe from its origins in the early 1980s to the present day. It is an extraordinary journey from the humble beginnings of Europe's first satellite TV channel, allowed to broadcast from point to point only (London to Malta) at a time when private reception of a satellite signal was illegal. Those early days saw cross-border TV channels fighting hostile governments, facing the antagonism of the broadcasting establishment and provoking the contempt of advertisers (Part 1).

The stars came into alignment for pan-European television (PETV) in the late 1990s when, this book argues, a transnational shift occurred in European broadcasting. The expansion of the cable and satellite reception universe enabled cross-border channels to develop distribution, digitization expanded networks' capacity and lowered transmission costs, and the development of broadcast satellite neighbourhoods eased the international transmission of TV signals. European legislation made transnational television legal, harmonized copyright law and clarified practices in collective rights management. European integration and the enlargement of the European Union facilitated the cross-border operations of media corporations and helped to expand their consumer market. The commercial environment became more favourable with a growing number of multinationals of all sizes with brands to market across Europe and consumers to reach across borders. The advertising industry restructured and large marketing groups acquired the size and scope to conduct pan-European campaigns. Public service broadcasters confirmed their commitment to international television and diversified entertainment conglomerates entered the PETV industry with the resources, scope and expertise to develop a successful multinational TV business. Broadcasters understood how to deal with an international audience and adapted their channels and organizational structure toward European cultural diversity. Network-centric TV operations were created that enabled management teams to articulate the local and the global by combining global efficiency and local flexibility (Parts 2 and 3).

Today, cross-border networks count among television's most prestigious brands and have become prominent in several genres such as business news, factual entertainment and children's television. In many European territories they rank among the leading TV channels. Where their ratings remain behind those of terrestrial stations, they compensate with strong brand equity and an ability to deliver specific and attractive demographics across frontiers to advertisers. And while terrestrial stations struggle in a changing industry, transnational TV networks contribute to transforming it. Many practices that have become standard in television first emerged from the pan-European TV industry, including horizontal programming, multi-stream revenue strategies, multi-platform distribution and comprehensive marketing partnerships with advertisers (Part 3).

The relationship between globalization and transnational television is an intricate one. The growth of multinationals and cross-border activities, the expansion of world trade and the internationalization of marketing all come into play to feed the growth of transfrontier television. In turn, transnational TV networks participate in the flows of communication and systems of exchange that feed into cosmopolitan modes of production, typical of industries such as fashion and music, and the worldwide integration in sectors such as finance. Thus globalization and transnational television mutually transform each other. Part 4 shows how globalization feeds off transnational TV networks, which in turn are transformed by globalizing forces. The conclusion draws parallels between three types of networks (transnational television, logistics and IT) and their reconfiguration by globalization.

The study of transnational television still throws up significant difficulties. The discipline of international communication has moved on since the exponents of the cultural imperialism thesis maintained that satellites constitute a 'threat' to the 'integrity of national cultures' and pondered whether nations could retain control over television 'in the face of foreign broadcasting'.[1] The end of the Cold War saw cultural nationalism recede, and recent literature on international television has slowly disentangled itself from a nation-centric framework. The most spectacular advances have been achieved in the realm of media aimed at migrants because of the transnational nature of these audiences.[2]

Nonetheless, the new research agenda has yet to be grounded on a firm theoretical basis and there is still need for a set of methodological and theoretical principles that would determine the shift in international communication away from the prison-house of a national perspective. We should listen, I suggest, to Ulrich Beck's calls to replace 'methodological nationalism' with 'methodological cosmopolitanism'.

The German sociologist defines the cosmopolitan outlook as an attempt 'to overcome methodological nationalism' that fails to grasp the ramifications of the process of globalization, which 'not only alters the interconnectedness of nation-states and national societies but the internal quality of the social'.[3] '[T]he challenge is to devise a new syntax' that can help us comprehend the interpenetration and juxtaposition of cultures, the interconnectedness of societies, the interdependence of nation-states and the blurring of boundaries.[4] This syntax is less a collection of concepts and methods than a perspective – or 'vision' – that avoids taking for granted the congruence between national societies and economic, social and political realities that have acquired a transnational dimension and which transform these societies from within.

The new conceptual space formed by the cosmopolitan outlook can help us step outside the nation-centric discourse that can no longer account for the cultural experiences created by transnational media. Since globalization and technology are remapping media spaces and markets, national television cannot be taken as a point of reference or as the benchmark against which all types of broadcasting should be measured. Transnational television contributes to an opening of national communications systems and makes them operate on four levels: the local, national, regional and global. These systems conserve their national dimension but it has become less overriding than when European governments dominated broadcasting against the wishes of consumers and the logic of markets. This remapping questions the relation between media and national territory and makes media systems more open and diverse than they have ever been.[5]

A second obstacle to the understanding of transnational television is that most communication scholars are honorary members of the Worshipful Society of the Local. They have decided that globalization is a tsunami that eradicates everything in its path and threatens local cultures. This approach artificially constructs an antagonism between the local and the global that does not need to exist. In the transnational media order the local has gained freedom and significance: technology has disembedded the local from place as it can travel anywhere. With the Internet and communications satellites, local media can be consumed across spaces and people are now able to read their local paper, watch their local TV channel or listen to their local radio station wherever they migrate or travel. In transnational television the local is as significant as the global. At corporate level, the ability to leverage both terms has become key to a successful commercial strategy. Cross-border TV networks are breaking down the opposition between the local and the global and have made each term an extension of the other. The local and the global are no longer terms in conflict: they inform and transform one another in a constant dialogue (Chapter 11).

This research uses two main sources. The trade press was consulted mostly for the historical part of the study. One title in particular, *Cable & Satellite Europe*, in its previous incarnation as a subscription-funded publication, was found to be an extensive and reliable source of information. However, this research privileges primary sources and an excess of 150 interviews were conducted between 2000 and 2008. Most interviews were face to face, some by necessity were telephone interviews to Europe and the United States, and a small amount via email. I spoke to pioneers of satellite television, high-ranking media executives (among them many chief executives and company presidents), and experts in international broadcasting such as copyright lawyers and trade journalists. I also spoke to satellite service providers, cable and DTH operators, advertising and marketing agencies, localization studios, research companies, copyright collecting societies and trade associations (see List of Interviewees). On a few occasions interviews were held off-the-record and in this case references are not supplied. I also had access to proprietary research supplied by media owners, research companies and trade associations.

PART ONE

IMPOSSIBLE BEGINNINGS

CHAPTER I

PIONEERS IN SATELLITE TELEVISION, 1982–4

This chapter retraces the early years of transfrontier television in Europe. In a sense, TV channels have always crossed borders because of the natural overspill of terrestrial television signals. However, communication satellites revolutionized television transmission in the early 1980s, allowing for the emergence of the first international channels. Pioneers in satellite television in Europe had to surmount formidable obstacles and very few were able to reap the rewards for the risks they took.

TRANSFRONTIER TELEVISION BEFORE COMMUNICATIONS SATELLITES

Channels began crossing borders when television was still firmly in the hands of nation-states and when governments expected public broadcasters to make a strong contribution to national culture. Thus the international reach of these channels was incidental to their main purpose. At first, it happened purely by accident when the television signal overspilled to neighbouring countries. Progressively, some signals were relayed terrestrially and then transmitted to local cable networks. It was a widespread phenomenon in all the small European countries, particularly those which shared a language with their bigger neighbours, including Austria, Belgium, Denmark, Ireland, Switzerland and the Netherlands. Germany's ARD and ZDF, France's TF1, Antenne 2 and FR3, and the BBC and ITV were the stations with the largest foreign audiences.

There was nothing accidental about the overseas audience of British stations: their signal was picked up by a huge terrestrial antenna near Calais, which was then transmitted by the French PTT (the former Post, Telegraph and Telephone administration responsible for telecommunications) to Belgian and Dutch cable networks. Until copyright agreements were signed in Belgium and the Netherlands in 1984 (Chapter 4), it was totally illegal and not very effective: whenever a tanker went along the Channel, the signal would disappear.

Before the fall of the Iron Curtain, the overspill of Western channels in Eastern Europe was not purely fortuitous either: high-power transmitters were positioned near the borders of East Germany, Hungary and Czechoslovakia.[1] Although the terrestrial signal from Western transmitters covered about 85 per cent of East Germany, the local authorities happily added ARD and ZDF to the cable networks when they discovered that 'citizens who could receive West German TV were less likely to want to emigrate to the West than those who could not': Western entertainment helped them numb the pain of living in a communist regime.[2] Like elsewhere in Europe, cable networks were built in part to respond to the popularity of 'foreign' TV channels, a fact that has been overlooked by the nation-centric accounts of television history.

The audience for overspill channels was significant, particularly in small countries. An early 1990s estimate suggested an audience share of 5 per cent across the whole of Europe. But while it was practically non-existent in the large countries, it reached up to 60 per cent in places like Ireland and Switzerland.[3] In these territories, foreign channels constituted most of viewers' choice. For instance, when the copyright agreement was signed in Belgium in 1984, 11 of the 15 channels on the cable networks came from abroad.[4]

CLT: a pioneering international broadcaster

Europe's sole international broadcaster of the pre-satellite era was the Compagnie Luxembourgeoise de Télédiffusion (CLT). Its predecessor, the Compagnie Luxembourgeoise de Radiodiffusion (CLR) had broadcast Radio-Luxembourg from the heart of the continent since the interwar years. Following the rebuilding of the station in the aftermath of the Second World War, the government of the Grand Duchy granted a television licence to the CLT – taking the new acronym for the occasion – on 1 July 1954. The broadcaster designed a francophone channel for Luxembourg, France and Wallonia. Transmission tests began in January 1955 and the official inauguration followed on 14 May. RTL TV was not only Europe's first purposely international TV channel but among the first advertising-funded stations.[5]

For many years, the over-the-air service, which broadcast from a transmitter near Dudelange, did not reach beyond the adjacent regions of

France and Belgium. Its distribution expanded in the 1970s when it began to be carried on the fledgling French and Belgian cable networks. Its popularity prompted the authorities in Wallonia to grant it a licence in the 1980s, and CLT split the channel in two. In Belgium, the broadcaster formed a joint venture with local press owners and launched RTL TVi (RTL Télévision Indépendante), which broadcast on local terrestrial frequencies. In France, the cable version of RTL TV also received a licence from the local regulatory body but the terrestrial version continued to broadcast from Luxembourg.[6]

The French government was suspicious of the CLT and always tried to curtail its independence. In the 1960s it occasionally cut the cable connecting the Paris-based studios of the radio service to the transmitter in Luxembourg. It put pressure on appointments of journalists and executives and tried to exert even more control after 1970, when French companies held nearly 60 per cent of the company's shares.[7]

THE EMERGENCE OF COMMUNICATIONS SATELLITES

Europe was only the third world region to place a television channel on satellite. The first satellite TV system was built by the Soviet state, which faced the challenge of distributing a TV signal across a territory that spread across 11 time zones. In the mid-1960s, the government realized that it was no longer practical to try to reach remote and sparsely populated areas with a terrestrial broadcast network. The Molnya communication satellite system became operational around the fiftieth anniversary of the Bolshevik Revolution, in October 1967. As the satellite signal was relatively weak, the ground stations necessitated dishes between 10 and 20 metres in diameter, and since the satellite was not geostationary, the antennas had to be able to track it in orbit.[8] Although the ground stations were costly, the system remained cheaper than a network of terrestrial transmitters, and by the end of the decade receiving stations had been installed all over the Soviet Union.

Molnya was supplemented by a more powerful and geostationary satellite system in 1976, the Ekran TV broadcasting system. The much stronger signal from the Ekran satellites reduced the system's receiving costs, enabling the authorities to install earth stations in some of the remotest parts of the Soviet empire. The Ekran system helped deliver central television to the least populated areas of the north, Siberia and Kazakhstan. In turn, it was complemented by the Gorizont satellite network, coupled to the Moskva distribution system, which the Russians commissioned to cover the 1980 Moscow Olympics. By the mid-1980s the three satellite distribution networks covered most of the Soviet territory and reached 90 per cent of its population.[9]

While the Russians built a satellite TV system for a national broadcaster, satellites were initially used by local cable channels in the United States. Satellite communications were pioneered by a Manhattan cable service called Home Box Office (HBO) founded by Charles F. Dolan and partly owned by Time Inc. In order to recoup some of the operating and programming expenses they decided to expand the service to other cable systems. HBO first reached 365 homes in Wilkes-Barre, Pennsylvania, on 8 November 1972, transmitting to their cable operator via microwave link. In September 1975, in order to broadcast a boxing match between Muhammad Ali and Joe Frazier taking place in the Philippines, Gerald Levin, who headed HBO, rented transponder space on a recently launched RCA satellite. HBO used the spacecraft to retransmit the match from Manila and make it available to a couple of cable networks in Florida and Mississippi, thus inaugurating the era of satellite cable networks in the USA. Levin subsequently took a loan from HBO's parent company to finance a long-term lease on the RCA spacecraft. When HBO was made available to local cable systems nationwide its distribution dramatically increased. By the mid-1980s, about 6,000 cable operators relayed HBO to a total of 20 million subscribers.[10]

Further south, a young man by the name of Ted Turner had inherited a billboard company following his father's suicide. He diversified the company to radio in 1968 and made his first purchase in television two years later when he acquired WJRJ-Atlanta, a struggling television station that he renamed WTCG. Turner felt inspired by Soviet satellites, and the possibilities of satellite distribution as demonstrated by Levin were not lost on him either. In December 1976, following authorization from the Federal Communications Commission (FCC), he began transmitting WTBS – as the station was now called – via satellite to cable operators. When Turner transformed a local station into a national network WTBS developed into the first 'superstation'.[11]

As cable expanded, the idea of a 24-hour news channel began to float around in the fledgling cable industry. Turner was first to take on a project that was presented to him by Reese Schonfeld in 1978. The executive promoted the channel to cable affiliates up and down the country, who keenly signed up to it. Cable News Network (CNN) was launched on 1 June 1980 with Schonfeld as president. International expansion quickly followed, beginning with Asia in 1982.[12]

From Satellite Television plc to Sky Channel

Ted Turner was the inspiration behind Europe's first satellite TV channel. Brian Haynes, a producer for Thames Television, was sent by the *This Week* programme to the United States in 1978 for a documentary on Turner who, he thought, had 'discovered satellites'.[13] Back in Europe, Haynes wished to start a similar service and received the support of Jim Shaw, a director at Thames Television's sales department, who saw it as an opportunity to sell international advertising. Looking for a satellite, Haynes came across the European Space Agency's (ESA) Orbital Test Satellite (OTS), which showed its capacity to transmit TV programmes during a demonstration at Wembley, North London, in September 1978. The ESA needed fresh money to keep the satellite running and was happy to rent a transponder to Haynes. Although an agreement was reached with the ESA, an authorization had to be granted from at least one of the Eutelsat signatories, the European PTTs that still held a monopoly over telecommunication (Chapter 4). Echoing the initial developments of wireless telegraphy earlier in the twentieth century, satellites were first designed for telecommunications purposes and, although the OTS footprint could be received anywhere in Europe (with a decent-sized dish), Haynes needed to designate a point B that he claimed he wanted to reach. All the Eutelsat signatories who were contacted refused to breach the monopoly over telecommunications relays and declined to downlink the channel's signal. Haynes looked at alternatives, including the British Forces in Germany and oil rigs in the North Sea and Gibraltar, until Malta finally agreed to it in late 1981. Their part of the deal was a free dish and the rights to rebroadcast football matches. With the Malta agreement and the Eutelsat clearance in his pocket, Haynes turned to British Telecom (BT), then part of the Post Office, to secure an uplink service. BT and the Home Office reluctantly agreed to it since a member of the European Broadcasting Union (EBU) – Malta – had requested a service from the ESA satellite.[14]

In London, Guinness Mahon, a merchant bank, helped raise risk capital. Thames Television pulled out of the project, anxious about the reaction of the British regulatory agency (the Independent Broadcasting Authority) and the effect it might have on its licence renewal. £4 million was successfully raised from a variety of investors, including Barclays, Ferranti (a British electronics company), the National Magazine Company (a Hearst subsidiary), and publishers DC Thomson in Britain and Mondadori in Italy. Broadcasting tests 'to Malta' began in 1981, in effect offering cable operators across Europe full view of the channel. They quickly showed interest. The official launch took place on 26 April 1982 with a regular broadcast of two hours a night. In addition to Malta, cable operators received the authorization to downlink Satellite Television's signal in two other countries: Finland and Norway. Approximately 116,000 households were able to receive Europe's first satellite TV channel on that first night. Very few of them were in Malta, for reason of technical delay, and more than half were found in Helsinki. Heavily cabled markets such as Switzerland, Belgium and Holland would soon open up. This launch took place in a very difficult context: there was no pan-European legislation, advertising regulations were not only very restrictive but different from one country to another, commercial television was banned in most countries and state monopolies prevailed in the telecommunication sector.

Satellite Television's programming was in English, light and entertaining. It was a diet of pop music, soap opera, cheap TV series and sport. English football was particularly popular in Scandinavia but broadcasts were stopped by request of the Football Association of Norway, who accused Satellite Television of emptying their stadia. Early advertisers included Coca-Cola, Philips and Unilever.[15]

Meanwhile, Rupert Murdoch had convened his companies' chief executives to his alpine retreat in Aspen, Colorado. There, John Tydeman told the 'newspaper tycoon' – as Murdoch was referred to at the time – that he ought to get a foot in the new media door. Upon his advice, Murdoch appointed a team in London which included Tydeman, Gary Devey from Fox Television in Australia and Malcolm Tallantire from Murdoch's press operations in the UK to look for new projects. After dabbling with the idea of a 'worldwide newspaper' delivered by satellite, they soon stumbled on Satellite Television plc. The existing shareholders were not hard to convince to part with their shares: Haynes had gone through the initial £4 million and needed £6 million more to carry on operations. By the summer of 1983 Murdoch had acquired Satellite Television for £1 plus debts. The mogul brought in a new management team and appointed Patrick Cox as first managing director. Cox was working at RTL and was trying to buy a satellite channel but the major shareholders, notably Havas, were dithering and he left. Cox was visiting his new boss in

New York and in his office came across the artwork for a project Murdoch had been forced to abandon. Murdoch had tried to set up a satellite service to compete with CNN, but the main US cable channels (notably HBO and Discovery) blocked him by moving to a new satellite and buying all the capacity. The project was called Sky Band and Cox suggested using it for the newly acquired channel based in London, which was duly renamed Sky Channel. Murdoch was primarily interested in the UK market but was forced to pay attention to the rest of the continent because it was there that cable networks were developing. Despite Murdoch's doubts about a pan-European service, he established Sky Channel as the leading satellite service of the 1980s.[16]

TV5 AND 3SAT: CONTINENTAL PUBLIC SERVICE BROADCASTERS JOIN FORCES

The second-oldest satellite channel in Europe and the current doyenne of transnational TV channels is the francophone TV5Monde, which started broadcasting as plain TV5 in February 1984. It dates back to 1974, when the French government decided to dismantle the state broadcaster (the Office de radiodiffusion-télévision française – ORTF) into seven companies, among them the channels TF1, Antenne 2 and FR3.[17] The ORTF had been designed to be, as General de Gaulle put it, 'the voice of the state in France and the voice of France in the world'.[18] France was still catered for since the government kept the state monopoly over broadcasting, but the country's overseas broadcasting presence suffered. The ORTF was the designated organization to set up all exchange and cooperation programmes with France's foreign partners. Once it was taken apart, not only was it difficult to reassign in a piecemeal manner the different missions to the new companies but the overseas partners no longer knew who to speak to in France. Patrick Imos, a diplomat, decided to pick up the pieces when he realized the role television could play in asserting French influence in the world. His first step was to set up a network of people in French embassies and cultural centres around the world in charge of audiovisual matters. These 'attachés audiovisuels' were responsible for opening contacts in foreign countries and promoting France's expertise and programming in radio and television.[19]

At a later stage, the fledgling communications satellites came to the attention of Imos, who understood the potential of the technology for television distribution. He designed a project of cooperation among five francophone public broadcasters: the three French public television channels (TF1, Antenne 2 and FR3), Wallonia's RTBF and the SSR from French-speaking Switzerland.

Although surprising considering France's international ambitions, there were very good reasons behind this assemblage of broadcasters. The TV5 signal would need the relay of the cable networks to reach an audience, and while cable had yet to take off in France, both Belgium and Switzerland were among the most heavily cabled countries in Europe. Furthermore, TV5 had no choice but to transmit from Eutelsat's first satellite, the European Communication Satellite 1 (ECS 1), which replaced ESA's OTS and became operational in February 1984 (Chapter 4). It had ten transponders, for which Eutelsat received 27 applications. France's best chance to secure a slot on this satellite was to request it in partnership with other European broadcasters. Promoting French language and culture was an idea that may have been attractive to the backers of TV5, but it was a case of making virtue out of necessity.[20]

The participating channels formed a Groupement d'intérêt économique – an administrative structure similar to that of Airbus – called Satellimages, headed by Jean Rouilly, an executive from Antenne 2. TV5 began broadcasting three hours a night with the launch of ECS 1, reaching the cable networks in Belgium, Holland, Switzerland and West Germany, and soon expanding to Scandinavia. From the outset, distribution was TV5's strong point. Cable operators welcomed the network because it was put together by public broadcasters and its programming was not outrageously commercial. It was free and did not carry commercials at the time, and so did not threaten local arrangements to share the TV advertising cake. The initial budget was modest and TV5 rebroadcast its partners' programming: Mondays and Thursdays were supplied by Antenne 2, Tuesdays by the SSR, Wednesdays and Sundays by TF1, Fridays by FR3 and Saturdays by the RTBF.[21]

In January 1986 a Quebecan consortium joined in, including the Canadian Broadcasting Corporation (CBC), private broadcasters and film companies. The Canadians energized the network by bringing a more commercial approach. They eventually produced their own signal that incorporated 60 per cent of the original feed which they sold for a good profit to cable affiliates in Canada and the United States. This signal opened up the all-important North American market but also created imbalances that TV5 executives were called to address at a later stage (Chapter 6).[22]

3Sat followed TV5 on the Eutelsat satellite later in 1984. It was backed by three public broadcasters, ZDF in West Germany, ORF in Austria and SRG in German-speaking Switzerland. The channel was headquartered at ZDF's studios in Mainz, and the German broadcaster, which provided 55 per cent of the programming, was firmly in charge. The Swiss contributed to 10 per cent of the output, the Germans being allegedly wary of the Swiss-German dialect. 3Sat began broadcasting to a few thousand cable homes in Germany on 1 December 1984 but reception proved difficult in Switzerland. As soon as the occasion arose, the channel moved to a German satellite, DFS Kopernikus, in order to improve reception.[23]

COMMERCIAL VENTURES FROM MAINLAND EUROPE

FilmNet: Europe's international film channel

FilmNet was created by the pioneers of pay television in the Netherlands. The project was started by Esselte Video International, a subsidiary of the Swedish conglomerate Esselte, and Rob Houwer, a prominent Dutch film producer. Before the channel began broadcasting they were also joined by ATN (Abonnee Televisie Nederland). ATN was a joint venture involving VNU, Holland's largest magazine publisher, and United International Pictures (UIP), a distribution company that grouped Hollywood majors MGM/United Artists, Paramount and Universal (and today is jointly owned by the latter two). UIP had dabbled with film channels in the early days of European cable TV before the majors questioned why they should invest in a 'medium that in the end would have to come to them for product anyway', as Houwer observed at the time.[24]

FilmNet launched in March 1985, transmitting from the transponder rented out by Esselte on ECS 1. It soon spread across Northern Europe, starting with a few cable nets in Belgium in December 1985, followed by Finland, Norway and Sweden in 1986, and Denmark shortly afterwards. FilmNet claimed 208,000 subscribers by the end of 1987, rising to 430,000 subscribers by the end of the decade. The number of connections was relatively small but FilmNet was a premium channel. At a cost of £10 a month for subscribers it was far more expensive than basic tier channels such as CNN and TV5.[25]

FilmNet was Europe's sole international film station at the time.

Switzerland's Teleclub made only a brief foray into Germany and France's Canal Plus would eventually embark on a European expansion drive but on a country-to-country basis. None of the British film channels, such as Premiere, ever succeeded in expanding to the continent (see below). For all its merit, FilmNet could not turn a profit and had lost £40 million by 1990. Esselte was defeated and put the channel on sale, which was picked up by Nethold. The new owner was a joint venture bringing together the South African pay-TV concern MultiChoice with Swiss-based Richemont, the luxury brand company. Nethold's chief executive officer (CEO), Johann Rupert, was eager to diversify his group into pay-TV and invested heavily in the sector. At one stage, the group's activities in pay-TV spanned 13 countries to reach 2.5 million subscribers. Nethold took FilmNet to more than 800,000 subscribers by the mid-1990s but that was still not enough to reach profitability. FilmNet's age-old problem was that only a minute fraction of households (around 2.5 per cent) with access to cable took a subscription. In early 1997, FilmNet was gobbled up by the giant of pay-TV at the time: Canal Plus. The French group progressively replaced the old name with its own brand, and FilmNet disappeared from the Benelux and Scandinavia (Chapter 8).[26]

New World Channel and World Public News

New World Channel was in the first batch of satellite channels in Europe. It started transmitting on 1 October 1984, sharing a transponder with TV5 on ECS 1. The channel was a Norwegian venture launched by Hans Bratterud, head of European Broadcasting Network, which operated a radio channel in Oslo. The backers of New World Channel were religious organizations which influenced the nature of programming. The channel built up a distribution of up to 100,000 houses across Finland, France, the Netherlands, Norway and Sweden before disappearing off the radar screen in the second half of 1986.[27]

World Public News (WPN) was the brainchild of Marc de Cock, the head of Independent Television Services, a Belgian company. WPN launched in April 1985 from the International Press Centre in Brussels and scheduled an eclectic mix of programming bought from broadcasters around the world. Despite the name, WPN contained little news and broadcast documentaries on a broad range of topics from culture to current affairs. The channel expanded to a few thousand houses in the UK before running out of money.[28]

UK CABLE PROGRAMMERS EXPAND OVERSEAS

Thorn EMI

In the early 1980s recently awarded cable franchises across the UK prompted the emergence of new programme providers. Some of these channels never ventured abroad but those that did rank among the pioneers of international television in Europe. A key player was Thorn EMI, a software-to-hardware British conglomerate created by Peter Laister when he merged Thorn with EMI, a film and record company, in the late 1970s. The group already had an interest in television manufacture and rental when it decided to become involved in cable and satellite television. The company had several content divisions that were eventually regrouped under the umbrella of Thorn EMI Screen Entertainment. Within this division a young American executive, Richard Wolfe, fresh from Warner Amex, started an operating unit called Thorn EMI Cable Programmes in which all three cable channels launched by the group were developed. These included a movie service briefly called Cinematel and renamed Premiere once the name became available and which remained in the UK during its brief existence; The Children's Channel, which in due course reached a handful of overseas markets; and Music Box, which was European from the start.[29]

Music Box was Europe's first music television channel. It began life as a programme slot on Sky Channel in February 1984 and became a fully fledged satellite channel on 12 July 1984, having received the UK's last transponder on ECS 1. Thorn EMI did not want to take on the risk alone so it became a joint venture with Richard Branson's Virgin Group, and Yorkshire TV taking a 5 per cent stake. The chief executive, Charles Levison, was a lawyer in the music industry and was appointed by the Branson side. Levison had been running WA Records in London between 1981 and 1983 and was liaising with Bob Pitman and other people at MTV in America. His idea was to start an equivalent station for Europe. His legal expertise was also crucial in framing and negotiating the extremely complex legal issues involved in music video copyrights and royalties. No legal framework existed and agreements with rights societies (of which there were many) and cable operators had to be written from scratch and reached on a case-by-case basis. Satellite coverage did not guarantee access to European cable operators. The Dutch cable networks were starting to fill up and the enterprising marketing director, Marcus Bicknell, was starting to receive requests for payment in exchange for distribution. These difficulties did not prevent Music Box reaching the second-highest European distribution (behind Sky) by the end of 1985, with 3.3 million connections spread over ten countries. Programming consisted mostly of pop videos – a British invention according to Levison – and programmes such as *Chart Attack* and *Gig Guide*.

As innovative as the programming was, the management was never able to break into profit and the channel had lost £15 million by 1986. Talks held in 1985 with MTV – not yet in Europe – were unproductive, and the channel was finally bought by a consortium of ITV companies. They relaunched it as Super Channel in January 1987 (Chapter 2).[30]

A company was created for The Children's Channel with four main shareholders: Thorn EMI, Central Television, British Telecom and DC Thomson. The managing director, Wolfe, was at the helm of the channel until 1993 despite ownership changes. Thorn EMI's bungled industrial strategy finally caught up with the group, which pulled out of the cable industry in spring 1986. Likewise, BT had a change of heart and withdrew from cable television, selling its interests in The Children's Channel in the late 1980s.

The Children's Channel was launched on 1 September 1984 in the UK but did not reach its first foreign market, Holland, before November 1987. A year later The Children's Channel was reaching cable systems in two other countries, Ireland and Sweden. The reason for this delay was lack of funding, which also prevented the channel from expanding its programming after 3:00 pm: a clear handicap for a station that should have reached children on their return from school. In 1991 The Children's Channel was taken over by Flextech, a company that was in the process of disinvesting from the oil industry to become involved in the media, and which kept the station on European cable nets for a while.[31]

WH Smith

WH Smith is a venerable newspaper distribution company with a chain of high street shops across Britain. In the early 1980s it decided to invest in UK cable channels, seeing the diversification as the logical progression from old to new media.

Screensport (or Screen Sport in its early incarnation) was among Britain's early cable channels. The company was founded by Bob Kennedy in 1983 and the cable sports network began broadcasting on 29 March 1984.

Kennedy's first partners were American and included the network ABC and the cable sports channel ESPN. The station was initially intended for the British market but soon ran into difficulties because of the dreadfully slow development of cable in Britain. In order to limit the channel's losses, Kennedy was forced to look to the continental market and signed its first deal in Sweden at the end of 1985. A year later, the channel had not made much progress on the continent: in addition to the 100,000 or so connections in Britain, Screensport could be seen in 45,000 Swedish and 1,000 Finnish households. The difficult financial situation prevented the channel from investing in attractive programming and the schedule was a mixture of obscure sports and overseas acquisitions. The station showed little live action, which was replaced with news, magazines and coaching programmes in various sports. The losses were mounting to several million pounds by the end of 1985 and the shareholders were growing tired of the repetitive cash calls. In the summer of 1986 WH Smith, who already had a 27 per cent stake in the channel, agreed to buy out ABC and take control of the station, which it integrated into its Cable Division.[32]

WH Smith had two other channels that progressively made their way to the European cable networks. The company managed the Lifestyle channel, which was initially controlled by a consortium involving WH Smith (47 per cent), two ITV franchise holders – Yorkshire Television and Television South – and DC Thomson (17.7 per cent each). Lifestyle, launched at the end of 1985, was a low-key channel aimed at 'housewives' and consisted primarily of repeats from the two ITV companies. It broadcast during the day only and shared a frequency with Screensport, which at first started transmitting at 5:00 pm.[33]

It was John Griffiths, the chairman of British Cable Programmes, who set the ball rolling for The Arts Channel in 1984. The project was picked up by a consortium led by WH Smith who invested £2 million in the station and launched it in September 1985, making it available to 3,000 subscribers in four cable franchises: Aberdeen, Coventry, Westminster and Glasgow. The schedule mostly consisted of recorded art performances, of which 25 per cent was classical music, 15 per cent opera, 7.5 per cent dance and 10 per cent drama.

With only 15,000 homes receiving The Arts Channel by mid-1987, Griffiths began to look beyond Britain for expansion. He thought that art performances would go down well with an international audience and developed his hope of becoming the 'cultural voice of Europe'.[34] He entered Sweden in late 1986, followed by Finland, Norway, the Netherlands and

Ireland. Only a few connections could be made in each of these countries, and with many cable operators overcharging for the channel, the number of viewers – when known – was embarrassingly low. To fulfil his ambition Griffiths desperately needed fresh funds, but with WH Smith refusing to inject more money into the project the future did not look promising.[35]

CONCLUSION

Within a couple of years satellite technology was making a big impact on the European broadcasting scene. Many satellite channels were distributed to cable networks within a single territory (UK: Premiere, The Children's Channel, MirrorVision; Germany: RTL Plus, Sat1; Switzerland: Teleclub) but quite a few had started crossing borders. Table 1.1 lists those that had distribution in three or more territories. It shows that Holland was the main cable market and Sky the channel with the largest international reach. This short period also witnessed the emergence of Europe's first transnational migrant TV channel: RAI, the Italian public broadcaster, uplinked a national station on ECS 1 in order to reach Italian expatriates and was available on a few cable networks in Belgium (Chapter 10).

Table 1.1: Distribution of satellite channels present in a minimum of three territories, December 1985 (in number of connected households)

	3Sat	Music Box	New World Channel	Sky Channel	TV5	Worldnet	WPN
Austria	194,000	/	/	200,791	9,300	/	/
Belgium	/	444,805	/	521,458	913,000	427,000	1,200,000
Denmark	/	175,567	/	543	500	540	/
Finland	/	138,253	5,551	156,088	36,000	/	/
France	/	1,025	1,027	2,927	50,000	1,027	/
Germany	844,000	538,227	/	779,563	230,000	/	/
Luxembourg	/	53,000	/	3,765	27,000	27,000	/
Netherlands	/	1,390,932	34,000	2,101,591	1,400,000	21,400	35,000
Norway	/	/	4,000	138,728	38,800	/	/
Sweden	/	75,477	53,891	80,850	55,000	/	100,000
Switzerland	12,000	376,408	/	693,884	180,400	2,900	/
United Kingdom	/	101,299	/	135,815	5,000	10,500	/
Total distribution	1,050,000	3,294,993	98,469	4,816,003	2,945,000	490,367	1,335,000

Source: Cable & Satellite Europe, December 1985, pp.28–9.
Data conventions: '/': not applicable.

CHAPTER 2

THE DIFFICULT EXPANSION OF EUROPE'S SATELLITE TV MARKET, 1985–9

New companies entered the field of international television in the second half of the 1980s. Those that crossed the Atlantic during this period (CNN, MTV and Discovery) never looked back and are among today's iconic brands in the industry. A few Europeans (Eurosport and Viasat) also laid the foundations for successful business. But many others did not have the wherewithal to survive in what remained a very difficult environment. The risks they took and the investments they made never paid off and their channels never saw out the end of the decade.

WORLDNET: NEO-CONSERVATIVES GET VOCAL AND AMERICAN PUBLIC DIPLOMACY GOES GLOBAL

The world's first global TV network was not CNN, as is often believed, but a TV network launched by the Reagan administration in the 1980s. The first half of the decade was a period of intense ideological rivalry between the two main protagonists of the Cold War. The substantial propaganda and counter-propaganda measures adopted by the Soviet Union and the United States involved broadcasting thousands of hours of radio programming in tens of languages across the world. The Russians placed particular emphasis on disinformation, such as claims that the American government developed the 'AIDS virus' as a biological weapon designed to kill Africans and that it was involved in selling baby parts in South America.[1] When Ronald Reagan came to power he upped the ante in ideological warfare by greatly increasing the budget of the government's main propaganda arm, the United States Information Agency (USIA). He appointed Charles Wick as director, a close friend but also a Hollywood agent, movie producer and Republican fundraiser who had an understanding of both Washington and the world of entertainment.

The Hollywood backgrounds of Reagan and Wick made them both aware of the suggestive power of images, explaining to a large extent USIA's strategic move towards television in the 1980s. A series of precursor events encouraged them to persevere in their efforts to launch a fully fledged satellite TV channel. In December 1981 David Gergen, the White House communications director, and three neo-conservatives (Ben Wattenberg, Michael Novak and Norman Podhoretz) decided to attract the world's attention to the repression of the Solidarity movement in Poland. The result was *Let Poland Be Poland*, a celebrity-packed Hollywood extravaganza that denounced the despotism of the Soviet-backed Polish authorities and which was aired via satellite to broadcasters around the world in January 1982.[2]

The following year, Russian jet fighters gunned down a Korean airliner which had drifted into Soviet air space with 269 passengers on board. In the ensuing diplomatic battle the Americans decided to produce a videotape based on the recovered transcripts of the Soviet pilots. The tape was played during a speech by Jeanne Kirkpatrick, US Ambassador to the UN, at a special session of the UN Security Council. The tape – albeit not entirely accurate – had the desired effect, forcing the Soviet government to admit their deed within an hour of it being played.[3]

During 1983 plans were being drawn up for interactive press conferences via satellite, an idea rumoured to come from Rupert Murdoch, a close friend of Wick. The format was chosen by Alvin Snyder, director of the Television and Film Service of the USIA since 1982, who suggested that these conferences be 'a two-way video transmission between a US spokesperson and foreign journalists asking questions from their home base'.[4] The idea was tested shortly after the US invasion of the island of Grenada, in the Caribbean. The military operation drew criticisms even from America's closest allies and it was decided to mount the first videoconference to defuse the situation. On 3 November 1983 a satellite feed linked up Jeanne Kirkpatrick, two Caribbean prime ministers who had pleaded for American intervention, and reporters gathered at US embassies in Bonn, London, The Hague, Rome and Brussels. Following the session's success, these electronic press conferences began to be held frequently, bringing together top American policy makers – ranging from Vice President George Bush to Secretary of State George Shultz – and European journalists.[5]

Worldnet, as the interactive system was called, was progressively expanded to other world regions and was also used to relay Reagan's speeches to live audiences in American embassies. These videoconferences attracted criticism from some quarters but allowed the Reagan administration to bypass the Washington press corps and delighted journalists who gained direct access to influential members of the American administration. They became important sources of news and in some cases major media events.[6]

Following phase one, Worldnet was developed into a daily global TV service on 22 April 1985. The feat of creating the world's first global TV distribution system was achieved by Alan Simpson, who had gained experience in electronic warfare with the Royal Air Force. He was working for Visnews (a joint venture between Reuters and the BBC that was also trying to develop a global TV network) when he became Worldnet's lead technical consultant. From his base in Suffolk he crisscrossed the world installing receiving stations in between the surveillance equipment scattered on the roofs of US embassies – visiting 125 locations in all, including China and the Soviet Union. Worldnet was also made accessible to the general public via relays to cable operators and broadcasters (Table 1.1). The distribution system was served by a network of 19 satellites – a record for the time – the backbone of which was formed by the Intelsat birds.

The equipment installed by Simpson was illegal in most countries because in the mid-1980s national PTTs still held the monopoly over satellite downlinks. In Europe he met stiff opposition from British Telecom, a powerful player who did not see eye-to-eye with the private dishes installed on top of US embassies. Surprisingly – considering the pervasive anti-Americanism of the French political elite – it was the French state telecom operator who finally agreed to relay the signal in Europe from its own transponders on ECS 1, ECS 2 and Telecom 1B.[7]

In its final version Worldnet transmitted up to four hours a day and diversified into three programming strands. Interactive videoconferences were held between American officials, journalists and opinion makers at up to 15 different locations. Educative programming encompassed the teaching of American English, documentaries and news reports on American life and culture. This material was copyright-free and copied, usually without being sourced, by countless broadcasters around the world. The entertainment strand was popular with audiences because it included prime Hollywood content such as Charlie Chaplin movies that Wick got free of charge thanks to his Hollywood connections.[8]

Worldnet did not survive the Reagan administration and the service was wound down by George Bush Sr and killed off by Bill Clinton. Once the Iron Curtain had fallen, the station had already fulfilled its mission. In the mid-1980s Reagan raised the stakes one last time in the ideological war with the Soviet Union and fabricated a hoax called the Strategic Defense

Initiative (SDI), better known as 'Star Wars'. Worldnet became a major publicity vehicle for SDI and went to great lengths to give it an aura of credibility. The station transmitted images of a missile blown up in full flight (the tests were fixed by the Pentagon), and organized international talk shows and numerous press conferences with leading SDI experts. It did a pretty good job of convincing Russia and the world that the Americans had the technology to stop missiles launched in their direction, and made a significant contribution to the end of the Cold War.[9]

PUBLIC BROADCASTERS VERSUS COMMON SENSE: THE EUROPA DEBACLE

The development of satellite television was a mixed blessing for public service broadcasters. In the 1980s they were adjusting to the recent emergence of commercial rivals following the break-up of state broadcasting monopolies in several European countries. On the one hand, satellite technology was being recognized as an exciting new medium that would provide an opportunity to disseminate the 'best' of European television to the 'widest possible European audience'.[10] But it was also perceived as a fresh threat to the public broadcasters' position, and they feared that the technology would allow commercial players to rewrite industry standards. Thus their early interest in satellite technology was as much prompted by their enthusiasm for the new technology as concern over competition from the commercial sector.[11]

Following TV5 and 3Sat, public broadcasters' most ambitious projects were organized under the auspices of the EBU. Their first project, Eurikon, was an experiment carried out on a broadcaster-to-broadcaster basis for five non-consecutive weeks in 1982.[12] Each of five EBU members – the IBA (UK), RAI (Italy), ORF (Austria), NOS (Netherlands) and ARD (West Germany) – transmitted to 15 countries for a week in turn. They tested the pan-European appeal of their programmes, tried to identify a 'pan-national editorial viewpoint' for their news services, and experimented with different methods of communicating simultaneously with a multi-lingual audience.[13]

Following the success of the experiment, six EBU members set up a fund and feasibility study and the Dutch government and several European institutions offered support. After lengthy negotiations and deliberations at the EBU, five broadcasters from the Netherlands (NOS), Germany (ARD), Italy (RAI), Ireland (RTE) and Portugal (RTP) launched Europa on 5 October 1985.

Europa (based at the NOS studios in Hilversum) started with a handicap since most of the heavyweight EBU members refused to get involved. The French Antenne 2 and FR3 and the German ZDF feared that it would jeopardize their own TV5 and 3Sat. Likewise, the BBC stayed away because it was not convinced by the quality of the project, plus it was involved with ITV's Super Channel and had plans of its own.[14] The absence of a British broadcaster was a major drawback in the channel's attempt to reach a European audience. To make matters worse, Europa was moulded in the public broadcasting ethos of its backers: it did not pay enough attention to audience tastes and broadcast too many highbrow programmes. The running costs were high (vast sums were spent on translation) and the channel reached too few homes to attract any significant advertising revenue. The Dutch broadcaster, which was unwilling to carry on assuming much of the financial costs, put its colleagues out of their misery and switched off the signal on 27 November 1986, 13 months after the launch.[15]

SUPER CHANNEL: THE ITV COMPANIES CROSS THE CHANNEL

In the mid-1980s the ITV companies saw the European television market opening up and their executives watched Sky's ever-expanding distribution with growing envy. They were told that Murdoch's operation was collecting £14 million advertising revenue per year – a gross overestimate – and decided they wanted a piece of the action. The ITV companies reached the conclusion that 'there was going to be a market for pan-European television advertising that would generate a profitable commercial channel'.[16] They began drafting plans for a channel in late 1985 and launched Super Channel to great fanfare, and with Prime Minister Margaret Thatcher in attendance, on 30 January 1987.

The ITV companies did not build a network from scratch. Thorn EMI had withdrawn from Music Box by 1986 and the shares were split between Virgin (60 per cent), Granada and Yorkshire Television (20 per cent each). The station had lost nearly £15 million but had built up a network of five million subscribers across Europe. A deal struck between the two companies worked as follows: Super would buy Music Box for £17.5 million and inherit its distribution network and precious transponder on ECS 1, and Music Box would provide facilities and music programming for Super. Super's shareholders were Virgin (15 per cent) and the 14 participating ITV companies.[17] Thames Television, an ITV company that had shown interest in satellite television, pulled out of the project. Thames was going through managerial changes but the key factor behind the withdrawal was company director Richard Dunn's correct assessment, at the time, that this pan-European advertising market was a chimera.[18]

The scheduling philosophy of Super rested on the idea that the channel should display the best of British programming. This translated into repeats from the ITV schedule and programmes bought in from the BBC. Super's most popular shows were *Allo Allo*, *Benny Hill*, *Kenny Everett*, *The Lotus Eaters*, *Survival*, *Spitting Image* and *Tales of the Unexpected*. On the whole, the channel was not a success on the continent. Unsolved issues with the unions (notably with the actors' body Equity) over international rights prevented the channel from delivering its promised schedule (Chapter 3). Its share of audience was well below that of Sky in European key markets and the ITV companies were subsequently accused of 'post-colonial arrogance [...] in expecting continentals to queue up to watch a Best of British channel'.[19]

The news was the most innovative part of the schedule and the only original bit. The first news bulletin designed for a European audience was produced by ITN – ITV's news provider – and was born in a Portakabin on the roof of their London building. The daily 9 o'clock news bulletin started with international news then business, followed by European stories, sports, travel news and European weather. Every aspect of the bulletin was devised for an international audience, from news selection to delivery. Anchorman John Suchet – who made his name first at Super – reckoned 'to knock around a third off the normal pace of a British newscaster'.[20]

With an annual budget of £20 million Super was, by a long way, the best-funded attempt at cracking the pan-European advertising market. The station's average programming cost reached £2,500 per hour, while Sky's never exceeded £2,000. News alone cost £16,000 an hour. The running costs far exceeded the revenue from advertising which amounted to £4 million in 1987. By the time Super executives had realized they were chasing a ghost market the station had lost £46 million.[21]

Super was put on the market, attracting interest from Sky and a consortium called Television Broadcasting Company (TBC), a venture involving Thames and Carlton Communications among others. The negotiations were fruitless and in the second part of 1988 the ITV companies began to pull out from the channel, letting Virgin become the dominant shareholder with a stake exceeding 40 per cent. When all else had failed an Italian industrialist took control of Super towards the end of 1988 with Branson remaining a sleeping partner. Pierluigi Marcucci had made a fortune trading plasma between Eastern and Western Europe and the reasons behind his involvement in Super have always been mysterious. He bought the channel for £1, assuming at first nearly £10 million of unpaid bills (later reduced to £2.5 million), while the ITV companies wrote off £55 million in debt.[22]

Marcucci ran Super on a shoestring. Programming costs reached a new low and did not exceed £750 per hour, which compared unfavourably to the hundreds of thousands of pounds that terrestrial stations could spend on some of their shows. In between multiple relaunches, Super shared a frequency with a shopping station and sold airtime to tele-evangelists. Despite a poor schedule the channel managed to expand its European distribution network to 31 million homes by the end of 1993. It was access to these cable homes that NBC bought in 1994 for £25 million, renaming the channel NBC Super (Chapters 7 and 9).[23]

EARLY BIRDS: THE FIRST AMERICAN CABLE NETWORKS TO CROSS THE ATLANTIC

CNN: a crusader comes to Europe

In the mid-1980s CNN was the first American channel to cross the Atlantic, starting a phenomenon that has continued unabated ever since. After the start of CNN on 1 June 1980, Ted Turner did not rest on his laurels. The channel began its international expansion in 1982, gaining access to Japan, Australia, Canada and parts of Latin America. In its domestic market CNN had access to nearly 30 million homes by the end of 1984. The number of permanent bureaux was expanded to eight outside the USA in locations such as Beirut, Cairo, Jerusalem, Nairobi, Tokyo and Moscow.[24]

Ted Turner, by now the chairman of a successful television network (Turner Broadcasting System – TBS) was a businessman first and foremost. But he was also an idealist whose liberal views were influenced by his friend and fellow Southerner, Jimmy Carter. Turner used to fly the UN flag outside his office in Atlanta well before committing US$1 billion of his own fortune to the United Nations. Like the Victorian idealists such as William T. Stead who preceded him in journalism, Turner wished to make the world a better place. It is with this mindset that he developed CNN, bringing it to Europe on 30 September 1985.[25]

Even though the European feed was serviced from Atlanta and the content originated in America, it differed slightly from the US version.

CNN material that could not get copyright clearance for Europe was replaced by items from CNN Headline News (launched in the USA in January 1982). The schedule presented a mix of news bulletins, magazines, and interview programmes such as *Crossfire* and *Larry King Live*. One of the highlights was *CNN International Hour* which broadcast daily at 9:00 pm and presented in-depth coverage of key regional issues by the network's bureaux. The signal was distributed via Intelsat V at 27.5 degrees West – not a particularly visible satellite – but large distribution was not the point. At first, CNN did not allow cable operators to relay its signal and reserved its service for hotels and broadcasters. The Dorchester in Hyde Park, London, was the first hotel to sign up for CNN. The station was made available to broadcasters via the news exchange of the Geneva-based EBU.[26]

In 1987 CNN began to build up its European distribution network. By mid-year it had about 150,000 connections, notably in Sweden, and was approaching the 1.5 million mark by winter 1988 through a strong presence in Belgium, Germany, the Netherlands and Norway. CNN's coverage expanded dramatically in August the following year when it accessed a Soviet satellite following lengthy negotiations with Gosteleradio, the state broadcaster. The Gorizont satellite transmitted on the C-Band producing a weak signal over an extremely large area, opening up at once Africa, the Middle East, the Indian subcontinent and Southeast Asia for CNN. The deal attracted the wrath of the US Federal Communications Commission, which threatened Ted Turner with his licence, but gave CNN near-worldwide coverage 24 hours a day, making the station the world's first *commercial* global TV channel. It was, above all, a political and technical achievement as the great majority of people had never heard of the channel and when they did, they rarely had the capability of watching it.[27]

Although CNN never really registered on Europe's commonly used audience measurement systems – especially before the first Gulf War in 1990–1 – the channel had a major influence on European broadcasting. It was the region's first 24-hour news channel and, as Bob Ross (CNN International's managing director) said at the time, it 'forced a concept of newsworthiness that is quite alien to Europeans'.[28] The idea has been embraced by several European broadcasters who have since launched news and current affairs services for their domestic audience.[29] In the field of international news, CNN's dominance became all too apparent during the first Gulf War. This prompted broadcasters and politicians to get their acts together and raise funds to finance (costly) news channels. These efforts led to the launch of the BBC's World Service Television in April 1991 and EuroNews in January 1993 (Chapters 6 and 9).[30]

MTV

The world's first all-music channel was the creation of an American company called Warner Amex, a joint venture between Warner and American Express. Warner Amex launched MTV (Music Television) in 1981, alongside Nickelodeon and the Movie Channel. MTV proved a great success with cable affiliates because the channel gave a boost to their image and attracted a young audience. Within five years the MTV signal was picked up by 4,000 cable operators who relayed it to 30 million homes nationwide.[31]

In the mid-1980s MTV and its sister channels were acquired by Viacom International, a diversified entertainment company that held interests in radio stations, cable networks and television production. Viacom itself was attracting the attention of corporate raiders and was eventually bought by Sumner Redstone, the owner of a cinema chain called National Amusements. The deal was finalized in June 1987 following a protracted battle between Redstone and Viacom management.[32]

MTV arrived in Europe a few months later and was officially launched in London on 1 August 1987. Despite its domestic success Viacom was not confident enough to venture alone in Europe and formed a joint venture with British Telecom (24 per cent) and Robert Maxwell (51 per cent). The channel launched to 1.6 million homes – a record at the time – across seven countries: the Netherlands, Germany, Sweden, Denmark, the UK, Switzerland and Finland.[33]

Although eagerly anticipated by young Europeans who had heard about the channel's prowess in the States, MTV was greeted with a certain amount of scepticism. Two music channels had already gone bust – Music Box and France's TV6 – although KMP Musicbox and Video Music were still serving the German and Italian markets. And the two leading pan-European channels, Sky and Super, already programmed a lot of pop music.

Once the worries about MTV's audience size and its ability to attract advertising were somewhat alleviated, the channel's pan-European strategy began to be questioned. Past failures and the inability of the few surviving international channels to show a profit had not gone unnoticed, and observers argued that the pursuit of a European audience would most certainly end in tears.[34] But these doubters did not see through to MTV's professionalism and hallmark blend of astute marketing, continuous audience research and cutting-edge programming. From the start MTV realized that European tastes were distinct and adapted the channel accordingly: within a year of being on air MTV Europe had entered into collaboration agreements with hip UK production houses and co-produced more than 2,500 hours of original programming, the equivalent of seven hours per day. Even though the station's initial attempt to 'transcend language barriers' – as an MTV executive put it at the time – with a single pan-European feed in English would prove futile, at least the channel had not alienated its audience with irrelevant American material.[35]

In the late 1980s it was MTV Europe's shareholders arrangement that briefly created problems. Robert Maxwell, as usual, was less than accommodating. He nurtured lofty ambitions in television and had restructured his interests in the field – spanning several countries – under a new company, the Maxwell Entertainment Group. In 1988 he replaced the more experienced Patrick Cox at the helm of his company with Mark Booth, a young American executive. Booth came from MTV USA and was the managing director of MTV Europe when he was poached by Maxwell. Maxwell intended to leave Booth as MD of MTV, a decision that incensed Viacom executives who saw it as an attempt by Maxwell to take control of the channel. With Redstone in charge at Viacom, Maxwell had picked on the wrong guy and the issue was resolved in Viacom's favour with the appointment of their candidate, Bill Roedy, to the position. In the early 1990s Viacom became the sole owner of MTV Europe. The company acquired the shares held by BT and bought out Maxwell – a few months before his death – for £39 million.[36]

Discovery

The third American channel to come to Europe was Discovery. The station was founded in 1985 by John Hendricks, who pursued the idea of dedicating a channel to the vast amount of documentaries overlooked by broadcasters. The new venture rapidly ran out of cash and Hendricks knocked on the door of a large US cable operator, TeleCommunications Inc (TCI). John Sie, a TCI executive, and John Malone, the company's chief executive, formed a consortium with three other cable operators, United Cable, Cox Communications and NewChannels Corp. In 1986 they bought a 56 per cent stake of Discovery for US$20 million and acquired the rest for $120 million three years later.[37]

Discovery became the fastest-growing channel in the history of US cable and had access to more than 35 million homes four years after its launch. Its appeal was compelling for cable operators: it brought an upmarket audience and enhanced the image of cable as a family educational tool. In addition, since the company could acquire documentaries at reasonable prices it charged a relatively cheap carriage fee.[38]

Discovery rapidly set its hallmark programming strategy. It ploughed as much money as possible into its schedule, sourced programmes around the world from a large range of producers, and based its selection on quality and local audience interest. The company signed deals with independent documentary makers and leading public service broadcasters ranging from the BBC to NHK.[39]

Discovery first ventured to Japan in 1987 and launched in Europe in April 1989 (followed by Asia and Latin America in 1994 and India the following year). The European channel was initially licensed to United Artists Programming, a UK-based affiliate of a major US cable operator, United Artists Entertainment. United Artists Programming, headed by Adam Singer, made several investments in UK cable channels in the early 1990s, notably in Bravo and the Learning Channel. It lost Discovery to TCI in 1993 when John Malone decided to take full control of European operations.[40]

Like MTV, Discovery immediately adapted to a European audience, buying and soon commissioning programmes from leading documentary producers. Compared with its performance in the home market, however, Discovery spread relatively slowly in Europe. Two years after its launch it was distributed in 1.4 million households thinly spread across the UK, Scandinavia and the Netherlands. Discovery realized the importance of adapting the schedule to local audiences in Europe at an early stage and began developing a separate feed carrying subtitles for Scandinavia in late 1992.[41]

THE BATTLE FOR EUROPE'S SPORTS CHANNEL

Screensport and the formation of the first European transnational TV network

When WH Smith took over Screensport in the summer of 1986 (Chapter 1), the new parent company renewed its efforts to expand the European reach of the channel. By autumn 1988 Screensport was available in 11 countries but its distribution remained weak with only one million connections (as compared to nearly 14 million for Sky). The management led by Francis Baron, WH Smith Television (WHSTV) managing director, realized that English was a hindrance to the penetration of Screensport on European cable networks and decided to split the feed into separate language versions. It began with France launching TV Sport in 1988 as a joint venture with the Générale des Eaux, the French utility company that would later form the backbone of Vivendi Universal. WHSTV repeated the operation in the Netherlands with SportNet and in Germany with SportKanal. By the end of 1990 WHSTV had formed The European Sports Network (TESN), which comprised four language versions – including Screensport in the UK – of the same video feed. TESN, in which the American sports channel ESPN had held a 25 per cent stake since 1989, fully owned Screensport but was a minority shareholder in the European channels. On the continent TESN's partners included Canal Plus and Générale d'Images, a Générale des Eaux subsidiary.[42]

TESN was the first – albeit rudimentary – transnational TV network to be set up in Europe and was the first attempt to adapt an international signal to the region's linguistic diversity. Early in 1991 TESN pursued the localization strategy further by launching a separate programming window in France. The French 'opt-out' – two hours every evening on TV Sport – showed local sports (including horseracing, boxing and volleyball) exclusive to this market.[43]

A few months later the leading force behind TESN was throwing in the towel. Despite years of investment WHSTV never showed a profit and WH Smith decided to stop experimenting with new media. A consortium composed of WHSTV's partners in the sports network and the American group ABC/Capital Cities – coming back after a five-year gap (Chapter 1) – bought the company's interest in TESN, Lifestyle and UK channel Cable Jukebox for £45.3 million in the summer of 1991.[44]

The consortium, which renamed the WHSTV properties the European Television Networks (ETN), was torn apart by differences on the strategy to follow. American shareholders favoured a pan-European approach for Screensport while the French planned to break up the network into local channels. Barely a year later the consortium was proposing a merger with a rival launched a few years earlier: Eurosport. The parties reached an agreement early in 1993. Under the terms of the deal Lifestyle stopped broadcasting on 25 January, followed by Screensport on 28 February. TF1 and Bouygues, the French construction group that bought TF1 in 1986, reduced their share in Eurosport to 34 per cent to accommodate Canal Plus and ESPN. TV Sport, the only surviving ETN feed, was now jointly owned by TF1 and some ETN partners, including Canal Plus, Générale d'Images and ESPN.[45]

With Screensport and Lifestyle two of the early proponents of European transnational television disappeared. But these channels had found only a marginal interest with the audience, partly because WH Smith brought the ethos of a newspaper distributor to television. These channels were managed by the bottom line, and while cost control is crucial it should not be at the expense of investment into programming. The WH Smith management never quite grasped that if their channels did not provide a decent schedule, viewers would migrate to those that did.

Eurosport

A project for an international sports channel went back as far as the early 1980s at EBU. When the organization experimented with Eurikon Jean-Pierre Julien, an EBU executive, advocated launching it as a sports channel. When the Europa project was discussed a few years later the EBU's sports committee again proposed to make it a sports station. The idea resurfaced in the same committee in 1987 in the wake of the Europa fiasco (see above). The driving force behind the channel was Vittori Boni from RAI, who was the committee's head.[46]

EBU members' interest in a sports channel was prompted by a wish for distribution of sports programming they had acquired but had not found time to schedule on their terrestrial channels. At stake for the EBU members was their relationship with sports federations and access to rights. These federations were increasingly reluctant to give or sell rights to broadcasters who would not schedule their competitions for the simple reason that advertisers will not commit to sports without exposure.[47]

Following approval for the project the EBU embarked on a search for a partner and selected Rupert Murdoch's News International at the end of 1987. It was agreed that EBU members would provide the programming and News International produce the channel and absorb the losses of the first few years. It was a considerable coup for Murdoch, considering that the EBU footage and rights catalogue were coveted by many commercial broadcasters. After being denied access to EBU material, WHSTV had filed a case against the organization even before the launch of Eurosport. WHSTV accused the EBU of operating as a cartel and breaching competition Articles 85 and 86 of the Treaty of Rome. Broadcasters rebuffed by the EBU included Super, CNN and Deutsches Sportfernsehen (DSF). The ensuing lawsuits threatened the viability of Eurosport until 2005.[48]

Unlike Europa, Eurosport benefited from wide support across the EBU, encompassing the heavyweight members. Sixteen EBU members signed the partnership agreement with News International on 23 December 1988, notably the BBC, Italy's RAI and the French TF1 and Antenne 2. For domestic reasons, ARD and ZDF could not immediately join the consortium but gave their support to the venture.[49]

Meanwhile, Murdoch was in the process of a complete overhaul of his European TV operations. Sky Channel may have been the leading pan-European channel in terms of distribution but the station was haemorrhaging money (Table 2.1). The ratings did not even reach 0.5 per cent on the continent, confirming the difficulties English channels had of breaking into foreign-language markets.[50] Sky did not attract anywhere near enough advertising revenue and Murdoch was growing increasingly disillusioned with the demands and insufficiencies of European cable operators. The launch of Astra in December 1988 – the first commercial communication satellite over Europe (Chapter 4) – gave him the opportunity he had been waiting for for a long time. Murdoch was desperate to seize a piece of Europe's largest TV advertising market.

On 5 February 1989 Murdoch launched Sky, his multi-channel pay-TV platform in the UK. He had little hesitation in swapping Sky Channel for Eurosport on European cable networks, giving the sports channel a solid head start in terms of distribution. Eurosport might have been available across Europe but its primary purpose was to complete Murdoch's line-up of channels, which comprised a new UK-only Sky Channel (later Sky One), Sky News – also launched on 5 February – and Sky Movies.

Sky Television's rival in the UK's direct-reception market was a consortium called British Satellite Broadcasting (BSB). BSB launched more than a year after the Sky package (on 29 April 1990) but went through £700 million far more quickly. The consortium was in dire straits within months and by the end of 1990 Murdoch had accepted a merger proposal from BSB's management. The BSB platform disappeared and Sky became BSkyB (British Sky Broadcasting). Among the stations that Murdoch inherited was BSB's Sports Channel, which he thought would be of greater interest to a British audience than his own Eurosport because of the vast amount of money poured into its sports rights.[51]

The Sports Channel was the station Murdoch wished to retain, and as he was about to sell its Eurosport shares the European Commission was delivering its verdict on WHSTV's complaint about EBU's trading practices. The Commission ruled that the EBU had breached competition laws by giving access to its sports material solely to Eurosport – a channel that included a commercial broadcaster among its shareholders – while continuing to deny access to EBU events to other commercial players. On hearing this Murdoch wrote off around £20 million in losses and closed the channel down on 6 May 1991. Three days later TF1, the French terrestrial commercial broadcaster, began its effort to revive the channel, which went back on air on 22 May.

The Commission was satisfied with the TF1 takeover: the French broadcaster was as commercial as News International but held EBU membership by virtue of its previous incarnation as a public service channel. Murdoch could be forgiven for feeling hard done by by a legal decision that led to the replacement of one commercial broadcaster with another.[52]

Bouygues – TF1's majority shareholder – joined TF1 in Eurosport by the end of 1991, its 31 per cent holding adding to TF1's 20 per cent share in the channel. Eurosport's ownership remained stable until its merger with Screensport in February 1993 (see above), at which point shares were split among TF1 (34 per cent), Canal Plus and ESPN (33 per cent each). Also in 1993, TV Sport – Screensport's French feed – was rebranded as Eurosport France. During the 1990s TF1 progressively bought out its partners to become the channel's sole owner. In parallel, Canal Plus became Eurosport France's main shareholder until TF1 acquired the channel in the early 2000s, linking it up with the main European feed.[53]

Eurosport travelled a rocky road but succeeded in establishing itself as Europe's leading thematic channel by the mid-1990s. It attracted 'more advertising revenue than all the other pan-European channels put together' – albeit an estimated modest £61 million – and its extensive multi-lingual voice-over service helped it break all distribution records.[54] In September 1995 the sports channel was broadcasting in eight languages to 65 million homes across 35 countries. It had sufficient appeal to viewers to risk the wrath of cable operators by demanding carriage fees, which constituted up to 40 per cent of its income.[55]

THE ARTS CHANNEL AND THE EUROPEAN BUSINESS CHANNEL

Eurosport was a rare success in what remained a difficult environment for international broadcasters, and at the end of the 1980s two channels ran into trouble. The Arts Channel was making slow progress in Europe with barely one million connections around 1987. Its audience was too small to attract advertising, although the channel won a few sponsorship deals to supplement its meagre income from cable operators. Early in 1988, the station was saved by a pension fund as it was about to shut down when managing director John Griffiths decided to share a transponder with Sky on ECS 1. The Arts Channel transmitted on Sky's frequency every evening between midnight and 3:00 am. Although it had to transmit on another channel during the day, it boosted its European distribution by more than 10 million homes. Murdoch used the respectability of arts programming to win favour among local authorities in Europe who were reluctant to allow Sky's mix of wrestling and pop videos onto their cable systems.[56]

A few months later the Arts Channel was taken over by United Cable Television Corporation (UCTC), an American company with interests in Discovery and Bravo (see above). UCTC's plan was to transform the Arts Channel into the European equivalent of Hearst's Arts and Entertainment (A&E) in the USA, a channel that mixed programming on the performing arts with drama and comedy. The plan was never implemented, partly because Griffiths did not share UCTC's vision for the channel. Viewing figures remained stubbornly low and negotiations for a takeover took place with Sky. When Murdoch withdrew Sky from Europe early in 1989 he was more interested in developing his own arts channel to complement the Sky package – predicting that advertisers would be attracted by an upmarket audience – and plans fell through. UCTC withdrew its investment, Griffiths failed to attract a new majority shareholder and the channel ceased transmissions on 14 April 1989.[57]

The first attempt to set up a business channel in Europe came from Switzerland. The Zurich-based European Business Channel (EBC) was the brainchild of John Winisdorfer. The venture was well funded, with Swiss backers holding nearly half the shares and the rest split between production company Blackbox, Jean Frey Verlag and CLT, among others.[58] Up to 120 staff worked at EBC, including 30 reporters and correspondents. Winisdorfer attracted personnel from top broadcasters in Germany and Britain. Both James Long, the EBC's business editor, and Will Hutton, the editor-in-chief, came from the BBC. Long's intentions were to provide a complete service from a pan-European perspective to the business community. He thought that existing business programmes were 'obsessed' by financial trading and stock markets and, inspired by the BBC's late-night programme *Newsnight*, wished to bring a current affairs approach to the genre.[59]

In 1989 the EBC started broadcasting two feeds for a few hours every morning, targeting professional investors during their working hours. The first, in English, was relayed by Sky and the other in German and relayed by RTL Plus. Financial difficulties surfaced before the EBC could expand its service into the evening. The expenses – the editorial budget alone was set at £6 million – far outstripped advertising revenue. EBC's problems were compounded by the failure of Europe's main satellite launcher, Ariane, in February 1990, delaying distribution plans, and the announcement of a joint venture between CNN and the *Financial Times*. Investors such as Bertelsmann and Time Warner could not be convinced to invest fresh cash in the channel, which ceased transmissions on 29 June 1990 owing £36.6 million.[60]

CONCLUSION

Table 2.1 shows the distribution of satellite channels in Europe in the first quarter of 1989, which proved to be a turning point in the history of the medium. The ITV companies had just withdrawn from Super Channel and Murdoch was pulling Sky Channel out of Europe. The table hints at the emergence of new markets such as Spain and Ireland but reveals a reception universe largely confined to Northern Europe.

SINGLE LINGUISTIC AREA SATELLITE CHANNELS

Satellite technology had enabled television channels to cross borders but not all stations that uplinked to satellites used them for that purpose. Eins Plus in Germany, TV Norge in Norway, Kindernet in the Netherlands, Canal J and Canal Jimmy in France, all pointed to a single market. Several stations emerged that opted midway between the national and the pan-European: they crossed borders but remained within the confines of a linguistic area.

The German-speaking market

From the early 1990s a host of TV channels began to serve German-speaking countries and surrounding territories. They predominantly targeted Germany and were in the hands of German companies, but they were also marketed in Austria and German-speaking Switzerland. In addition to 3Sat (Chapter 1), RTL Plus, Sat1 and Pro 7 were available terrestrially in Germany and on cable and satellite in the other two countries. These channels could also be seen in the Italian Tyrol, the Netherlands, Belgium, Denmark, Scandinavia and Central Europe.

Sat1's foundation goes back to PKS (Programmgesellschaft für Kabel und Satellitenfernsehen), a channel that began transmitting on ECS 1 in 1984. This station was the brainchild of a syndicate led by PKS itself, which was a subsidiary of Leo Kirch's film distribution company and that involved two German publishers, FAZ and Otto Maier. The channel was relaunched as Sat1 the following year when the circle of magazine publishers was

Table 2.1: Full-time distribution of international satellite channels present in five or more territories, first quarter 1989 (in number of connected households)

	Arts	Children's Channel	CNN	FilmNet	Lifestyle	MTV	Screensport	Sky Channel	Super Channel	TV5
Austria	359,000	/	/	/	/	/	/	359,000	415,000	22,000
Belgium	1,710,000	/	827,000	80,000	/	2,255,000	/	1,710,000	1,800,000	1,540,000
Denmark	526,000	/	163,000	8,000	1,000	459,000	1,000	526,000	500,000	339,000
Finland	421,000	/	/	14,000	/	226,000	2,000	421,000	400,000	215,000
France	109,000	/	21,000	/	/	171,000	90,000	109,000	50,000	95,000
Germany	4,332,000	/	307,000	/	1,450,000	1,313,000	1,450,000	4,332,000	4,300,000	4,821,000
Ireland	316,000	250,000	8,000	/	272,000	262,000	272,000	316,000	300,000	27,000
Luxembourg	87,000	/	/	/	/	/	/	87,000	100,000	65,000
Netherlands	3,818,000	530,000	665,000	92,000	47,000	2,205,000	47,000	3,818,000	3,700,000	3,338,000
Norway	383,000	/	145,000	8,000	25,000	318,000	25,000	383,000	400,000	182,000
Spain	218,000	/	/	/	/	/	/	293,000	32,000	60,000
Sweden	620,000	101,000[a]	63,000	90,000	40,000	738,000	40,000	620,000	525,000	619,000
Switzerland	1,468,000	/	11,000	/	/	179,000	18,000	1,468,000	1,200,000	727,000
United Kingdom	302,000	138,000	36,000	/	183,000	191,000	207,000	302,000	180,000	13,000
Total distribution	**14,669,000**	**1,019,000**	**2,246,000**	**292,000**	**2,018,000**	**8,317,000**	**2,152,000**	**14,744,000**	**13,902,000**	**12,063,000**

Sources: *C&SE*, February 1989, pp.72–3 and August 1989, pp.68–9.

[a] Figure represents Scandinavia.

Data conventions: '/': not applicable.

expanded to Bauer, Burda, Holtzbrinck and Springer, among others. The news was produced by Aktuell Presse Fernsehen, a group that brought together around 150 newspapers. The news bulletins presented in a relaxed style were well received but the schedule lacked coherence: all ten partners of Sat1 had decided to retain their independence and remain responsible for the programming of their own weekly slot.[61]

The scheduling problems were resolved with a series of reshuffles that progressively replaced informative programmes with PKS's large quantities of American movies and TV series, but the volatile nature of the organizational arrangements caught up with the channel. In 1989 Kirch attempted to take over the station and the ensuing battle between the film magnate and the opposition, led by the Axel Springer group, nearly brought the channel down. By now Sat1 had achieved 17.5 per cent of audience share, just behind ARD but ahead of RTL Plus, its main commercial rival. The warring parties had too much to lose and found an arrangement that accommodated Kirch's dominance.

From Germany, Sat1 became available via satellite in Austria in 1986 and in Switzerland the following year. By 1992, the year it launched separate programming windows for these two countries, it had established 800,000 connections in Austria and 730,000 in Switzerland, a significant proportion of TV households in two relatively small markets (Table 2.2).[62]

The origin of RTL Plus also goes back to 1984. After its success in Belgium with RTL TVi, an offshoot of RTL's original francophone service (Chapter 1), CLT formed a joint venture with Bertelsmann in 1984 to launch RTL Plus in Germany. At first, RTL Plus broadcast over-the-air from Luxembourg to the Saarland, Rheinland-Pfalz and Nordrhein-Westfalen, before expanding its reach via ECS 1 in August 1985. It was given terrestrial frequencies by the German authorities in 1988, following which the channel reached profitability. The programming strategy of Helmut Thoma, RTL's CEO, was simple: to adapt US networks' formats to the German market. It paid off in 1993 when RTL Television – RTL Plus's new name – became Germany's most-watched channel. In Austria and Switzerland the station established half-a-million and one million connections respectively by 1990, and doubled its reach in each country by the mid-1990s (Table 2.2).[63]

Two other German channels gained some distribution across borders. Eureka, a general entertainment station based in Munich, was renamed Pro 7 (or ProSieben) when Gerhard Ackermann sold 49 per cent of his shares to the Kirch family early in 1989. Tele 5 was Germany's fourth commercial channel and was launched with the backing of Silvio Berlusconi in August 1987.[64]

In the early 1990s all these channels transmitted from German and European broadcast satellites (DFS Kopernicus, TV Sat 2 and Astra 1A) – in addition to German terrestrial relays – and were available across Europe. However, only two stations developed a multi-territory strategy in the German-speaking market: ProSieben and Sat1 localized their satellite feeds in Austria and Switzerland, where they launched daily programming windows that exist to this day. (Today both stations are part of the ProSiebenSat.1 Group.) RTL opened up a Swiss advertising window in January 1993 but abandoned the project and subsequently remained faithful to the principle of country-specific channels.

Scandinavia

The definition of a Scandinavian market was initially problematic. Was there enough cultural similarity and economic integration among the Nordic countries to justify a pan-Scandic strategy? Question marks arose over the degree of commonality between languages spoken in Sweden, Norway and Denmark. In the two smaller countries, there were concerns about losing local identity to a regional whole such as Scandinavia.[65] However, one Swedish entrepreneur did more than anybody else to prove the doubters wrong: Jan H. Stenbeck.

Kinnevik was an industrial conglomerate established in 1936 with a wide range of interests that spanned activities such as steel and iron production, farming, forestry, real estate, transportation and insurance. When Stenbeck took control of the family business in 1977 he further diversified the group into media and telecommunications. He could see a huge opportunity that was too good to miss: Sweden, but also Norway and Denmark – a combined market of 18 million people – were without commercial channels and television advertising. In 1986 Stenbeck established ScanSat, a wholly owned Kinnevik subsidiary, headquartered in London and headed by Jan Steinmann, in order to oversee the group's television activities. On 31 December 1987 the company launched TV3 from Camden, North London, using an Intelsat satellite to reach Scandinavia, transferring to Astra 1A as soon as it became available. The London uplink offered many advantages, not least the ability of circumventing Swedish legislation that banned advertising-supported channels. From the start the channel was a multi-lingual service offering programmes in any of Scandinavia's three languages with subtitles for the other two.[66]

TV3 was a great success with audiences and advertisers. It attracted nearly £10 million in advertising revenue in its first year and its distribution was

Table 2.2: Distribution of single-linguistic area channels, December 1992 (in number of connected households)

	3Sat	Pro 7	RTL Plus[a]	Sat1	SVT1, 2	Tele 5	TV3	TV4[b]	TV1000
Austria	800,000	750,000	570,000	800,000	/	900,000	/	/	/
Denmark	/	620,000	/	/	/	/	920,000	/	11,000
Finland	/	/	/	/	500,000	/	/	/	/
Germany	11,500,000	16,000,000	11,600,000	11,000,000	/	10,690,000	/	/	/
Norway	/	/	/	/	430,000	/	700,000	174,000	50,000
Sweden	/	/	/	/	/	/	2,001,000	1,476,000	240,000
Switzerland	1,000,000	730,000	1,400,000	730,000	/	/	/	/	/
Total distribution	13,300,000	18,100,000	13,570,000	12,530,000	930,000	11,590,000	3,621,000	1,650,000	306,000

Source: CG-SE, December 1992, pp.56–7.
[a]Figures for September 1992.
[b]Figures for September 1992.
Data conventions: '/': not applicable.

immediately much wider than that of pan-European channels in Scandinavia. The channel hit two million connections by the end of 1989 and 3.5 million by the end of 1992 (Table 2.2). TV3's impact in Scandinavia was not confined to commercial success since it forced the Swedish government to adapt its broadcasting policy and authorize television advertising.[67]

The group would eventually launch other free-to-air commercial channels, such as TV4 and TV6, but first it diversified into pay-television. As the largest private investor in the Société Européenne des Satellites (Chapter 4), Kinnevik had a second transponder to fill on Astra 1A and launched TV1000 on 27 August 1989. It was a premium channel charging the equivalent of £10 per month, with programming similar to that of HBO in the United States mixing TV series, movies and sports. It reached 300,000 subscribers in 1992, half the number of its more established competitor, FilmNet (Table 2.2).[68]

TV1000 was a transformative project for Kinnevik and a new subsidiary Viasat was formed in 1989, with the responsibility of managing the group's fledgling pay-TV interests. In 1994 Kinnevik brought all its media concerns under one roof, forming the Modern Times Group (MTG), which was floated three years later on the New York and Stockholm stock exchanges. MTG built up its own direct-to-home satellite platforms in the Nordic region and the Baltic states under the Viasat brand (Chapter 4). It expanded the TV1000 offering to six channels (e.g. Action, Classic, Family, Nordic) and launched six Viasat-branded stations (Viasat Sport, Crime, Nature, Explorer, History and Music). All these are multi-territory channels that are present across the Nordic region and several other markets in Europe.[69]

Another cross-border venture was the Nordic Channel, a small station launched in 1989 by a husband and wife who had gained experience at SVT, the Swedish public broadcaster. The majority shareholder was Matts Carlgren, a timber producer who controlled the channel through his production company, Karissima. Nordic was essentially a Swedish station but it gained a foothold in Denmark, Finland and Norway in the early 1990s. It was bought by a Luxembourg-based company called Scandinavian Broadcasting System – today part of ProSiebenSat.1 – towards the end of 1991, who brought it back to Sweden.[70]

Like ARD in the German-speaking territories, Sweden's public broadcaster SVT reached beyond its home market. Following Norway, it established distribution in Finland and Denmark during the first half of the 1990s, reaching a combined 1.8 million homes in these three countries by 1996, nearly half its total cable and satellite distribution.[71]

CHAPTER 3

THE END OF A CHIMERA?

By the early 1990s international TV channels were no longer seen as having much future in European broadcasting. Paul Barker and Tim Westcott summed up the prevalent mood in the industry when they stated:

> With pan-European television an idea that has gone out of fashion, Europe remains a fragmented market for satellite television, in which the experience of the past few years has tended to enhance rather than dissolve boundaries between national and language markets.[1]

Many pan-European channels had failed: Sky Channel (1983–9), Music Box (1984–6), Screensport (1984–93) and Lifestyle (1985–93), Europa (1985–6), the Arts Channel (1985–9), ITV's Super Channel (1987–8) and the European Business Channel (1989–90) were the most prominent names in a list of casualties that included many smaller ventures and stillborn projects. Thorn EMI, the ITV companies, British Telecom, WH Smith and News International were among those investors that had lost money in pan-European television.

Successive pan-European audience surveys stubbornly pointed to the evidence: faced with increasing competition from commercial stations targeting single territories or language-specific markets, the ratings of English-language channels remained way below those of national channels. Even MTV, one of the few international stations seen as a success, was assailed by emerging local rivals such as France's MCM and Germany's VIVA.[2]

The two leaders of the European pay-TV industry were shunning international feeds altogether in favour of national channels. Once News International retreated to Britain and got underway a satellite platform serving a single market audience, profits quickly followed.[3] On the continent Canal Plus, which launched in France in 1984, dominated pay-TV television. It was expanding from market to market by establishing local channels with ad-hoc partners (Chapters 8 and 10). The company was recording a profit and the European expansion of André Rousselet's group was soon compared to Napoleon's *grande armée*.[4] For once, industry analysts agreed, transnational satellite television had little prospect on the continent.[5] Several factors explain the difficulties encountered by European television until the mid-1990s.

A RESTRICTED RECEPTION UNIVERSE

At the root of the problem was the size of the reception universe that international TV channels tried to reach. Direct-to-home satellite reception was still reserved for a few boffins and transnational stations were restricted to the cable market. In the 1980s this market was confined to Northern Europe and essentially comprised Austria, Belgium, Britain, France, Germany, Luxembourg, the Netherlands (for a long time the biggest cable market in Europe), Switzerland and Scandinavia. In two key territories, France and Britain, the number of cable connections did not exceed a few hundred thousand because both countries messed up their cable development plans. (The British government was not interested in supporting cable companies and the French one nearly killed the industry by providing help but trying to control it.)

All told, 25 million European homes were connected to cable in 1991, a fraction of the 132 million TV households in Western Europe.[6] In addition, not all cable systems carried cross-border TV channels. Before the publication of industry directories, international broadcasters had to root out from some obscure place cable operators susceptible to carrying their channels. As Richard Wolfe, developing the distribution network of Music Box in Europe at the time, remembers:

> There was no infrastructure in each of the markets for soliciting the cable operators. Barclay [Duston] and I would traipse around the medium-sized towns of Belgium, Holland and Switzerland in a rented car. In some cases we would have a phone number of the local electricity company (in many cases the same as the cable operator) but sometimes we had nothing. On arriving at such a town we would follow the pylons to the main switching site or look for the gas tanks of the local utility combine. Sure enough, in a Portakabin in the gas works we would find some charming local employee who was Mr Cable Operator. Our war-cry was 'give us a channel'; more often than not, he did so.[7]

The cable industry was very fragmented and this operation had to be repeated many times to cover a territory. All early international stations built up their continental distribution in pretty much the same manner. Furthermore, the capacity of analogue networks was limited to between 18 and 24 channels. At first, cable providers welcomed new broadcasters with open arms but by the late 1980s they were in a position to cherry-pick the stations they wished to carry, making it even more difficult for international TV channels to secure access on their system.[8] Thus the reception universe – let alone the actual viewership – was far too small to bring a decent amount of carriage fees and was too thinly spread across Europe to attract advertising. Under these conditions Sky Channel did well to reach a peak distribution of 15 million connections, a record for the 1980s (Table 2.1).[9]

A RESTRICTIVE LEGAL FRAMEWORK

When international TV stations began to broadcast they faced a restrictive legal environment. Before the movement towards deregulation and liberalization gathered pace in Europe, legislation contained many entrenched monopolies and reflected protectionist policies. In addition, the pace of technological progress was such that policy makers and legislators needed time to adapt to existing regulations.

In the early 1980s commercial television was still forbidden in most European countries. Britain's ITV, Luxembourg's RTL and Monaco's Télé-Monte Carlo (TMC) were the notable exceptions. It was a time when political and cultural elites expected public broadcasting to contribute to the formation of the national culture. They were designed to uphold the nation's imagined cultural boundaries and were central to the modernist intent of engineering a national identity and consciousness.[10] State broadcasting monopolies, enshrined in the law books of most European nations, were in place to ensure that nobody would interfere with this design.

When satellite television developed in Europe, the predominant fear was that it would help the private sector, and multinational media corporations in particular, to get a foothold in national markets and thus adulterate those carefully crafted national identities.[11] Cable operators were occasionally prevented by their governments from carrying 'foreign' satellite feeds on their systems. In Belgium, an official sealed the TV mast of a cable operator in a vain attempt to interrupt the TV signal.[12] Governments opened up to commercial television when they realized that the potent combination of commerce and technology was unstoppable. By the end of the 1980s commercial satellite television was generally accepted in Europe – sometimes after lengthy court battles – but that did not stop some local authorities and governments from raising other obstacles against foreign broadcasters. International broadcasting was not yet completely legal, but the debate that would lead to the European Community's Television Without Frontiers Directive (TVWF) a few years later had begun (see below).[13]

There can be no doubt about the role played by international broadcasters in the deregulation process. Liberalization was bound to happen but transfrontier stations brutally confronted governments with the issue and forced the pace of the movement. Kinnevik and RTL were among the companies who used 'flags of convenience' to broadcast as out-of-country channels and circumvent local regulations in Scandinavia, Germany and the Netherlands.[14] Faced with the giant footprints of communications satellites, national borders were beginning to look fragile and superfluous.

Although European markets progressively opened up, many obstacles remained for international broadcasters. Before the implementation of the 1989 TVWF Directive, international TV channels needed to go through a lengthy process of authorization with governments. Officials rarely knew how to deal with these requests and passed them from one ministry to another. Once the appropriate department had been pinned down and assuaged, the consent of the national PTT operator was also needed to downlink the signal.[15]

For the first few years, private satellite reception was illegal without a PTT licence. Once in 1984 Televerket, the Norwegian PTT, stopped a signal downlink from exhibitors at a trade fair because they did not have the required authorization. Regulation changed across Europe in 1985, paving the way for private satellite TV reception.[16]

Local authorities could complicate the matter further. On the continent, municipalities frequently owned the cable networks they had installed or subsidized – even when they were run by private companies – and could decide what they carried. Many of them paid little attention as long as satellite channels were controlled by a few British eccentrics or low-profile companies. When someone like Murdoch came knocking on their door politics kicked in and some councils began to have second thoughts. Conservative municipalities in Bavaria objected to Sky's fare of wrestling and pop music; left-wing councils in the Netherlands objected to Murdoch's political outlook. Channels such as Discovery and MTV ran into similar problems, reflecting the difficulty of the situation when satellite television's legality had not yet been fully ascertained.

THE BATTLE FOR NEIGHBOURING RIGHTS AND COPYRIGHT

Issues surrounding rights were among the most problematic for the cable and satellite TV industry in the 1980s. Two distinct types of rights must be distinguished: the neighbouring rights are held by performers such as actors, authors, composers and photographers (thus also called performing rights), while the main copyright is usually held by producers and distributors of audiovisual works. Rights agreements determine where, when and how many times a programme can be shown and can have a determining influence on the fate of a channel.

The international nature of cable and satellite broadcasting created a complex range of issues that took years of court battles and jurisprudence to solve. At first, cable operators rejected demands for rights clearance from rights holders. They argued that cable was only a technical support for retransmission and that rights holders would be paid twice if they acceded to their demands. In the early 1980s, in a court case opposing Hollywood majors and the Dutch Cinema Association to the cable operator of a Dutch town (Amstelveen), the Dutch Supreme Court decreed that cable retransmission constituted a new public communication and thus was subject to rights obligations. Similar verdicts were delivered across Europe. It was ruled that cable operators would have to seek agreements with rights holders' professional associations and collecting societies, which had been formed precisely to help cable companies identify and remunerate them. Performing rights were collected by the local societies who would retain a fee and retrocede the rest to the (usually foreign) rights owners. Copyright issues began to be handled by a producers' international organization in 1981, the Geneva-based AGICOA.[17]

The first satellite TV channels were caught up in several controversies. In November 1983, as France's president François Mitterrand was visiting the Netherlands, the Amsterdam cable operator KTA thoughtfully installed TV5 on its system. Before transmissions had even started, the Dutch performing rights society (Bureau voor Muziek Auteursrecht – BUMA) brought KTA to court, arguing that the cable company was acting like a publisher and therefore had to pay music copyright fees for TV5 broadcast in the Netherlands. KTA retorted that TV5 had already paid fees to the French rights society (Société des Auteurs, Compositeurs et Editeurs de Musique – SACEM), who did not object to retransmission in the Netherlands. Before the dispute was settled the affair had rung alarm bells at Sky. It became one of the first international stations to sign a series of agreements with performing rights societies across Europe, starting with the Netherlands, Belgium, Austria and Switzerland.[18]

The affair illustrated the need to establish a protocol for rights agreements in Europe. The first collective arrangement was signed in Belgium in 1984. The contract involved three parties: the professional association that represented Belgium's 40 cable operators (RTB), the broadcasters whose signal they retransmitted, and two collecting societies acting for the rights owners. Holders of performing rights were represented by the Belgian performing rights society (Société Belge des Auteurs, Compositeurs et Editeurs de Musique – SABEM) and copyright owners were represented by AGICOA.[19] RTB agreed to retrocede 15 per cent of its income (about £13 million) to foreign rights holders. Fifty-four per cent was split between SABEM and AGICOA and the rest was shared among broadcasters from five countries. Of the remaining 46 per cent, the British share (which covered BBC1, BBC2 and ITV) amounted to 25 per cent. The BBC, for instance, having received two-thirds of this 25 per cent, could claim to have obtained '66% of 25% of 46% of 15%' for the Belgian relay of its two channels, or about £1 million.[20] Similar agreements were reached across Europe, starting with the Netherlands the following year, but uncertainties over rights remained.

Problems with performing rights agreements compounded the difficulties of several satellite channels. ITV and the BBC, who both supplied programming to Super, had signed agreements with Equity, the actors' union in Britain. Equity fretted over the amount of repeat programming and the impact it could have on its members' employment. The original contracts were only for a certain number of showings and a certain number of territories. When Super was about to begin transmissions, the broadcasters realized that either they did not have the European rights or, when they had the rights, it would cost them a fortune to allow the programme to be transmitted across the continent. As a result, both ITV and the BBC were pulling out programmes from Super's schedule at the last minute and the channel never really lived up to its promise of showcasing the 'best of British' programming.[21]

Another clause in the small print of the contract between Equity and the two broadcasters stipulated that lead actors' consent had to be given for all repeat broadcasts. If any one of them refused, the programme could not be shown. This added to Super's woes because as a consultant later explained: 'If they [the actors] had appeared years ago in *Doctor Who* as a disfigured alien they weren't very keen.'[22]

Rights acquisitions by satellite broadcasters were hampered until the legal issues surrounding rights were clarified by the 1993 SatCab Directive (Chapter 4). Until then, the Hollywood majors had a 'policy of not selling to TV channels which deliberately cross frontiers'.[23] The exception was Paramount, who signed a deal with Sky in October 1983 only because – like Murdoch – one of their executives was Australian and he decided to use Sky's pan-European feed to showcase Paramount products and re-run programmes they could no longer sell anyway.[24]

The structure of the film rights market also went against satellite broadcasters. In order to maximize their earnings the American movie studios sold their rights to agents who acquired them for anything from a single territory to a whole region. These agents retailed the rights market by market, with the rights ending up in different hands in different countries. Rights became locked in a tangled web of contracts and it was virtually impossible for a satellite broadcaster to obtain rights clearance across Europe (see also Chapters 4 and 11). A particular stumbling block was Germany where the leading film distributor, Leo Kirch, used to negotiate exclusive rights for his stations directly from Hollywood studios. Nothing could be transmitted across Europe if it could be picked up in Germany because Kirch had the rights, killing off in one stroke the ability to transmit Hollywood programmes by satellite.[25]

THE DEARTH OF THE PAN-EUROPEAN ADVERTISING MARKET

When the first satellite TV stations launched in Europe there was an unsated demand for advertising airtime. Approximately 27 channels accepted commercials in Europe in 1984 and nearly all were in the hands of public service broadcasters who doled them out in driblets. Four countries banned advertising altogether: Belgium, Denmark, Norway and Sweden. An estimate placed the demand for airtime at twice the amount that was on offer.[26]

When satellite channels first appeared, advertisers held on to them like a life raft. The first commercial was booked by Unilever for Impulse deodorant on Haynes' Satellite Television, followed by multinationals ranging from Coca-Cola and Philips to Shell and Kellogg. It quickly became apparent to these companies that pan-European television was a medium particularly ill-suited to advertising FMCGs (fast-moving consumer goods). Most multinationals did not return to international TV stations, who ultimately saw very little of their advertising money. Research in 1988 estimated that the pan-European TV advertising market was the equivalent of 1.5 per cent of the British market or – according to a 1991 study – about the combined advertising revenue of ITV and Channel 4 for a month.[27]

Three advertising agencies were initially interested in pan-European television: Foot, Cone & Belding (today Draftfcb), McCann Erickson and J. Walter Thompson. They were all quick to spot a range of issues. Too few companies had a need for the pan-European coverage offered by channels like Sky and Super. Brand names changed across the continent, as did packaging and product cycle. Most multinationals devolved marketing to their local affiliates, who passed on the advertising budget to a local agency. Very few campaigns were suitable for international treatment, and to place a message on pan-European television an advertising agency had to coordinate marketing strategies across Europe. This localized marketing structure was typically adopted by two big advertising spenders, Nestlé and Unilever, and they had practically no means of running a centralized advertising campaign.[28] As Toby Syfret, former head of new media research at J. Walter Thompson and Ogilvy & Mather, summarized:

> Either budgets allocated to pan-European broadcasts were constrained by the client's difficulty in securing a central budget; or proposals that looked good were not acted upon because the client had no mechanism for taking a central decision; or local agency opposition defeated a consensus. From the client angle, nothing would seem to work worse than the quite common practice of going cap in hand to local offices in order to stump up their contributions. Some want the campaign, others are sure to prefer to invest in domestic media, quite possibly urged on by the local agency, which does not want to see part of its natural budget disappear, and so on. The end result is frustration for all concerned.[29]

Satellite channels did not have the flexibility of offering local advertising windows (Chapter 5). Clients could not block out a country where, for instance, their product had yet to be introduced. Pan-regional coverage was a waste if they were present in only a handful of territories. The distribution of audiences was another matter for concern. As far as they could be measured, satellite channels reached vastly different audiences in both size and demographics from one country to another. A channel could reach a young audience in high numbers in a country like the Netherlands and an older audience in fewer numbers in Germany, where cable penetration was not as extensive.[30]

Political and cultural issues were also a matter of concern. Advertising regulations differed markedly from country to country. Some banned advertising for children and others banned children in commercials.[31] While advertising for tobacco was prohibited everywhere, a range of products such as alcohol faced a variety of legal restrictions. When advertising itself was not regulated, consumer markets for products such as pharmaceuticals differed from country to country.

These impediments to pan-European marketing campaigns restricted the pool of international advertisers to well below the 200 or so multinationals that possessed international brands.[32] These limitations resulted in a soft market for pan-European TV advertising that explains many of the financial difficulties facing satellite channels in the 1980s.

SPREADING RISKS BUT CREATING PROBLEMS: CONSORTIUM BROADCASTING

The early era of transfrontier television was plagued by a type of ownership structure that often resulted in 'consortium broadcasting', as the phenomenon may be called. Investing in cable and satellite television entailed costs and risks that few companies were willing to take alone and thus most early cross-border TV channels involved consortia of shareholders. Consortium members participated in strategic decisions and sometimes collaborated in day-to-day management. Public broadcasters joined forces for TV5, 3Sat and Europa. Joint ventures were behind most commercial channels, notably Super Channel, all the Thorn EMI and WHSTV stations and even MTV until Viacom bought out its partners (Chapter 2). Eurosport – and EuroNews at a later stage (Chapter 6) – were two cases of collaboration between public and commercial broadcasters.

The problem with joint ventures is that they often themselves became the prime source of risk. Not all consortium members have the same objectives, resources, expertise, managerial culture and organizational heritage. Conflicts among members arose regularly and the management was unable to implement a plan based on a long-term strategy. When a key shareholder pulled out, it destabilized the whole enterprise. Joint ventures tended to be risk-averse in an industry that demands a high dose of calculated risk taking. The advantages of a simplified ownership structure were highlighted by Robert Thomson, a senior executive at TCI (the backbone of today's Liberty Global), in the following terms:

> You need an ownership structure that can give you owners who are willing to take risks and who don't blink. In our company there is a control group which owns a majority of the voting shares. We don't have to look over our shoulders and worry about take-over artists or focus on short-term profit. We are able to take the risks we need to.[33]

It is no coincidence that as the industry matured, consortium broadcasting declined to become a rare form of ownership. Today, most cross-border TV channels are controlled by a single or dominant shareholder, enabling a clear and independent management structure and delivering better entrepreneurship (Table 8.3).

THE HOUSE THAT RUPERT BUILT

The commercial hitches of the early transnational TV channels should not detract from their many achievements. They were pioneers in many ways and brought about a series of innovations in the European television industry. Sky introduced the American technique of horizontal programming consisting of scheduling the same show, TV series or type of programme every day or every week at the same time.[34] This technique brings coherence and clarity to a channel and is today commonly used throughout Europe.

International broadcasters brought a new business model to Europe in low-cost television. They may not have had the programming obligations of public service broadcasting, relying heavily on cheap imports, but they also knew that a schedule cannot be built solely around acquisitions and thus produced their own programmes. The solution for stations like Music Box, The Children's Channel and Sky was to produce at a fraction of the cost of their better-heeled rivals and make programmes for a few hundred pounds an hour. The cheap production costs may have been reflected in the range and quality of programming but satellite channels had very low overheads. While the average public service broadcaster typically employed well above 10,000 people, Murdoch – the biggest employer in the satellite business – had 150 people working for him at Sky.

Satellite broadcasters have been a major force in Europe's changing television landscape. They introduced competition when state broadcasters did not want any, prompting the latter to launch a massive rearguard action to repel the newcomers. A period of intense lobbying began in national parliaments and Brussels, coinciding with the drafting of TVWF Directive, with some public broadcasters allegedly spending more on legal fees than satellite broadcasters did on their entire operation.

Satellite broadcasters offered choice when viewers had none. At a time when state broadcasting appeared to be more interested in pandering to politicians and obeying the diktats of the local cultural elite, public satisfaction did not figure high on their list of priorities. They neglected daytime scheduling and entire sections of the population, e.g. children and youngsters. When five public broadcasters tested their programming philosophy with Europa, none of them had noticed that most Europeans' idea of a relaxing evening in front of their TV set did not extend to Bulgarian opera and Russian ballet. While state broadcasting was dabbling with concepts such as national identity and social cohesion, satellite focused on serving TV viewers. By being more attuned to people's needs, satellite TV channels helped transform a business centred on the nation-state into a more market-friendly industry.

Unsurprisingly, satellite television was not to everybody's taste. The guardians of European culture, a formidable alliance comprising 'moral crusaders, government quangos and self-interested national broadcasters', raised arms at once against the new channels.[35] Virulent press campaigns were waged against satellite broadcasters accusing them of bringing 'Coca-Cola culture' into Europe and spreading moral filth. Melvyn Bragg, pundit and presenter of arts programme *The South Bank Show*, said at the time:

> Soon the satellites will begin bombing us with soft porn and vile action of all sorts, while the world's media megalomaniacs will be able to beam their 'messages' into our garden furniture dishes.[36]

Since Northcliffe, the cultural elite has been learning to live with the popular press and today they are learning to live with cable and satellite television, having failed to spread moral panic. Meanwhile the public, hungry for alternatives, has welcomed the new broadcasting.

PART TWO

THE COMING OF AGE OF PAN-EUROPEAN TELEVISION

CHAPTER 4

USHERING IN A NEW ERA: EUROPEAN REGULATION AND SATELLITE TECHNOLOGY

The obituary of transfrontier broadcasting was written prematurely. Over the course of the 1990s the obstacles that nearly brought down international channels began to recede. The satellite TV industry matured and consolidated. Newcomers who had tried to enter the television industry via the pan-European route had left the market. The broadcasters who persevered learned from their mistakes and redesigned their channels. Above all, the regulatory, commercial and technological environment that emerged during this decade radically changed the prospects of the pan-European television industry. This chapter focuses on those regulatory and technological elements that enabled cross-border TV channels to thrive in Europe.

THE REGULATORY FRAMEWORK

Twenty years of regulation: from Television Without Frontiers to the Audiovisual Media Services Directive

The European authorities were led to legislate on international TV transmissions because of developments in technology and the emergence of satellite channels. Two European institutions competed for the opportunity to provide the legal framework for satellite television. The Council of Europe proposed a draft convention in 1987. Its text espoused the cause of a protectionist clique that included France, Belgium and Italy, and sought to contain transfrontier broadcasting as much as possible. It was also hostile to commercial interests: it proposed advertising restrictions to within programme breaks (i.e. excluding sponsorship) and a ban on commercials on satellite channels that targeted specific markets (for example, those dubbed in Dutch on Sky Channel). It introduced a quota system which stipulated that at least 60 per cent of broadcasting time had to be devoted to European works and requested that satellite channels comply with the broadcasting standards of the country of reception, in effect putting the fate of cross-border channels in the hands of national governments.[1] Advertisers and commercial broadcasters, led by the ITV network, rang the alarm bells. Timothy Renton, the British broadcasting minister, voiced their concerns and won some concessions that appeared in the final draft of the Convention.[2]

Parallel to the Council of Europe's attempts to curb the fledgling industry, the European Commission had renewed its own earlier efforts to produce a broadcasting directive. The Television Without Frontiers Green Paper was published in 1984 and a draft directive followed in May 1986. Long and bitter negotiations took place for three-and-a-half years, opposing a tiny group of liberal-minded countries led by Britain against the larger protectionist camp headed by France. The Directive 89/552/EEC was finally signed by the foreign ministers of the European Union's Member States at a meeting in Paris on 3 October 1989. Although the Directive shared a number of clauses with the Convention, the Commission's text was more liberal than the Council's. The Commission worked under the guidance of previous laws that sought to establish a single market in Europe, including the 1957 Treaty of Rome and the 1986 Single European Act. The Commission's overall aim was to encourage the free flow of cable and satellite channels in Europe and ultimately form a common market for broadcasting.

Effective lobbying from the advertising industry and commercial broadcasters (united under the aegis of the Association of Commercial Television – ACT) managed to remove the most stringent advertising rules. Included at the insistence of the British representatives was a proviso that took the sting out of the quota system. Article 4 paragraph 1 stipulates that broadcasters have to reserve 'a majority proportion of their transmission time' for European works, but only '*where practicable and by appropriate means*'. The French reluctance to drop their demand for compulsory quotas was overridden by their desire to see the directive adopted under their presidency of the European Union.[3] In effect, the practicality clause enabled cross-border TV channels to broadcast across Europe on the simple promise to work towards the 50 per cent target, which some have yet to reach. Above all, Article 2 paragraph 2 established the legality of transfrontier broadcasting in Europe by stipulating that:

Member States shall ensure freedom of reception and shall not restrict retransmission on their territory of television broadcasts from other Member States for reasons which fall within the fields coordinated by this Directive.

Transmissions can only be suspended by a Member State when a channel 'seriously and gravely infringes' upon those provisions that protect minors and prohibit the 'incitement of hatred on grounds of race, sex, religion or nationality' (Article 2 paragraph 2a and Article 22). The text established the prevalence of the channel's country of origin for jurisdiction purposes, and in practice it enabled broadcasters to transmit a signal across Europe holding a single licence issued by the country in which they are based. The TVWF Directive, implemented in 1991, was ground-breaking in as much as it was liberal in character and was the world's first international agreement on transfrontier broadcasting.[4]

The 1989 Directive led to problems of application, most notably concerning the country of jurisdiction. In the mid-1990s several court cases arose when a few regulatory authorities prohibited certain cross-border channels from transmitting on their local cable systems. An argument regularly put forward was that these broadcasters were established in another Member State with the sole aim of circumventing the legislation of the country of reception.

The 1989 piece of legislation was revised in 1997 and Directive 97/36/EC set to clarify the country of jurisdiction. Jurisprudence having established that 'a Member State that doubts the correct control of the law by the host Member State may take that state to the Court of Justice of the European Communities for violation of the Directive', the 1997 Directive confirmed the country of origin as the place of jurisdiction but clarified the criteria of establishment.[5] Article 2 paragraph 3b stipulates that

if a broadcaster has its head office in one Member State but editorial decisions on programme schedules are taken in another Member State, it shall be deemed to be established in the Member State where a significant part of the workforce involved in the pursuit of the television broadcasting activity operates.

Nikolchev and Lange, two legal analysts, observed that these clarifications – known as the principle of jurisdiction – failed to solve jurisdictional conflicts since 'national laws will continue to give expression to different standards and as a result broadcasters will continue to have an incentive for *forum shopping*'.[6]

The second revision of the TVWF Directive was initiated in 2003 by public consultation to extend its scope to online and non-linear audiovisual services. Renamed the Audiovisual Media Services Directive for the occasion (AVMS), the new legislative text was approved by the European Parliament on 29 November 2007. For the first time product placement in films, series, sports and light entertainment programming was authorized, although Member States could opt out. Media service providers were encouraged to develop their own codes of conduct regarding food advertising in programmes aimed at children. Broadcasting quotas remained unchanged and were extended to on-demand services.

After the 2003 initiative, the protectionist Member States seized the opportunity offered by the consultation period to contest the principle of the country of origin as sole place of jurisdiction. Had several of them succeeded in regulating a transfrontier audiovisual service, this would have severely restrained the activities of cross-border TV channels and may have spelt the end for the PETV industry. Despite their sustained efforts, the new legislative act maintained the rule of one place of jurisdiction and preserved the freedom to provide TV services across borders. However, it added a supplementary derogation if it could be proven that a broadcaster had targeted a Member State and established itself in another Member State 'in order to circumvent the stricter rules [. . .] which would be applicable to it if it were established within the first Member State' (Article 3 paragraph 3b). It also complemented infringements to Article 22 of the 1989 Directive with a series of provisions pertaining to respect for human dignity, protection of the environment and public health (Article 3e).

The 'SatCab' Directive

The more technical aspects of transfrontier satellite broadcasting and cable retransmission were dealt with by another directive. Satellite broadcasting was hampered by copyright issues since programme rights had to be secured in each and every country touched by a satellite's footprint. Cable operators had to gain rights clearance with so many rights holders that many were overlooked and did not receive appropriate remuneration for the retransmission of their works. Some operators decided simply to ignore rights owners altogether, who were frustrated by unpaid fees. Conversely, the holders of neighbouring rights, such as actors, had the ability to block entire European transmissions.

The European authorities sought to harmonize Europe's copyright regime and set up a pan-regional framework governing the rights and copyright related to satellite broadcasting and cable retransmission with Council Directive 93/83/EEC, which was adopted on 27 September 1993. The 'SatCab' Directive – as it came to be known – built on existing global licensing agreements between cable operators and rights holders that were first signed in Belgium and in the Netherlands in the mid-1980s (Chapter 3).

The copyright management system created by the SatCab Directive involves four partners. *Content creators* can hold various rights attached to a programme, notably copyright if they are the producer and neighbouring rights if they are performers, musicians or script writers. With a few exceptions, they have to assign a *copyright collecting society* to manage these rights on their behalf. *Content aggregators*, such as TV channels or broadcasters, must clear all the rights associated with a programme and negotiate with collecting societies, or sometimes the rights owners themselves. Likewise, *content distributors* (cable operators, satellite platforms, etc.) must acquire all necessary third-party rights involved in the channels and content they retransmit.[7] Broadcasters, for instance, can take part in negotiations involving up to seven issues:

(i) Whether the rights will be transferred to them [the broadcasters] or that they will rather be granted a licence to use the work, performances and/or commercial phonograms for a certain period of time or at a certain number of occasions; (ii) The period of time for which the rights are acquired; (iii) How many times communication to the public will be allowed; (iv) The territories for which the rights are acquired; (v) The exploitation model (Free TV vs. Pay TV vs. on-demand); (vi) the possible exclusivity of the right and (vii) the payment scheme.[8]

The great merit of the SatCab Directive is that it made collective rights management compulsory. Article 9 stipulates that copyright owners and holders of related rights can only 'grant or refuse authorization to a cable operator for a cable retransmission [. . .] through a collecting society'. By preventing rights owners from exercising their rights directly and individually with cable operators, the Directive removed the threat of anyone being able to block the cross-border transmission of a programme. It protected cable operators against individual claims from rights holders, but guaranteed the latter fairer and more widespread distribution of revenue.[9]

Satellite operators did very well out of the Directive since it stipulates that *when a signal is encrypted* they do not need to acquire rights for all the territories touched by the satellite's footprint, only in the country of origin. However, the problem with this piece of legislation is that it is not technology-neutral, as cable operators still need to clear rights for every territory in which they broadcast. The SatCab Directive abided by the famous Article 11bis of the Berne Convention that introduces the concept of retransmission rights: when a cable operator picks a channel and distributes it on its network the Berne Convention defines this as a rebroadcast, i.e. a new communication, and 'when this communication is made by an organization other than the original one', then this organization must obtain rights clearance again.[10] But this is an issue of greater relevance for national TV channels that are rebroadcast in several territories than for pan-European TV channels. In principle, broadcasters like Discovery or Eurosport acquire rights for all the territories they need at the outset.

Both the TVWF/AVMS and the SatCab Directives helped the progress of international broadcasting in Europe. In their great wisdom, the European authorities refrained from the temptation to reinvent the wheel and rather built upon the practices and agreements prevailing in the pan-European television industry.[11] These directives did not iron out all the problems related to international audiovisual services: Europe's television market is still fragmented and Europe's copyright regime is far from being harmonized.[12] However, European regulation managed to remove legal uncertainties and close up the most glaring loopholes. Uniquely in the world, many countries have found a common ground on transfrontier broadcasting and have created a regulatory framework that 27 governments must abide by.

EXPANSION OF THE RECEPTION UNIVERSE

A few other factors came to the rescue of the PETV industry in the 1990s, not least the exponential growth in the number of households connected to cable and satellite. Although 18 million households were connected to cable in 1989, this had grown to 95 million with access to either cable or satellite ten years later. By 2006, 138 million homes across 32 countries in Eastern and Western Europe could watch cable or satellite channels (Table 4.1).[13]

Table 4.1: Cable and satellite TV market in Europe, 2006 (in millions of households)

	TV Households	Cable/Satellite
Western Europe	164.7	97.7
Eastern Europe	114.4	40.5
Total	**279.0**	**138.1**

Source: Eutelsat.

This expansion considerably enlarged the *reception universe* of cross-border TV channels. In the constricted European reception universe of the 1980s, Sky Channel did well to reach 15 million homes. The first transnational TV network to break through the 100 million mark was MTV in 2004. By 2007, five cross-border TV channels reached an excess of 100 million homes and the average distribution of the top 26 transnational TV channels was 57.6 million households (Table 7.1).

Several factors explain the eightfold increase of cable and satellite homes between 1989 and 2006. The fall of the Iron Curtain and the enlargement of the European Union opened up television markets in Central and Eastern Europe, creating a large European audiovisual *space* (not market) of 279 million TV households. By 2006, 114 million of these homes were in the former communist countries, of which 40 million had access to cable and satellite. The gap between the total number of TV households and those connected to cable and satellite has constantly narrowed over the years. Table 4.1 shows that in 2006 about half of European homes were able to receive cable and/or satellite channels. Finally, satellite technology came into play. Communications satellites transformed the distribution and reception of TV channels with their ability to broadcast thousands of channels from a single orbital location and beam them directly into the homes of millions of viewers.

TWINKLE TWINKLE LITTLE STAR: TELEVISION AND THE EUROPEAN SATELLITE INDUSTRY

Eutelsat and the ECS programme

Europe's first satellites were developed by the European Space Agency (ESA), an organization created by the merger of two fledgling European space programmes in 1973. It was ESA's Orbital Test Satellite (OTS), launched in 1978, that relayed the first TV channels over Europe in 1982, starting with Satellite Television plc (Chapter 1). The ESA also instigated the European Communication Satellites programme (ECS), which would eventually be managed by Eutelsat. The latter was an organization purposely founded in 1977 by European states and the PTTs to develop Europe's satellite telecommunications system. Under an agreement signed in 1979, the ESA procured the satellites (the main contractors included British Aerospace, Matra, AEG-Telefunken and Thomson-CSF) and provided the technical expertise to run the system.

The first ECS satellite was launched in June 1983 and was positioned at 13 degrees East, where it became operational in mid-February 1984. The entire capacity of ECS 1 was immediately filled with TV services (Chapter 1). ECS 2 was launched later in 1984 but ECS 3 was lost with the failure of Ariane flight V15, the European launcher, in September 1985. The series was completed with ECS 4 (1987) and ECS 5 (1988).

The ECS series had on average ten operational transponders and could relay up to ten television channels. ECS 1 was entirely devoted to TV signal relays and the other spacecraft were used for a mix of broadcasting and telecommunications purposes. When the capacity on ECS 1 was three times oversubscribed it became clear that video applications would constitute a large slice of the communications satellite market. However, none of the satellites of the ECS family was designed for video distribution. Like the OTS, ECS spacecraft were intended for the relay of telecommunications signals, i.e. *point-to-point applications* such as public telephony and data transmission.

The technology that is sent on board satellites tends to be conservative. Satellite operators adopt a 'safety-first' policy since it is difficult to fix a spacecraft that is on a geostationary orbit 36,000 km from earth. Satellite technology development cycle is slow. Several years elapse between the definition of a satellite programme, the procurement process and negotiations with manufacturers, the design and manufacturing of the spacecraft, to its launch into orbit. Thus the size of the video market caught Eutelsat by surprise and it took the organization nearly a decade to be in a position to respond.

The Hot Bird position and the principle of co-location

Eutelsat began preliminary studies for its second satellite system in 1981. The Eutelsat II series was designed with television distribution in mind and the spacecraft were given more power and greater capacity (16 transponders). Narrow bandwidth and shaped beams were developed to improve ground reception. Eutelsat II F1 was launched in August 1990 (positioned at 13 degrees East), followed by two other craft in January and December 1991 (10 and 16 degrees East) and Eutelsat II F4 in July 1992 (7 degrees East).[14]

The Eutelsat II series was a commercial success with well over 30 channels occupying the transponders of the four spacecraft by 1993. But the scattering of the satellites across four orbital slots was becoming an issue. This was the legacy of the telecommunications era, when a single satellite was positioned at each orbital spot. The problem was made worse by the organizational structure of Eutelsat.

Eutelsat was an intergovernmental organization where much of the power resided in the hands of the 25 Member States and the satellite operator's signatories, the members' national PTTs. The Member States' Assembly of Parties determined the organization's overall policy and the Board of Signatories elected the director general, voted the budget and dealt with procurement and operational issues. Eutelsat had little contact with its customers: signatories leased their share of capacity to clients of their choice and then provided them with services such as uplinking and downlinking, usually at an extortionate rate. Thus the Eutelsat signatories sold capacity on the II series with little coordination and, as a result, the TV channels were relayed from a variety of orbital slots spanning 7 to 16 degrees East.[15]

Some of the organization's clients in the broadcasting industry expressed concerns about this. If their TV channels were to transmit from one slot, cable operators, collective antenna owners (e.g. hotels) and the public could access these stations with a single dish.

An important category of customer began to agitate in this direction and pressed for reform. The Bruges Group brought together five public broadcasters involved in satellite television (Deutsche Welle, EuroNews, RAI, RTP and TV5). The group sent an open letter to Eutelsat director general, Jean Grenier, in February 1993, asking for capacity reservation to be centralized to enable their channels to regroup on 13 degrees East as soon as practically feasible.[16]

Eutelsat listened closely to the group's requirements but had more pressing reasons that compelled them to build up their own position. One of them was spectrum optimization. As the demand for capacity evolved, the staking of satellites on an orbital location began to make sense. Co-location enabled the full frequency band to be optimized and increased the number of channels that could be hosted at one position. From a reception point of view, co-location offered viewers access to a greater variety of TV channels with a dish pointing towards a single position.[17]

Above all, a formidable competitor had emerged in the Société Européenne des Satellites (SES), which in fact was the first to understand the necessity of co-location. Co-location demands the ownership of all frequencies on a position and Pierre Meyrat, SES CEO between 1986 and 1994, sent his own team to the International Telecommunication Union (ITU) negotiations of the late 1980s to make sure that he secured all the frequencies at 19 degrees East. Once these were safe, SES began staking up broadcast satellites at the position, threatening to pull the rug from under Eutelsat's feet in the satellite TV market (see below).[18]

Eutelsat responded by building up the 13 degrees East position with the launch of Eutelsat II F6 in March 1995. The co-location of Hot Bird 1 – as the satellite was named – with Eutelsat II F1 (see above) brought the number of transponders at the same position to 32. Hot Bird 1 enabled the satellite operator to offer extra capacity to existing clients and attract a new clutch of channels including Arte, MTV Europe, TVE Internacional and MCM Euromusique.[19] Hot Bird 2 and Hot Bird 3 followed in November 1996 and September 1997 respectively, and the series had reached Hot Bird 9 in 2008 (below).

It is a convenient position for Eutelsat. In the analogue era the risks of signal interference were significant and the organization controlled the orbital slots on either side of the Hot Bird position (10 and 16 degrees East).[20] Having accumulated so much delay in the video market, Eutelsat was keen to develop a position not too far from the one that SES was building at 19 degrees East in order to facilitate the reception of both signals with a dual-feed receiver (known as Low Noise Block downconverters – LNBs). The proximity of the locations enabled Eutelsat to sponsor the manufacture of the dual-feed LNBs with the aim of facilitating their adoption by consumers. A market for dual-feed LNBs still exists (Chapter 10) but they have not proved as essential to Eutelsat's survival in the video market as was first thought. Hot Bird became a successful location in its own right, even though it did not come soon enough to save the organization disappearing from a market it had helped create.

Société Européenne des Satellites (SES): 'Fernsehen ohne Grenzen'[21]

The remarkable tale of SES contains as many unpredictable twists, heroes and villains as the intertwined storylines of a soap opera. Between 1959 and 1979, the ITU organized a series of conferences that allocated radio frequencies worldwide. The 1977 World Administrative Radio Conference (WARC), which was attended by 111 delegations at the ITU headquarters in Geneva, apportioned the frequency bands assigned to satellite broadcasting (11.7–12.2 GHz for Europe, the Middle East and Africa). Following an approach agreed at previous gatherings, the 1977 WARC allocated frequencies according to an 'a-priori plan' that aimed to give all ITU members 'equitable access' to radio frequencies and geostationary orbital slots. Based on this principle, the WARC 77 agreement attributed to each nation a portion of the geostationary orbit and associated frequencies. European countries received on average enough capacity for five satellite TV channels each.[22]

The government of Luxembourg was looking at alternative sources of revenue and employment for its declining steel industry when it decided to seize the opportunity offered by the WARC 77 allocations. Luxembourg was home to Europe's sole international broadcaster of the pre-satellite era, CLT (Chapter 1), which had the expertise to develop such a project. CLT had started working on LuxSat but came to a standstill because of opposition from France and West Germany, who saw CLT as competition for their national satellite communication systems. Their neighbours also opposed the idea of a commercial – and foreign – broadcaster transmitting over their territory. Luxembourg was powerless to prevent CLT from ditching the project because the majority shareholders were French companies who knew better than to irritate their government.

The Luxembourg government drew up alternative plans. In the summer of 1982 Prime Minister Pierre Werner formed a new team, enlisting help from a veteran of the Nixon administration, Clay 'Tom' Whitehead. As head of the Office of Telecommunications Policy, Whitehead helped formulate the 'open skies' policy that opened up the US satellite market to the private sector in the early 1970s. He was later managing director of Galaxy, the satellite TV distribution division of Hughes Communication, before becoming chief consultant of Luxembourg's new satellite venture, GDL (Grand Duchy of Luxembourg).[23] Other key people included Paul Heinerscheid, who had spearheaded the Duchy's previous satellite effort, Adrien Meisch, Luxembourg's ambassador to the USA, his wife Candace Johnson, Roland de Kergolay, former EU ambassador to the USA, and Meinhard Carstensen, a member of Dresdner Bank's managing board. They were joined in November 1983 by a task force that Werner appointed to lay the financial infrastructure and the project's legal foundation.

It took nearly two years for this force to prepare the ground and register the frequencies at the ITU. Meanwhile, Whitehead's team was touring Europe scouting for clients and backers for GDL. The project was ready by May 1984 and its management was handed to Coronet, a company controlled by Whitehead. However, the venture fell apart a few months later. Whitehead had failed to raise enough capital and it had become apparent to his partners that he was pursuing his own agenda. The authorities of the Duchy felt that he was trying to keep control of the company via complex legal structures and was coveting too much stock. GDL and Coronet parted company in September 1984.[24]

Coronet's problems were compounded by sustained French and German pressure on the Duchy. Realizing that Luxembourg was not giving up, both countries offered Luxembourg participation in their respective satellite systems and France even proposed – for a hefty fee – to host the RTL channels on its future spacecraft, TDF 1. Once this failed, the French resorted to underhand tactics and CLT shareholders went round Europe talking potential investors out of the GDL/Coronet project.[25]

It fell to Jacques Santer, Werner's successor in July 1984, to relaunch Luxembourg's satellite venture. A new team was formed that included several old hands (Corneille Bruck, Raymond Kirsch, de Kergolay) and Daniel Johanneson, the president of Kinnevik (Chapter 2). New financial and legal foundations were arranged and Santer, completing Whitehead's work, was able to finalize agreements with investors. The list of 11 initial backers included Kinnevik and seven banks (notably Dresdner and Deutsche Bank), who were joined at a later stage by three ITV companies, Thames Television, Television South West and Ulster TV. The Société Européenne des Satellites (SES) was incorporated in March 1985, with Bruck as chairman and de Kergolay his deputy. SES had about ten employees at this stage, a fraction of the people who worked at Eutelsat and PTTs' satellite departments. Technical expertise was provided by Telesat of Canada. By the end of the year, when the company placed an order for its first satellite, Europe finally realized that Luxembourg meant business.[26]

As if dealing with France and Germany was not enough, SES had to bear an onslaught from Eutelsat and its signatories. SES was a threat to the European organization's monopoly and its director general, Andrea Caruso, who had had a long career at intergovernmental leviathan Intelsat, was not inclined to view a private competitor with any sympathy. He predicted disaster for SES, citing the cost of launch insurance and European PTTs' hostility. The latter refused to cooperate and rebuffed SES's requests for technical coordination. Caruso thought that if the PTTs' European central body decided to wage war against SES because it caused 'economic harm to Eutelsat', there was not much Luxembourg could do to save its project.[27] And when he learned that SES had purchased a satellite from American manufacturer RCA Astro (soon to become GE Astro Space), it was too much for him to bear:

> If you consider the enormous amount of money paid by Eutelsat to ESA to develop a European space technology and the amount of cooperation that has gone on by European PTTs, it is just impossible to understand how someone, simply for the purpose of making money, could get an American satellite and harm an organisation which has been freely set up. It is even more inconceivable that a government with a strong commitment to Europeanism, such as Luxembourg's, could support such a venture.[28]

In fact, SES had looked into European satellites but found that European manufacturers specialized in high-power spacecraft that could carry only five TV channels, which was not considered enough to make the venture a commercial success. Even without obstruction from various parties the venture was undeniably risky for investors and programmers alike. SES was an unknown quantity in the satellite industry and had yet to order a back-up bird. Those who booked capacity early could not be certain that the satellite would be used by enough TV channels to become an attractive proposition for viewers.[29]

It is at this point that British Telecom (BT) came to the rescue. BT was a key signatory to both Eutelsat and Intelsat, but unlike its European peers it began privatization in the early 1980s. BT was based in London where many channels, mostly from North America, were looking for international distribution across Europe. The telecom operator, which had made several investments in fledgling cable channels (Chapters 1 and 2) and was heavily involved in the satellite industry through its telephony and data business, sensed a market opportunity. It first approached Eutelsat and suggested it procure a craft specifically built for the distribution of multi-channel television. The Paris-based organization was not interested on the grounds that it would not own and control the satellite in the way it controlled everything that happened in the satellite market in Europe. Reaching an impasse with Eutelsat, BT approached SES and found a company that shared its views. They agreed that there was a market for a medium-power satellite that would trade off the quality of signal and size of the antenna for the ability to squeeze a greater number of channels into the available bandwidth. SES had an orbital slot and the capability of procuring a satellite, but needed a partner that had a foot in the television distribution market and would be able to manage the relationship with Eutelsat. Thus a joint venture was formed under which the satellite operator would develop, procure and launch the satellite, and BT would build ground facilities and sell 11 of the 16 available transponders.

BT had no problem finding customers for the transponders, four of which were immediately sold to Rupert Murdoch on a long-term lease, but had to expend a lot of energy and influence trying to coordinate the SES satellite system (called Astra) with that of Eutelsat. BT had to ensure that the two systems would not interfere with one another and also demonstrate that Astra would not cause significant economic harm to Eutelsat. BT eventually assuaged Eutelsat's fears by holding its leases on its transponders so that the satellite operator would not be left with the financial burden of having empty capacity if broadcasters transferred from Eutelsat onto Astra (which they eventually did). Without BT's political clout and financial resources, SES would have been able to launch its satellite, but it is unlikely that it would have gained access to the European TV distribution market.[30]

The first Astra satellite (1A) was scheduled to be launched in March 1987 but the failure of the European space rocket, Ariane, in December 1986 delayed the launch to December 1988. When the spacecraft became operational in February 1989, it would change European broadcasting for ever.

SES: a paradigm shift

Luxembourg was not the only European country with satellite ambitions. Following the WARC 77 allocations, many governments launched ambitious communications satellite projects. France's TDF, Germany's TV Sat, the Nordic countries' Tele-X and the British and Italian Olympus were 'direct broadcast by satellite' (DBS) ventures designed to distribute television signals directly to viewers. All these projects were national in scope and were designed to boost the flagging fortunes of domestic electronics industries. Technological nationalism comes at a price and these ventures guzzled vast amounts of taxpayers' money. The satellites were high-power spacecraft capable of up to 230 watts transmission per channel and were complex and expensive to build and use. Some of these birds were eventually launched but all proved to be overengineered white elephants that failed to attract any lasting interest from viewers and programmers. By the time

SES had launched its first satellite, their bid for national glory was long gone and lost in space.[31]

European governments hoped to retain control of the satellite industry through Eutelsat. They also intended to carry on controlling what Europeans watched through the cable networks owned by municipalities (Chapter 3). Local authorities often acted as gatekeepers and to some extent ruled the channels that these systems carried. These plans were swept away when the Astra class rewrote the rules of television distribution and reception.

BT's help was fortuitous but several other factors contributed to SES's success. Clay Whitehead and Pierre Meyrat were the first to realize that medium-power satellites were powerful enough to transmit TV channels. These satellites were lighter, cheaper and could transmit many more channels in the same bandwidth. Rapid progress in receiving technology improved LNBs' sensitivity and enabled them to pull a good picture out of a weak signal. SES's Astra signal could be received with an antenna no larger than 90 cm in diameter, a perfectly acceptable size for the mass market. SES showed that high-power satellite beams were no longer needed, making European governments' DBS satellites obsolete.

SES was a truly transnational project. The outlook of the senior management team was international and investors came from seven countries. The company was not nailed to a territory, it was flexible and free to move where opportunities arose: at first the Astra beam was pan-European but after Rupert Murdoch showed interest it was reoriented towards the UK. Murdoch wanted to tap into the British TV advertising market and Astra helped him to do so.[32]

Above all, the medium-power satellite opened up direct-to-home (DTH) satellite reception in Europe, enabling broadcasters to overcome the bottleneck of cable distribution. DTH accelerated the development of pay-TV in countries that were poorly cabled, notably in Southern and Central Europe. In addition, DTH gave programmers better – and sometimes direct – access to the consumer market. Murdoch, like other channel providers, repeatedly branded cable operators as 'middle men' that got between him and his customers.[33] Direct-to-home reception put an end to the monopoly of cable companies in the delivery of multi-channel television. These companies provided a service but were perceived as gatekeepers that took an undue share of revenue. Astra revolutionized television distribution in Europe, rolling back governments' involvement in the communications satellite business and forcing Eutelsat and cable networks to be more responsive to market forces.

Building up Europe's broadcast neighbourhoods

Having positioned its first satellite at 19.2 degrees East, SES pioneered co-location by placing there a second satellite (Astra 1B) in March 1991. They followed it with ten spacecraft between 1993 and 2008, making 19.2 degrees East Europe's premier position for direct-to-home TV services. Six satellites operate from this position today and six have either been relocated or decommissioned (Tables 4.2 and 4.3). When the resources at 19.2 degrees became insufficient, SES began building capacity at 28.2 degrees East and launched Astra 2A in August 1998 to serve the British and Irish DTH market. The satellite operator had begun planning for this orbital location in 1996 but met opposition from Eutelsat, who claimed to be interested in an adjacent orbital slot at 29 degrees East. An acrimonious dispute was resolved when both parties agreed to split the available frequencies at this location, enabling SES to launch Astra 2B and 2D in September and December 2000.[34] In 2008, SES began building up a new position at nearby 31.5 degrees East, moving Sirius 2 there (see below) and renaming it Astra 5A (Table 4.4).

Once agreement was reached, Eutelsat positioned Eurobird 1 at 28.5 degrees East to serve the DTH market in Germany and the UK in 2001. Two other spacecraft, Eurobird 2 and 3, were subsequently positioned in adjacent orbital slots, at 25.5 degrees and 33 degrees East respectively. The Eurobird fleet was completed with Eurobird 4 (formerly Hot Bird 3), positioned at 4 degrees East, and Eurobird 9 (Hot Bird 2), relocated at 9 degrees East in May 2007 (Table 4.8). The entire Eurobird fleet is designed to complement the Hot Bird system, but 9–10 degrees East is being developed as a key position for the video market in Europe with a focus on high-definition television. This orbital slot has the advantage of being close to the Hot Bird neighbourhood, allowing dual-feed antennas to receive radio and TV channels from both locations.

Eutelsat's main position remains Hot Bird, where four satellites are currently sited, with one more spacecraft scheduled for 2009 (Tables 4.6 and 4.7). Similar to Eutelsat's strategy at 10 and 13 degrees East, SES is building resources at 23.5 degrees East, which combines with its historic location at 19.2 degrees East. Two satellites are already there and the third is scheduled for launch in 2009 (Table 4.5). The location serves the DTH market in the Benelux and five countries in Central Europe and is designed to combine with 19 degrees East to create a 'virtual universal orbital position for Europe'.[35] Using Astra's dual-feed LNBs, consumers can access with a single dish the whole range of TV channels located at the two positions, in addition to new media services such as IPTV (Internet Protocol Television), content-on-demand and interactive television.

The Hot Bird and Astra positions are Europe's two leading video neighbourhoods. At the end of 2006, the Hot Bird position broadcast about 1050 channels to an audience of 121 million homes in Europe, North Africa and the Middle East. Hundreds of broadcasters transmit in excess of 1800 stations from the Astra positions to a DTH audience of 45 million homes and a total reception universe of 109 million European TV households.[36]

There are a few other important video neighbourhoods in Europe. Five degrees East looks at the Baltic countries, the Nordic region, Central and Eastern Europe. The broadcasting position is run by SES Sirius, a company that is 90 per cent owned by SES and 10 per cent by the Swedish Space Corporation. SES Astra and SES Sirius operate three spacecraft at this orbital slot: Sirius 3 and 4, and the redeployed Astra 1C.

Telenor, the Norwegian media and communication group, has developed One degree West as a broadcasting position primarily serving the Nordic region, Central and Eastern Europe. It operates three satellites here, Thor 2, 3 and 5 (with Thor 6 scheduled for 2009), and leases capacity on Intelsat 10-02. In Europe, satellite broadcasting services are also offered by Intelsat (various positions), Hispasat (30 degrees West) and Greece's Hellas (39 degrees East).

Table 4.2: The Astra constellation at 19.2 degrees East: relocated and decommissioned satellites

	Astra 1A[a]	Astra 1B[b]	Astra 1C[c]	Astra 1D[d]	Astra 1E[e]	Astra 2C[f]
Launch date	December 88	March 91	May 93	November 94	October 95	June 01
Manufacturer	GE Astro Space[g]	GE Astro Space	Hughes	Hughes	Hughes	Boeing Satellite Systems[h]
Transponder capacity	13	13	18	18	18	32/28

Source: www.ses-astra.com.

[a] Decommissioned in December 2004; [b] Decommissioned in July 2006; [c] Relocated at 5.0 degrees East; [d] Relocated at 23.5 degrees East; [e] Relocated at 23.5 degrees East; [f] Relocated at 28.2 degrees East; [g] Formerly RCA Astro; [h] Formerly Hughes Space and Communications.

Table 4.3: The Astra constellation at 19.2 degrees East, 2008

	Astra 1F	Astra 1G	Astra 1H	Astra 1KR	Astra 1L	Astra 1M
Launch date	April 96	December 97	June 99	April 06	July 07	Nov 08
Manufacturer	Hughes	Hughes	Hughes	Lockheed Martin[a]	Lockheed Martin	EADS Astrium
Transponder capacity	20	28	32/28	32/28	31/27	32

Source: www.ses-astra.com.
[a] Formerly GE Astro Space.

Table 4.4: The Astra constellation at 28.2 degrees East and 31.5 degrees East

	Astra 2A	Astra 2B	Astra 2C	Astra 2D	Astra 5A[a]
Launch date	August 98	September 00	June 01	December 00	November 97
Orbital slot	28.2° E	28.2° E	28.2° E	28.2° E	31.5° E
Manufacturer	Hughes	EADS Astrium	Boeing Satellite Systems	Hughes	Alcatel
Transponder capacity	32/28	30/28	32/28	16	26

Source: www.ses-astra.com.
[a] Previously Sirius 2.

Table 4.5: The Astra constellation at 23.5 degrees East

	Astra 1D	Astra 3A	Astra 3B
Launch date	November 94	March 02	Q4 09
Manufacturer	Hughes	Boeing Satellite Systems	EADS Astrium
Transponder capacity	18	20	52

Source: www.ses-astra.com.

Table 4.6: The Hot Bird position at 13 degrees East: relocated and decommissioned satellites

	Hot Bird 1[a]	Hot Bird 2[b]	Hot Bird 3[c]	Hot Bird 4[d]	Hot Bird 5[e]
Launch date	March 95	November 96	September 97	February 98	October 98
Manufacturer	Alcatel Space Industries	EADS Astrium[f]	EADS Astrium	EADS Astrium	EADS Astrium
Transponder capacity	16	20	20	20	20

Source: www.eutelsat.com.
[a]The last satellite in the Eutelsat II series (F6), deorbited;
[b]Relocated at 9 degrees East and renamed Eurobird 9;
[c]Relocated at 4 degrees East and renamed Eurobird 4;
[d]Relocated at 7 degrees West and renamed Atlantic Bird 4;
[e]Relocated at 25.5 degrees East and renamed Eurobird 2;
[f]Formerly Matra Marconi Space.

Table 4.7: The Hot Bird position at 13 degrees East, 2008

	Hot Bird 6	Hot Bird 7A	Hot Bird 8	Hot Bird 9	Hot Bird 10
Launch date	August 02	March 06	August 06	November 08	1Q 09
Manufacturer	Alcatel Space Industries	Alcatel Alenia Space	EADS Astrium	EADS Astrium	EADS Astrium
Transponder capacity	32	38	64	64	64

Source: www.eutelsat.com.

Table 4.8: The Eurobird fleet

	Eurobird 1	Eurobird 2[a]	Eurobird 3	Eurobird 4[b]	Eurobird 9[c]
Launch date	March 01	October 98	September 03	September 97	November 96
Position	28.5 degrees East	25.5 degrees East	33 degrees East	4 degrees East	9 degrees East
Manufacturer	Alcatel Space Industries	EADS Astrium	Boeing Satellite Systems	EADS Astrium	EADS Astrium
Transponder capacity	24	20	20	20	20

Source: www.eutelsat.com.
[a] Formerly Hot Bird 5; [b] Formerly Hot Bird 3; [c] Formerly Hot Bird 2.

Shopping centres in the sky: Europe's community satellites

The capacity of Europe's leading video neighbourhoods has increased exponentially over the past decades. The number of transponders per satellite has grown from around ten in the 1980s to up to 64 today. The biggest boost to satellite transmission capacity has been the digital revolution. Digitization is based on multiplexing, which is a ground-based activity. When a satellite receives a signal it simply changes the frequency, amplifies it and sends it back. Since spacecraft do not distinguish between analogue and digital, when TV signals were digitized in the 1990s, entire satellite fleets could be converted to digital retransmission. The compression rate of MPEG-2, the digital compression standard for full motion video, enables broadcasters to package around ten digital channels per transponder, where one analogue channel fitted previously. This is how hundreds of TV and radio stations can be broadcast from a single satellite today, let alone an orbital slot.

Digitization has helped reduce network expenses for broadcasters. On average, the tenfold compression rate has lowered transmission costs by a factor of six (digital channels still incur costs related to uplinking, downlinking and other ground services). Though generally cheaper, transponder prices vary greatly. In the premium video neighbourhoods developed by SES and Eutelsat a transponder can cost between €3 and €4 million a year. Satellite operators have been able to resist price pressure on these positions because of their value to broadcasters. The greater number of TV channels hosted in an orbital slot, the more the latter attracts viewers who orient their dishes toward it. In turn, the more dishes directed at a position, the greater audience it consolidates and the more attractive it becomes to broadcasters. The Hot Bird and Astra fleets are considered *community satellites* because they have built a 'dish community' that acts as a magnet for broadcasters.

The most common analogy of the broadcast neighbourhood is the shopping centre. The factors that keep the crowds coming to a shopping mall – and uphold the lease rates – are the combination of shops, the presence of an anchor tenant (e.g. a large supermarket) and facilities (e.g. parking, road access). Similarly, a broadcast neighbourhood with a large selection of channels, anchor tenants such as key content distributors (e.g. Sky) and good ground facilities is invaluable to any broadcaster. It is this environment that provides the broadcaster access to its audience and helps to justify the premium fees charged by the satellite operator. For instance, if a broadcaster wants to reach the British satellite TV market – or even the British pay-TV market for that matter – its only option is to lease capacity on the Astra constellation at 28.2 degrees East because nearly 9 million Sky subscribers have their dishes pointing in this direction.[37]

Satellite service providers

The international transmission of TV channels has been furthered by the emergence of satellite service providers. These companies have developed unique expertise in satellite TV distribution and provide an interface between satellite operators and broadcasters. They buy transponder capacity in bulk, lease it, provide uplink and downlink facilities, and offer encryption technology and all the other ground-based services that allow broadcasters to expand their international distribution. Companies in Europe include the Italian TeleSpazio, the Israeli RRSat and Siemens Business Services Media, which bought the BBC transmission operations in the early 2000s. While Siemens is building the terrestrial infrastructure to become a key player, the two market leaders remain GlobeCast and Arqiva (formerly BT Media & Broadcast).

GlobeCast, a France Telecom subsidiary, was founded in April 1997 following the consolidation of France Telecom's regional broadcast operations (including London-based Maxat) and a series of acquisitions such as the American Keystone Communications. This process enabled the French company to form a 'network of networks' that has the ability to deliver content almost anywhere in the world. The network is managed via 20 offices and 15 teleports and technical operation centres located worldwide. GlobeCast leases, and sometimes operates, about 50 distribution platforms spread across ten satellite systems.

This satellite capacity is connected to terrestrial transmission resources. GlobeCast's proprietary fibre optic network connects Paris, London, Milan, Rome and Madrid to four American cities (New York, Washington, DC, Miami and Los Angeles). The US system is linked to Singapore, and from there the cables run to Tokyo and Sydney. For the parts of the world GlobeCast does not reach the company signs partnership agreements with other fibre providers. However, clients expect GlobeCast to own and control most of its network in order to ensure reliability. This is why, for instance, in October 2007 BBC Worldwide chose the French operator to transmit its new fully localized entertainment channels into Poland, India, Hong Kong and Singapore.[38]

Arqiva, based in Hampshire, UK, acquired British Telecom's satellite broadcast services business, BT Media & Broadcast, in spring 2007. It is the only other player able to leverage a fibre optic network of near-global reach, BT having spent decades building it. Arqiva's network can carry a signal from Europe to America and, via Los Angeles, to Singapore and Hong Kong. It has four teleports and earth stations in Britain, three in Europe and two in the United States.

It is this former BT division that pioneered the *hybrid network solutions* that combine fibre and satellite transmission capabilities and which are now routinely offered by satellite service providers to broadcasters. *Programme contribution* applications, which consist of bringing a signal from point A to point B (as opposed to point to multi-point), are increasingly carried by fibre optic cables. Terrestrial networks are cheaper than satellite transmissions but less reliable. Cable networks are rarely 100 per cent redundant (i.e. being able to offer completely separate paths to a signal) and remain vulnerable at single points of failure: for instance, if the duct that carries two fibres in the circuit catches fire, both paths can be lost. Errors, human or otherwise, can occur at switches or gateways where cables meet. Because of the way the digital video broadcasting standard works, a network failure of a millisecond can translate into a 30-second picture loss when the signal reaches the set-top boxes.

Satellites remain competitive for point to multi-point *programme distribution*, or the network's 'last mile' when the signal reaches its final customers. Europe's main distribution satellites are those positioned in the premium broadcast neighbourhoods described above. For instance, in order to put a French channel like EuroNews on the Sky platform, the signal would be brought by fibre optic from Lyon to London, where it would be uplinked to Astra 2C at 28.2 degrees East. An Asian client like CCTV 9 can have its signal brought by fibre from Hong Kong to London and have it uplinked to a distribution satellite such as Hot Bird for European coverage. When fibre is not available, contribution satellites offer a not too costly alternative. Capacity on these satellites is cheaper than on the distribution ones because they are not located at premium positions and they usually deliver television signals to cable headends only. For instance, Eutelsat's W and Atlantic Bird satellites are used for contribution purposes only and are positioned to offer intercontinental connectivity.[39]

A few broadcasters with high cross-border transmission needs such as Al Jazeera English and CNBC have constructed their own global fibre optic networks. As an international business news channel CNBC operates in real time most of the day. Within 24 hours CNBC Europe transmits from London and picks up the American and Asian feeds according to where the financial markets are open. During daytime CNBC Europe also establishes multiple connections with its sister channels for insights and short news reports. In addition, the financial station has static cameras in banks and trading floors spread around Europe that it connects to for brief periods (Chapter 9). CNBC Europe books occasional satellite capacity to establish the European connections but relies on its own intercontinental fibre network for international transmissions.

The barriers of entry to satellite transmission have constantly been lowered over the past decade and today satellite TV distribution systems are used by a wide array of broadcasters reaching all kinds of audiences across borders. As mentioned above, digitization has driven down network costs because a TV channel transmitting in MPEG-2 (and increasingly MPEG-4), the digital compression industry standard, needs about a tenth of a transponder. Bandwidth efficiency gains have been accompanied by progress on the ground-segment side as teleports and technical operations centres have improved in terms of flexibility and capacity.

Satellite service providers have helped open up and democratize satellite capacity in Europe. They have contributed to lowering the costs of satellite transmissions and their expertise has enabled many small broadcasters to start international distribution. GlobeCast's uplink facilities and lease capacity on Hot Bird provide a gateway to Europe for over 100 channels. Many clients are public and private broadcasters from developing countries transmitting channels like Adjara TV (Georgia), Channel Punjab, Tamil TV Network or Yemen Satellite TV. For large customers, satellite service providers offer the possibility of outsourcing transmission capabilities and allow them to focus on their core business.

DTH distribution, multi-territory TV content distributors and transnational television

The expansion of DTH satellite reception remains one of the industry's most striking developments in recent years. It has played a key role in the European distribution of cross-border TV channels, and although barely 20 years old it has grown faster than cable from the outset. This trend is reflected in two sets of data: Hot Bird reception and the total cable and satellite reception market in Europe (Tables 4.9 and 4.10).

Table 4.9: Hot Bird reception in Europe: Cable and satellite trend (in millions of households), 1994–2006

	1994	2000	2001	2002	2003	2004	2006
Cable	41.1	61.2	64.4	65.2	66.5	67.9	73.5
Satellite	8.2	24.7	29.8	35.2	39.8	44.9	47.5
Total	49.3	84.4	92.8	98.7	104.2	110.5	121

Source: Eutelsat.

Table 4.10: Total cable and satellite reception market in Europe (in millions of households), 2002–6

		2002	2004	2006
Western Europe	*Cable*	49.6	49.6	52.1
	Growth in %	/	0.1	4.8
	Satellite (DTH/ SMATV)	38.7	42.5	47.7
	Growth in %	/	9.0	10.9
Eastern Europe	*Cable*	20.1	25.6	30.1
	Growth in %	/	21.4	15.0
	Satellite (DTH/ SMATV)	7.8	8.7	10.7
	Growth in %	/	9.9	18.7
Total	*Cable*	69.7	75.2	82.2
	Growth in %	/	7.3	8.5
	Satellite (DTH/ SMATV)	46.5	51.2	58.4
	Growth in %	/	9.2	12.3

Source: Eutelsat.

Today, quite a few DTH platforms display an impressive number of subscribers: towards the end of 2007, Sky (UK) had 8.8 million subscribers, Sky Italia 4.3 million, Premiere in Germany had 4.2 million, CanalSat (France) 5.3 million, Spain's Digital Plus had more than 2 million and Portugal's TV Cabo about 1.5 million. In addition, numerous smaller DTH platforms are popping up all over Europe's emergent territories such as Cyprus, Bulgaria, Romania, Hungary and Ukraine. In the more mature markets, some DTH operators specialize in low-cost bouquets or target specific populations. One such example is TV Vlaanderen, which serves the Flemish-speaking area and Flemish speakers living outside Flanders.[40]

Some platforms belong to multi-territory broadcasters and content distributors. News Corporation has significant holdings in BSkyB, wholly owns Sky Italia and became Premiere's largest shareholder when it acquired progressively about a quarter of the stake in spring 2008. Canal Digital started life in 1997 as a pay-TV platform jointly launched by Telenor and Canal Plus in Scandinavia. Since 2002 Canal Digital is solely owned by Telenor, the Norwegian media and telecom operator, and has expanded its operations to Finland. In December 2007 the company distributed pay television to just above 3 million subscribers in the Nordic region. Canal Digital is available via digital terrestrial television and cable but more than two-thirds of its customers receive their pay-TV channels via DTH or collective antennas (SMATV).[41] The region's second DTH provider is Viasat Broadcasting, which is a division of Sweden's Modern Times Group (MTG) (Chapter 2). Viasat runs DTH platforms in four Nordic countries, the three Baltic states and Ukraine. Late in 2007 there were 846,000 Viasat subscribers in the Nordic region and 133,000 in the Baltic states.[42] UPC Broadband is the European content distribution arm of Liberty Global and is present in ten territories, predominantly in Central Europe.[43] The UPC platforms totalled 9.7 million video subscribers in December 2007.

Since the Internet is emerging as a mode of TV distribution, most multi-territory content distributors have added IPTV to their systems. However, DTH has clearly emerged as the preferred method of distribution over cable. While UPC is predominantly a cable operator and Canal Digital offers both cable and DTH, Sky and Viasat shun cable altogether (Table 4.11).[44]

Table 4.11: Multi-territory content distributors in Europe, 2007

	BSkyB, Sky Italia	UPC Broadband	Canal Digital	Viasat
Geographical spread	3 territories	11 territories	4 territories	8 territories
Total number of video subscribers	13.1 million	9.7 million	3 million	1 million
Mode of delivery	DTH, IPTV	Cable, DTH	Cable, DTH, IPTV	DTH, IPTV
Proprietary multi-territory TV brands	Notably Sky- and Fox-branded channels	Extreme Sports Channel and eight Zone-branded stations	Canal Plus (Nordic)	TV1000 series and Viasat-branded channels

The fast growth of DTH platforms and operators has been extremely beneficial to transnational TV networks. For the purpose of television distribution, DTH holds many advantages over other technologies and especially cable. European cable has traditionally been a fragmented industry: most countries were carved up by the hundreds of local cable operators serving a region or a couple of small towns. None of these cable operators had the resources (many struggled with debts) to engage in substantial commercial and promotional activities. Where cable was conceived as a public utility, operators acted more as gatekeepers than promoters of 'foreign' TV channels (Chapter 3). Even though the cable industry has been consolidating for many years and today includes multi-territory players like UPC, most cable operators still lack scale and scope.[45]

In the mid-1990s when capacity was tight on analogue cable systems most international channels were squeezed out of the basic-tier package, greatly reducing their access to audiences and therefore advertisers. Sometimes cable operators only acquiesced to broadcasters' demands for carriage fees after threats of withdrawal and lawsuit. DTH technology simplified the supply chain and offered broadcasters better access to the market. Most DTH operators are integrated companies that can handle all the different aspects of pay television from encryption to subscription management and content provision, giving them the expertise and incentive to push pay television in their market.

Satellite platforms are able to offer a far greater variety of channels to viewers than cable systems. DTH operators were first to digitize their platforms, liberating vast amounts of bandwidth and giving them the opportunity to stack up channels in order to appeal to diverse communities of interest. In addition, cable operators were 'ill-equipped to handle premium or optional packages' and lacked a 'genuine tiering policy'.[46] Cable operators usually offered a two-tier pay structure, basic and premium. The premium tier offered a medley of channels but little extra choice in terms of family entertainment. DTH operators introduced a more sophisticated tiering policy, expanding a range of options for subscribers (e.g. children's, sport, documentary) that facilitated the take-up of pay and premium channels.

The capacity and marketing expertise of DTH operators opened up a range of opportunities for international content owners. These operators, anxious to increase choice for their customers, welcomed transnational broadcasters with open arms. They, in turn, started filling high-capacity satellite bouquets with channels that targeted various audience segments. The technological future of television distribution might be opening up with the arrival of new technologies but there is no doubt about the contribution that DTH has already made to the development of transnational television.

CHAPTER 5

THE ADVENT OF TRANSNATIONAL ADVERTISING[1]

The financial shape of many transnational TV networks improved with the upturn of the pan-European advertising market in the 1990s. The pool of international advertisers expanded as multinationals adjusted their marketing strategy to the challenges and opportunities of globalization. The advertising industry restructured, creating media buying agencies with specialist knowledge of pan-European television and the network to run transnational advertising campaigns mixing local and global objectives. Cross-border TV stations began to offer flexible local advertising windows that suited the multi-territory needs of advertisers.

GLOBALIZATION, EUROPEAN INTEGRATION AND PAN-REGIONAL ADVERTISING

As explained in Chapter 3, early attempts to use pan-European TV channels to promote fast-moving consumer goods (FMCGs) were inconclusive. Their subsequent absence from PETV prompted many observers to place question marks over the medium's viability and prospects. But over the following decade, international stations found new clients and FMCGs were replaced by products and services that were better adapted to international campaigns.

European market integration and the growth of multinational companies have led to a surge of products and services sold on a multi-territory basis. An increasing number of banks (for example HSBC, ING and UBS) and insurance companies (Allianz, AXA, Zurich) have activities that are transnational in scope. This trend is gathering pace in the services sector because of the growth of cross-border mergers and takeovers in Europe.[2] PETV is a useful platform for products that need little adaptation from one market to another, such as music, films, electronic games and consoles, computers and mobile phones. It is also popular with products that have a cosmopolitan appeal such as the luxury brands of the fashion sector.

The number of international brands is growing every year. The names of products that used to differ from territory to territory are being standardized. In new sectors (e.g. energy drinks, mobile telephony) brands internationalize at the very beginning of their life cycle (e.g. Red Bull, Vodafone). These brands will always use local media for efficiency purposes and reach consumers in great numbers. But some of these multinationals have realized how cross-border advertising allows them to develop their brands homogenously across a region and achieve consistent brand image and positioning. They also appreciate that a presence on transnational television can add international appeal to a brand. As a result, integrated pan-regional marketing structures are emerging with executives taking decisions at international level. Even though most advertising budgets are still decided locally, an increasing number of centralized accounts are being set up with money put aside for pan-European television. Thus, the number of advertisers on PETV steadily climbed throughout the 1990s to reach a few hundred today.[3]

Table 5.1 shows PETV spending by sector. Tourist boards and hotel chains (travel & tourism), banks and insurance providers (services), airlines (transport) and media and entertainment companies (culture & leisure) are among the most frequent PETV advertisers. Cross-border stations are also frequently used for corporate campaigns. Companies that have figured among the top advertisers in pan-European television in recent years include Adidas, Nokia, Philips, Samsung, UBS, Toyota and Vodafone.

Table 5.1: Top ten sectors by spending on pan-European television, 1999–2007

1999	2001	2003	2005	2007
Publishing	Automotive	Publishing	Travel & tourism	Travel & tourism
Travel & tourism	Culture & leisure	Automotive	Telecommunications	Services
Transport	IT	Telecommunications	Transport	Transport
Culture & leisure	Telecommunications	Travel & tourism	Culture & leisure	Telecommunications
Services	Services	Services	Services	Culture & leisure
Clothing & accessories	Travel & tourism	Culture & leisure	Publishing	Clothing & accessories
Sports equipment & sportswear	Sports equipment & sportswear	Media information	Energy	Energy
Telecommunications	Media information	Clothing & accessories	Clothing & accessories	Corporate
Drinks	Publishing	Drinks	Corporate	Information media
Computer printers	Clothing & accessories	IT	Sports equipment & sportswear	IT

Source: TNS Media Intelligence in *M&M Guide*.

Many companies advertising on PETV are in cutting-edge sectors that are particularly sensitive to an economic downturn. Thus cross-border TV channels' advertising revenue suffered in the early 2000s following the events of 9/11 and the burst of the Internet bubble. After a peak at approximately €628 million in 2002, the advertising income of Europe's leading PETV channels dropped to €419 million in 2004, before picking up again in 2005 and reaching an estimate of €672 million in 2007.[4] These figures are a fraction of the money spent on national media but represent a marked improvement from the late 1980s when total pan-European advertising spending was measured at the modern equivalent of €31 million.[5] In addition, the figures only take into account advertising campaigns that take place in at least three countries. This leaves aside local spending which accounts for most of the advertising on some PETV networks (see below).

From a media buying perspective, transnational television can be used in two ways. The 'umbrella strategy' consists of booking PETV as a complement to local campaigns. A multinational company with budgets in a handful of European countries may aim to complete its European coverage via PETV, typically in Central and Eastern Europe. Another reason to opt for this strategy is to run local and regional ad campaigns concurrently. This type of campaign implies a marketing strategy that has both local and regional objectives. In this case PETV contributes to the communication of the brand at international level. While local advertising concentrates on driving sales, a pan-European campaign can reinforce a brand and refine its positioning. A car manufacturer can promote its models locally and outline the values of the brand at regional or global level. Toyota, among others, has become adept at this type of campaign, which can be qualified as transnational because such campaigns are not merely international but mix the local with the global. This strategy is sophisticated and can be difficult to implement because it involves a high level of coordination between the agency's international department and the local office, and among the local offices themselves.

The umbrella strategy is for corporations that have the luxury of having both local and international budgets. But PETV is not the preserve of transnational conglomerates and is also booked by companies that have small advertising budgets. Not only are the rates for a 30-second advertising slot relatively cheap on PETV (Table 5.2), but the medium is cost-efficient as the rate per thousand viewers is well below that of national stations. Thus small advertisers can reach key European territories through transnational television at a fraction of the price of national media. Tourist boards, airline companies and banks from emerging markets and the European Union's newer members count among PETV's regular clients.[6]

Table 5.2: Selection of rates for a 30-second advertising slot, 2007

Channel	Period/Programme	Time	Price (€)
BBC World News	Global Evening Peak	19:00–24:00	4,278
CNBC Europe	Morning	06:00–12:00	2,250
CNN[a]		19:00–20:00	5,390
Discovery	Primetime	20:00–24:00	3,100
EuroNews	Evening peak	19:00–24:00	3,450
Eurosport[b]	Average		4,500
Extreme Sports	Primetime	18:00–24:00	500
Fashion TV	International feed		1,900
National Geographic	Primetime	17:00–24:00	1,465
Sky News	Peak	19:00–24:00	2,195

Source: M&M Guide 2007, p.66.
[a-b] 2006 prices.

THE RESTRUCTURING OF THE ADVERTISING INDUSTRY

Among the many evolutions that benefited transnational television in the 1990s is the restructuring of the advertising industry. Over the past decade a series of factors in the media sector induced full-service agencies to break up into creative shops and buying groups. The formation of global media conglomerates was accompanied by a consolidation of the media buying capacity in the advertising industry. Large groups such as OMD, Universal McCann or MindShare that purchase airtime and space in bulk have enough power to negotiate volume-linked triggers bringing discounts and other benefits. They are also able to discuss marketing partnerships that can involve content development and cross-border exploitation. And in a few instances they can sign framework agreements that involve separate divisions of a conglomerate. In addition, the advertising industry faces an increasingly complex media environment due notably to the multiplication of content platforms and audience fragmentation. Media buying agencies have three advantages where PETV is concerned. Being global, these agencies can handle the accounts of multinationals likely to be interested in international advertising. For instance, Mediaedge:cia has 118 offices in more than 80 countries, and OMD is present in 90 markets with about 110 offices. They are in a good position to understand the benefits that cross-border TV channels can bring to a regional or global campaign, and they have the resources to build up their specialist knowledge of new media such as PETV.[7]

Media buying agencies expanded their international departments as relationships with PETV owners developed. Carat, the agency owned by Aegis, has probably the largest international department in London, with over 100 staff spread across three floors. Twelve people alone are involved in the planning and buying of pan-regional television. It is a stark contrast to the recent past when 'the international used to be something you would almost do in the basement [and] you would have three people who might buy a page in *Time* sometimes'.[8] All the international departments of London's top media buying agencies are expanding, with an average size of between 40 and 60 people. Some agencies have smaller departments because they incorporate their international specialists within client teams (Table 5.3).

LOCAL ADVERTISING WINDOWS

A great limitation of international stations in the 1980s was that they could only offer pan-European exposure. Capacity was too sparse on analogue satellite systems for channels to be able to split their feed at a viable cost. Furthermore, legislation was in place to protect local advertising markets. Before the implementation of the 1989 TVWF Directive, several countries forbade international TV channels from carrying commercials specifically aimed at their market (Chapter 3). Understandably, there was little demand for pan-European campaigns. Most advertisers that paid interest to international advertising were present in three or four markets, not the entire continent. Very few messages can be beamed across a whole region without adaptation. The same product can be at different stages of its life cycle from one territory to another. Cars, for instance, rarely get launched in all markets at once. Different variants of the same product can be launched in different territories. Typically, car manufacturers might launch a cheap version in Central and Eastern Europe while selling a premium model of the same car

Table 5.3: PETV's top buying agencies (ranked by *M&M Guide*'s billing estimates), 2003–6

Agency	Billing 2003 (€M)	Billing 2004 (€M)	Billing 2005 (€M)	Billing 2006 (€M)	Holding company	Major clients
Zenith Optimedia	24	28	29	32	Publicis	Allied Domecq, British Airways, HP, Hyundai, Lexus, Puma, Toyota, Whirlpool, Zurich
MediaCom	24	24	29	32	WPP	Dreamworks, Emirates, Nokia, RBS, Shell, Tourism Australia
Media Planning Group	19	18	17	26	Havas	Air France, Accor Hotels, BNP Paribas, Dassault, Delta, Lacoste, Orange, Société Générale
Carat	27	29	26	25	Aegis	Adidas, Disney, EU Anti-tobacco, Lego, Philips, Tourism Australia, Toyota
Starcom	21	23	24	24.5	Publicis	BT Global Services, Johnnie Walker, Oracle, Twentieth Century Fox, UBS
MindShare	20	20	21	24	WPP	BP, Gillette, HSBC, IBM, Jaguar, Land Rover, Motorola, Nike, Rolex
Mediaedge:cia	20	18	17	24	WPP	Accenture, Sony, Sony Ericsson, UIP, Visa, Xerox
OMD	7	13	13	18	Omnicom	Apple, Blackberry, Elizabeth Arden, General Electric, Vodafone
Universal McCann	14	13	14	14	Interpublic	ExxonMobil, Microsoft, Intel, UPS
Initiative	16	12	12	13	Interpublic	Credit Suisse, Egyptian Tourist Board, Samsung
Columbus (Eurolab)	2	2	2	2	/	Domino's Pizza, Hornby
BJK&E	1	1.5	2	1.5	WPP	*Financial Times*, Systems Capital Management

Sources: M&M Guide 2003–6; holding companies: *Campaign – The Top 100 Agencies*, 22 February 2008, p.12.

in Western Europe. Some industries, such as pharmaceuticals, face many different regulations across territories and a pan-European campaign is strictly off-limits. European cultural diversity makes it difficult for the same message to remain efficient, let alone relevant, across different markets.

These barriers began to fall when cross-border TV channels split their pan-European feed and started inserting commercial breaks for one or several territories. The pioneers in local advertising windows were CNN and MTV, who began offering local advertising to Germany in 1992. Commerzbank was one of CNN's first local sponsors, the bank's spokesman explaining the attractiveness of the deal as follows: 'we finance 11 per cent of Germany's foreign trade, and it's important for the bank and its customers to keep abreast of breaking news elsewhere in the world'.[9]

In the course of the 1990s local advertising grew in popularity and PETV channels continuously expanded the number of ad windows on offer. BBC World News, CNN, Eurosport and France 24 are among the only stations not to offer local ad inserts today, reflecting the fact that clients now book these channels in order to build up the international appeal of their brand. Highly localized European networks can offer as many local ad windows as they have local channels (Chapter 11). The rest offer anything between one to 15 local ad inserts (Table 5.4). Most channels pick the UK – Europe's biggest TV advertising market – followed by any of the other four key territories (Germany, Italy, France or Spain). Stations also tend to open ad windows in the markets where they do well: Fashion TV offers local inserts in Russia, Travel Channel in Poland and TV5Monde in the three francophone territories. Local advertising inserts do not necessarily coincide with language and programming localization (Chapter 10).

Local advertising windows have opened up a realm of possibilities for advertisers, who can book PETV flexibly and are no longer required to buy pan-regional. Clients can buy a local campaign and advertise in one country, opt for an international campaign and select a group of territories, or buy a whole pan-European campaign. Advertisers can also run locally produced advertising spots simultaneously across Europe, ensuring that a pan-European campaign remains relevant to all markets. Advertisers in the FMCG sector frequently employ this method since tailoring is an effective marketing strategy and aspects of their product (such as packaging) may differ from one country to another. Pan-European campaigns can also be staggered in time. Advertisers can start a campaign in the Netherlands in June, run it in Scandinavia in July and carry it through across Europe over

Table 5.4: Selection of advertising windows on PETV channels, 2007

Channel	Local advertising windows
Arte	France, Germany
Bloomberg	France, Germany, Italy, Spain, UK
Boomerang	France, Hungary, Italy, Nordic (Denmark, Norway, Sweden), Poland, Romania, Spain, Turkey, UK
Cartoon Network	France, Hungary, Italy, Nordic (Denmark, Norway, Sweden), Poland, Romania, Spain, Turkey, UK
CNBC Europe	Germany, UK
Discovery	Benelux, Central and Eastern Europe, Denmark, France, Germany, Hungary, Iberia, Italy, Nordic (Finland, Iceland, Norway), Poland, Romania, Russia, Sweden, Turkey, UK
Extreme Sports	France, Poland, Portugal, UK
Fashion TV	Russia, UK
Hallmark	Bulgaria, Hungary, Italy, Poland, Romania, Russia, Scandinavia, Turkey
Motors TV	France, Germany, UK
National Geographic	Benelux, Denmark, France, Germany, Hungary, Italy, the Netherlands, Poland, Portugal, Romania, Russia, Scandinavia, Spain, Turkey, UK & Ireland
Sky News	UK/Ireland
Travel Channel	Poland, UK
TV5Monde	Belgium, France, Switzerland

Source: M&M Guide 2007, pp.64–5.

the following months. Another frequent situation is that an advertiser may want to isolate a country where it cannot be seen for legal or business reasons (Vodafone, for example, cannot advertise in France), or already runs a separate campaign that would clash with its international message.

From a media owner's perspective, local ad windows have enabled cross-border channels to compete for local advertising budgets. Most PETV channels sell local advertising through offices or representatives spread across the continent. For the children's channels (Cartoon Network, Jetix, Nickelodeon), Discovery, National Geographic and MTV, local advertising represents three-quarters or more of their total advertising income.

DELIVERING AN AFFLUENT AUDIENCE

Most PETV channels attract a more upmarket audience than that of terrestrial stations. It is the case for all the documentary channels, Fashion TV, Travel Channel and Eurosport. The news channels (Chapter 9) cater for an even more upscale and business-oriented audience: figures show the average CNBC viewer has an income over €107,000 and a net worth of €615,000; and 30 per cent are senior managers.[10]

A battery of surveys tracks down this lucrative but elusive audience at pan-European level (see below). The leading one is the European Media and Marketing Survey (EMS), which measures European audiences in terms of *reach*, which is defined as *the number of people having seen at least once a specific programme or spot over a defined period* (daily, weekly or monthly). Table 5.5 shows the weekly reach – the industry standard – of a selection of PETV channels over the last 12 years in the EMS *universe*.

The universe of the largest EMS survey concentrates on Europeans living in the top 20 per cent of the population by income, about 40 million individuals (13 per cent of the total population). The revenue threshold varies from country to country but averages €50,000. The EMS universe's representative sample of about 15,500 usable respondents is spread across 19 countries.[11]

Thus Table 5.5 shows that, for instance, 42.2 per cent of the respondents within the 2007 EMS universe have watched for at least two minutes one of the PETV news or business channels during the week preceding the phone interview. This translates into an estimated audience of some 16.7 million Europeans for these channels alone, while PETV's weekly reach totalled almost 26 million people in 2007. These scores are far higher than those of the pan-European business press. In 2007 the reaches of pan-European dailies ranged from 0.3 per cent (*Wall Street Journal Europe*) to 1.4 per cent (*Financial Times*). Among magazines, *The Economist* stands at 1.9 per cent and *Time* at 2.7 per cent.[12] While the PETV figures are going up, those for the print titles have been falling for the past decade. It is arguably not fair to compare exposure to a TV channel that can last a fleeting moment to that of a press title that requires the reader's undivided attention. Nonetheless, it dawned on media buying agencies in the early 2000s that the reach of television was far superior to that of the press, and the news and business PETV channels established themselves as the medium of choice to reach upscale audiences.[13]

The unique audience profile of news and business PETV channels presents several advantages. These stations offer minimum audience wastage

Table 5.5: PETV weekly reach in EMS regular universe of 40 million Europeans, 1996–2007 (in percentage of viewers within this universe)

Channels	1996	1997	1998	1999	2000	2001	2002	2003	2004	2005	2006	2007
BBC World News	1.8	2.3	3.3	4.4	5.7	6.3	6.6	7.8	9.7	11.4	11.9	11.6
Bloomberg	/	/	0.6	1.7	2.0	3.7	5.2	4.6	5.0	5.7	6.1	6.1
CNBC	/	0.5	2.0	3.9	4.5	5.3	6.1	5.6	5.8	7.0	7.1	6.7
CNN Int.	16.5	15.1	15.5	16.1	18.2	17.2	19.5	17.0	18.5	19.0	19.2	17.5
EuroNews	12.1	11.2	12.1	13.3	16.5	16.0	15.2	15.0	15.0	16.9	17.8	18.0
Sky News	3.7	8.1	9.5	9.5	10.5	10.7	10.2	9.7	12.2	14.2	14.7	15.3
News/business	**26.8**	**27.3**	**29.2**	**31.0**	**35.7**	**35.8**	**37.4**	**36.2**	**38.4**	**41.1**	**42.9**	**42.2**
BBC Prime	1.6	1.5	2.3	2.8	2.7	3.1	3.3	1.9	2.3	0.9	0.9	0.8
Deutsche Welle	1.7	1.8	1.8	1.9	2.2	2.5	1.6	1.4	1.6	1.7	1.7	1.8
Discovery	6.1	7.0	8.4	9.2	10.4	12.5	12.9	13.7	14.1	16.1	18.1	18.4
Eurosport	31.4	33.0	32.5	33.2	33.3	34.3	30.8	28.9	27.5	31.1	32.4	31.3
Fashion TV	/	/	/	1.3	1.5	1.8	2.0	1.7	2.2	2.3	1.9	2.1
MTV	14.5	12.1	13.5	14.1	15.6	16.0	16.7	15.6	23.4	27.9	27.8	27.8
National Geographic	/	/	/	/	6.0	8.0	9.0	9.7	11.0	12.6	13.9	14.7
Travel Channel	2.0	2.0	2.3	3.1	3.7	4.3	4.6	4.7	/	6.3	6.7	6.7
TV5Monde	6.6	5.3	5.4	5.1	6.5	6.6	6.5	6.3	6.7	7.1	7.4	7.2
General PETV	**41.7**	**41.5**	**42.6**	**43.8**	**46.8**	**49.0**	**47.9**	**47.0**	**50.0**	**55.3**	**56.7**	**57.2**
PETV weekly	49.3	48.9	49.8	51.0	54.5	56.4	56.4	55.6	58.8	63.3	65.2	65.9

Source: EMS Guide 2007, pp.20–8.

Data conventions: '/': not applicable.

to advertisers who wish to reach a corporate audience, either to advertise a product or deliver a corporate message. There is no point in a luxury car manufacturer advertising on terrestrial television because it would be paying for millions of viewers who cannot afford its cars. News and business channels are perfect for advertisers such as luxury goods manufacturers, technology firms and service providers to the corporate elite who would rather talk to the people who count than count the people they talk to. These stations also offer an advertising environment that is adapted to an affluent and business audience. Commercials for corporate campaigns are not squeezed in between ads for accident insurance helplines and debt consolidation companies.

News and business PETV channels are high-value media brands with which advertisers like to be associated. Channels like BBC World News and CNN are well regarded by their audience. They are perceived as trustworthy, stimulating, up-to-the-minute in terms of reporting and 'ahead of the game' with their comments and analysis.[14] When something significant happens in the world, the international news TV channels are where this audience turns to because it appreciates that these stations have *access* to places and key people. They know that these channels can report from anywhere on the planet as opposed to merely relaying what other channels say. Global newsgathering capabilities, objective coverage and reporting based on what the audience needs to know bring credibility and a certain aura to these channels (Chapter 9). These attributes rub off on the brands that advertise on these stations and are monetized on the international advertising TV market.[15]

BEYOND SPOT ADVERTISING: CROSS-FORMAT AND CROSS-PLATFORM MEDIA DEALS

PETV channels have pioneered non-spot advertising. They must try harder than terrestrial stations to attract advertising clients and they benefit from the looser regulatory framework of cable and satellite. Programme sponsorship used to be the staple of non-spot advertising but many more options are available to advertisers today. Corporate profiles are one- to two-minute clips in which a company, region or country makes a presentation. With ad-funded programming, a broadcaster agrees to produce and air a programme paid for by an advertiser on a mutually agreed topic. Ad-funded programming ranges from one- to two-minute vignettes to debates and full-length documentaries. In recent years, EuroNews has produced vignettes for Toyota and Canon, a debating forum for Shell (*Comment*) and a series of four-minute programmes for UBS, *Musica*, that bring news about concerts and festivals in Europe. CNBC has run a documentary series on pensions for HSBC (*Live long & prosper*), in addition to shows for clients like Hewlett Packard (HP) and Cisco. BBC World News has produced a programme on world cultures for Samsung and MTV a reality series, *Meet or Delete*, for HP. Once guidelines have been agreed, the editorial rests in the control of the broadcaster. Credibility is a major asset for these channels and none of them would risk airing material that would breach the trust viewers place in them.

Integrated communication solutions prepared by PETV stations combine several media, including on-air, online, mobile, press and events.

Conglomerates like Time Warner manage to offer multimedia deals with titles that belong to the group (e.g. CNN and *Time* magazine). As well as the usual on-air facilities, Jetix's online opportunities expand to games, promotions and bespoke websites. The station offers merchandizing and licensing opportunities and can involve advertisers with magazines and events, such as the pan-European annual Jetix Kids Cup. Fashion TV's forte is the on-the-ground presence it can offer to clients through events such as the Fashion TV Model Awards and Fashion TV parties. Some of the most intricate deals are put in place by MTV's advertising team, Viacom Brand Solutions, which can tie up on-air activities ranging from spots, competitions and co-branded messages to programme sponsorship with a multimedia campaign and on-the-ground promotional activities that can take place at ad-hoc events or the MTV Awards show.

On air cross-format advertising presents several advantages for PETV clients. Ad-funded programming enables them to become part of the channel, not merely to advertise on it. As they often sign long-term deals with broadcasters (six months to a year) they benefit from their association with a strong media brand. They can articulate their own brand in different fashions and approach the audience with material that is relevant to them. Integrated communication solutions that combine several platforms allow advertisers to involve the audience even more actively and build up an intimate relationship with them, especially when interactivity plays a part in the package.[16]

RESEARCH: FORGING A PAN-EUROPEAN UNIVERSE

Audience research has always been a matter of concern for cross-border TV channels because their international coverage necessitates comparable data on a cross-country basis. When they first began broadcasting in the 1980s, not all European countries had set up national audience measurement systems. Where these instruments were running – called people meters – they did not properly take into account cable and satellite stations. PETV channels had to commission their own research in order to have data to show to advertisers.

The earliest cross-border audience survey was commissioned by Sky in November 1985 and the first concerted effort came less than two years later. Petar (Pan-European Television Audience Research) was commissioned in

1987 by eight sponsors (among them Sky, Super, Screensport, RTL, Sat1 and McDonalds) and covered Europe's main cable markets: Austria, Belgium, Denmark, Finland, the Netherlands, Norway, Sweden, the UK and West Germany.[17]

Petar was a ground-breaking piece of research but did not live up to its clients' expectations. The number of sponsors first climbed to 16 but dwindled to four in 1991 and to one for the last three editions (1992 to 1994). It was an expensive exercise for stations that had yet to turn a profit. Petar also revealed ratings that were sometimes embarrassing for the sponsors. At a time when cross-border TV channels were still broadcasting in English, this survey highlighted the language barriers that prevailed in Europe.[18]

In the 1990s, people meters started taking multi-channel television into consideration and producing data of some relevance to international broadcasters. Although many of these broadcasters began to subscribe to these surveys – and increasingly do so today – problems remained as national metering systems were not harmonized and the resulting data were not comparable on an international basis. To this day, these systems are run by separate companies (Auditel in Italy, Médiamétrie in France, TNS in Spain, BARB in the UK, Gallup in Scandinavia, SKO in the Netherlands or GfK in Germany) who face different market realities and make independent methodological decisions.[19] In addition, national audience measurement systems, although accurate, are not tailored to the specific needs of cable and satellite channels. The minute-by-minute recording of nationwide audiences is not relevant for channels that pursue viewers with very specific demographics. People meters do not register out-of-home viewing figures and do not generate data suitable for audience profiling.

It was to answer the particular needs of PETV stations that an Amsterdam-based research company called Interview launched the European Media and Marketing Survey (EMS) in 1995.[20] The survey was built around industry requirements and was co-designed by commercial sponsors. It was devised to allow comparative analysis on a cross-market basis and generate attitudinal data for audience profiles. EMS is a *recall* survey done by telephone interviewing, the initial questions screening respondents to check if they belong to the EMS universe (see above). The average sample size of the EMS surveys since 1995 is about 16,000 respondents across 16 countries, and fieldwork started in Poland, Hungary, the Czech Republic and Russia in 2006.

A couple of surveys have an even more restrictive universe. EMS Select targets the top 3 per cent of the population in terms of income, a universe

that comprises eight million Europeans who in many cases earn at least
€80,000 per year.[21] The European Opinion Leaders Survey (EOLS, formerly
the European Business Readership Survey) has a universe size of only
31,713 individuals and a sample size of 2,021 respondents (2007 figures).
It focuses 'on those at the very pinnacle of position and influence in business,
government, media and academia'.[22] This includes department and section
heads of EU Commissions, high-ranking embassy staff and the most senior
executives working for corporations listed in the Global Fortune 500 with
turnover exceeding US$4 billion.

Recall surveys are considered less reliable than people meters by media
buyers. Some advertisers claim that these surveys can overestimate an audience
by up to a factor of two: people pretend they were tuned to some aspirational
channel, say CNN, while they were watching re-runs of ten year-old
American sitcoms. In addition, recall surveys have difficulties determining
the length of time people watch a particular channel and thus while advertisers
can approximate a channel's reach they are never quite certain that viewers
have seen their commercials. Despite these concerns, EMS has become a
reference in the PETV industry and the survey is sponsored by the leading
international broadcasters and media buying agencies.

The upscale universe of EMS remains unsuitable for cross-border
channels with a young audience. They subscribe to people meters in some
markets, but for comparative purposes advertisers and media owners must
turn to PeakTime, a Paris-based company that aggregates and homogenizes
data from national metering systems. PeakTime is also able to extrapolate
viewing figures at European level on the basis of the data collected in the
countries where a channel is measured.[23]

The PETV industry consumes an increasing quantity of qualitative
surveys. Stations' heads of research have realized that they do not know
enough about how people watch and interact with their channels. BSB
Media is among the new crop of companies that specialize in qualitative
studies, studying how viewers use and value the channels they watch.[24]

A growing amount of research done in the PETV industry is now
proprietary, being conducted or commissioned by the media owners for
their own use. Broadcasters monitor the impact of advertising campaigns
that air on their channels and commission surveys in order to refine their
own brand. For instance, the CNBC research team conducts in-depth
interviews and monthly focus groups with segments of their audience to
get feedback on programming and the CNBC brand. They have a panel of
viewers with about 500 respondents answering a questionnaire at regular

intervals. They also run ViewerTrack, a quarterly online survey based on a database of 7,000 email addresses. They get about 700 replies to queries about what their viewers are watching, what they think about it and what they would like to watch. There are also questions about advertising awareness and brand tracking. This research improves the accountability of the station towards advertisers. More importantly, it allows CNBC to define and position the station according to how viewers engage with the channel.[25]

There is a growing appetite for qualitative data because media owners and advertisers have realized that, in the age of interactivity, knowing how people engage with their brands is as crucial as counting pairs of eyeballs. Other research issues remain partly because international and comparative research is by nature difficult to conduct. For instance, some advertisers are calling for new research avenues, notably comparative studies between local and pan-regional media.[26] Nonetheless, considerable progress has been achieved over the past decade, a time during which PETV channels have constantly innovated and sought solutions to their research problems.

CONCLUSION

It is not the role of pan-European or even transnational advertising to supplant local advertising. Certain products in the FMCG sector require a creative style (e.g. the use of humour or irony) that does not translate well at international level. PETV does not fit the objectives of all international ad campaigns and terrestrial television remains an efficient way of reaching people in great numbers in a national market.

But PETV channels have travelled a long way over the past two decades to offer a focused proposition to advertisers. Their improved ratings enable them to deliver audiences with interesting demographics. They reach the young, the affluent, the corporate and sometimes a mix of all three. Many of these channels are trusted and well regarded by their viewers. The sheer number of PETV stations enables advertisers to pick the channel that best suits their campaign brief and target specific audiences that congregate towards a certain genre.

Even if PETV channels were to stand still, the world is moving in their direction. European market integration and globalization are trends that are affecting businesses across all sectors. These trends are forcing companies to rethink their organizational structure and international marketing strategy.

The 'international' is no longer a faraway land but part of everyday business life and is transforming the very fabric of most companies. In order to thrive in such an environment business needs to coordinate flows of people, capital and products across borders. PETV channels enable multinationals to reach consumers across markets simultaneously. They help them to define brands internationally and achieve consistency across markets. Local windows offer the opportunity for clients to decide how they want to run a pan-regional campaign and cherry-pick the territories in which they want to advertise. This flexibility enables advertisers to adapt advertising campaigns to marketing strategies that mix the local and the global, a distinct advantage in an age when the success of a company can be determined by its understanding of the exigencies of both terms and its ability to hold them in balance.

CHAPTER 6

PUBLIC BROADCASTERS: COMING TO TERMS WITH THE NEW MEDIA ORDER

The foundations of transnational television's current growth and prosperity were laid down in the 1990s, but the first half of the decade was a quiet period for the industry. Following the commercial difficulties of the 1980s, few candidates for international broadcasting were left standing. The period presented public service broadcasters with a window of opportunity during which they launched several cross-border TV channels. This chapter catches up with TV5 and 3Sat (Chapter 1), and then examines all the public channels launched in the 1990s. Finally, it analyses the challenges faced by public media owners as international broadcasters today.

TV5MONDE

The 1990s was a period of expansion for TV5. The channel established itself as a limited company in 1990 when TV5's funding partners became shareholders of Satellimages TV5. In the following years a few changes occurred among TV5's partners. The French public channels that separately held stakes in the network consolidated into France Télévisions. New shareholders arrived, notably Arte and Réseau France Outre-mer (RFO), France's overseas TV distribution and production network. Today the French shareholders hold approximately 66 per cent of the stock, while the rest is in the hands of the Swiss and Belgian public broadcasters (SSR and RTBF), and a consortium of Canadian and Quebecan broadcasters and producers. These partners offer programming to TV5 but 90 per cent of the budget (€90 million in 2008) is covered by the five participating governments: France (which alone assumes 84 per cent of the funding), Switzerland, Canada, Quebec and Belgium. The remaining 10 per cent of the budget is provided by TV5's revenue from advertising and carriage fees.

In the 1990s TV5 expanded its reach by launching feeds in Africa, Asia and America. The station eventually acquired global coverage and became one of the world's best-distributed networks. Today it has the second-highest distribution in Europe (110 million households – Table 7.1) and reaches 180 million homes worldwide. It covers Europe with two feeds: one for the francophone territories, launched in 1999, and another for the rest of the continent.

As mentioned in Chapter 1, the Quebecans were more commercially minded than the other TV5 partners. They produced their own channel split into three feeds that they sold across the American continent (Canada, USA and Latin America). Although 60 per cent of the channel's content came from Satellimages TV5, the company never received a penny for it. In October 2000, after two years of difficult negotiations, the five backing governments agreed to restructure TV5 and transfer all the signals to the new company: TV5Monde. The Quebecans kept TV5 Québec Canada but the feeds for the United States and Latin America/West Indies went back to Paris.

Late in 2007, French President Nicolas Sarkozy launched a review of France's external audiovisual policy in order to make it more effective. The following year an umbrella company, France Monde, was created in order to coordinate activities and resources at TV5Monde, France 24 and the international radio network Radio France Internationale (RFI). France Monde's first chairman is Alain de Pouzilhac (also France 24's chief executive) and its managing director is Christine Ockrent, the veteran journalist. TV5Monde's international partners initially expressed strong reservations about the set-up because they feared the French were planning to hijack the francophone broadcaster to become 'la voix de la France'. Faced with widespread opposition, the French government diluted its reforms and an accord was reached in April 2008.[1]

TV5Monde primarily rebroadcasts its partners' programming but it has its own budget, personnel (250 people), newsroom and identity. Since the 2000 reform, TV5Monde has a strong news strand and produces up to ten daily bulletins. The network has always tried to avoid a French-centric view of the world and most of its bulletins are produced for a specific regional feed. TV5Monde also produces weekly magazines covering Africa, world affairs, the economy, science and culture.

TV5Monde's profile is higher in regions such as the Middle East and Africa, where it has access to rights in sport and drama that it cannot clear in Europe. French movie producers have no interest in selling rights to the network in countries like Belgium and Switzerland, a natural constituency for their fare. TV5Monde remains at the heart of the French-speaking world because it brings different francophone communities together and enhances the knowledge and understanding of the francophone culture.[2]

3SAT

The three German-speaking public broadcasters that started one of Europe's oldest satellite services (ZDF, ORF and SRG – Chapter 1) were joined by ARD in 1993. About 75 per cent of 3Sat's schedule is provided by these four, of which 66 per cent comes from ZDF and ARD, 25 per cent from ORF and the remaining 9 per cent from SRG. The rest of the programming is produced specifically for 3Sat (usually by ZDF).

The broadcaster's mission is to be the channel for science and culture. It broadcasts a mix of news (i.e. the news bulletins of the participating broadcasters), magazines, documentaries, movies and dramas. Its flagship shows are *Kulturzeit*, a daily culture magazine, and *Nano*, a 30-minute science magazine. Like Arte (see below), 3Sat promotes a different type of television viewing and takes particular care with the coherence of its schedule that is organized around themes. It can broadcast up to 24 hours of programming focusing on an artist, actor or culture.

3Sat crosses borders but remains focused on Germany, Austria and German-speaking Switzerland, where it has near-universal coverage. Although the station is available in Europe through Astra, it does not try to reach non-German speakers. But the channel promotes the culture and language that bind the three German-speaking countries together.[3]

DEUTSCHE WELLE TELEVISION: FROM VOLKSMUSIK TO POPXPORT

Deutsche Welle has been an international broadcaster since 1953, transmitting radio programmes in up to 29 languages around the world. When it upgraded to television it turned to an organization set up for propaganda purposes during the Cold War: Radio in the American Sector (RIAS). RIAS was part of the United States Information Agency (USIA) from 1955 and broadcasted beyond the Iron Curtain to East Germany and other communist nations. In the late 1980s, under the leadership of Charles Wick, the USIA director, RIAS added a television channel to its operations (Chapter 1). When the Cold War ended, RIAS-TV lost its *raison d'être* and Deutsche Welle took over its staff and headquarters in Berlin. Deutsche Welle Television (DW-TV) began broadcasting in April 1992 and its objectives were later refined by the Deutsche Welle Act of January 2005.

The station's schedule is organized in the same way as that of BBC World News but with a language rotation between German and English every hour. Its news bulletin starts every hour on the hour and the back half-hour is devoted to magazines and documentaries covering the economy, politics, culture, lifestyle and European affairs. Together with Deutsche Welle's radio and online services, the channel promotes German language and culture and takes a German perspective on world affairs. DW-TV primarily aims at an international audience, although it keeps in touch with expatriates via the German-speaking hour.[4] Magazines like *Made in Germany* (business), *Discover Germany* (tourism) and *Kino* (German movies) promote local industry. With the same objectives in mind, a programme that was popular with German expatriates, *Volksmusik*, was replaced by *PopXport*, a showcase for German pop music.[5]

ARTE: ENGINEERING FRANCO-GERMAN CULTURE

Arte's origins lay in the wide-ranging collaboration programme between France and Germany begun in 1963. Circa 1984 both governments had reached the planning stage for their own cultural channel, then, the idea of a joint station arose two years later. The project was officially announced by President François Mitterrand and Chancellor Helmut Kohl at the 52nd Franco-German Summit – no less – in November 1988. In October 1990 the French Republic and eleven German Länders (responsible for broadcasting in Germany) signed a treatise establishing the legal foundations of Arte. The channel began broadcasting via satellite to cable operators in France and Germany on 30 May 1992.

Three broadcasters were involved in the negotiations: the French cultural channel La Sept, launched in 1989, and the two German public stations, ARD and ZDF. In order to ensure parity between the two countries, ARD and ZDF formed Arte-Deutschland, which became an equal partner in Arte with La Sept. The legal structure chosen for Arte – called a Groupement Européen d'Intérêt Economique in European law – ensured maximum autonomy for the two partners. Negotiations were lengthy and difficult because they brought together two countries with two conflicting broadcasting models. The Germans delegate broadcasting matters to regional authorities and place emphasis on cultural diversity, while the French broadcasting policy has statist and nationalist overtones and is centrally controlled from Paris. French news media and journalists remain close – some say subservient – to political personnel, while in Germany a Chinese wall separates the two professions. Thus the German partners proceeded with extreme caution and agreed to a deal only when assured that their independence was guaranteed.[6]

The existence of Arte owes more to diplomacy than public demand. The channel was supposed to strengthen the Franco-German alliance, which used to be considered the engine of European integration. The station was promoted by those in politics who never accepted that resilient national cultures can stand in the way of European cohesion. They recognized that for Europe to prevail as a political entity people would have to feel more European and that a European culture would have to be fabricated *ex nihilo*. Television seemed a reasonable place to start, a view expressed, among others, by Arte president Jérôme Clément in 1992:

> In order to change mentalities, the mindset, and create the conditions for a true united Europe, a currency, an army corps, and directives, as good as they can be, are not enough. Not even a treatise. A common imagination is needed [in order to] think Europe together. The Germans, the French, the Italians, the Spanish and all the others, even the British, should learn to look at and think about the world together, and show it together to their compatriots.[7]

Similar views were reiterated more than a decade later by Christoph Hauser, Arte's head of programming, who stated in 2006 that the channel's objective was to give Europe 'a soul'.[8] Based in Strasbourg since October 2003, Arte signed several co-production agreements with European broadcasters between 1995 and the early 2000s, including the BBC and Sweden's SVT. Three public broadcasters, RTBF in Belgium, TVP in Poland and ORF in Austria, have become associate members. But for all its European fervour, Arte remains essentially a binational organization with the French and Germans solely in charge of the channel's destiny. And although Arte has widespread coverage in six countries (Austria, Belgium, France, Germany, Switzerland and the Netherlands) it draws most of its audience from France and Germany.

Arte's programming is exceptionally eclectic and is highbrow without being conformist. A new thematic schedule was developed between 2004 and 2006 around history and society, art and music, cinema and fiction, and knowledge and discovery. Each genre is inclusive – cinema, for instance, encompasses silent movies, short films, portraits of directors and interviews with film stars. The concept of the themed evening is core to the brand and takes place up to three times a week, expanding on a topic in current affairs, politics or culture. A topic such as women and politics can be treated with a documentary on a contemporary female politician and a movie on an illustrious monarch from the past. Arte's political objectives might be far-fetched, but it cannot be denied that the station has a schedule that is highly distinctive and more original than any commercial broadcaster could deliver.

EURONEWS

The European Broadcasting Union drew up plans for an all-news channel in the late 1980s. Like the BBC (see below), its calls for public funding fell on deaf ears until CNN rose to prominence during the Gulf War in 1990–1 and the project received financial support from the European Parliament, several governments and participating broadcasters. At first, subsidies lay at the heart of the station's funding, so much so that the channel's commercial income was initially budgeted at only 20 per cent of total revenue.[9]

EuroNews went on air on 1 January 1993 and was backed by about 12 EBU members led by a first tier of shareholders comprising France Télévisions (holding 20.9 per cent of shares), RAI (17.0 per cent) and Spain's RTVE (15.7 per cent). The running costs rapidly proved too high for the European backers and broadcasters. In 1995 the French government somehow managed to convince Alcatel to become the first private investor and acquire 49 per cent of shares through a subsidiary.[10] The French conglomerate took advantage of a strategic review to pull out soon afterwards and the shares were left on the market with no takers. They were picked up by ITN for £5 million in January 1998, starting an ill-fated joint venture between the British news provider and France Télévisions, the main shareholder. The French public broadcaster's incoming president, Marc Tessier, took against ITN. He resented the fact that a station based in France was run by the 'infidel English' and thought the European news channel stood in his way, occasionally comparing it to a piece of chewing gum stuck to his shoes.[11] He was planning his own domestic news channel and wanted to be involved in the government's project for an international news channel that would eventually become France 24 (Chapter 9).

The relationship between the two partners deteriorated to the point that Stewart Purvis, ITN's CEO, decided to cut his losses and leave. Not only did Tessier discourage potential partners but he refused to buy back ITN's shares. After six months of legal wrangles, France Télévisions agreed to buy ITN's shares for €1, representing a huge shortfall for the British company.

Today EuroNews is a much stronger commercial proposition: only 7 per cent of its budget (€30 million) is covered by subsidies, the rest of its income being derived from advertising and sponsorship (30 per cent), fees received from the participating 22 public broadcasters that can air the channel on their frequency (40 per cent), co-production agreements with the European Union (20 per cent) and carriage fees from cable operators. RTR (Russia), with 15.2 per cent of the shares, and SSR (Switzerland), with 9.1 per cent, have joined the group of first-tier shareholders.

EuroNews's main weakness has always been its location. The station established itself in Lyon when the shareholders received what they thought was an attractive offer from the local authorities. The decision proved an unfortunate strategic blunder: once stuck in this sleepy provincial town EuroNews was relegated to the periphery of Europe's power network and fell prey to the strike-happy French unions. Since Lyon was preferred to Munich, both German public broadcasters (first ARD and then ZDF) pulled out of EuroNews, cutting off the channel from its largest television market in continental Europe. To make matters worse, Lyon's local authority reneged on many of its promises made to EuroNews.

Despite this handicap EuroNews has been a great success with European viewers. Its unique ability to broadcast in eight languages made it Europe's most-watched international news channel in 2007, ahead of CNN (the previous leader), Sky News and BBC World News (2007 EMS survey, Table 5.5). The concept of delivering European news to Europeans works well in the age of increasing regional integration. EuroNews provides up-to-the-minute news bulletins that cover politics, business, finance, sport, weather and breaking news from a European perspective. Complementary programmes cover the arts, cinema, fashion and travel (*Le Mag* and *Agenda*), business and finance (*Economia* and *Markets*) and European affairs (e.g. *Europa*). *No Comment*, launched in the ITN days, is an award-winning signature programme that airs the day's striking images without commentary. (See Chapter 9 for analysis of EuroNews's programming and news coverage.)[12]

THE CHRONICLES OF THE BBC
IN THE SATELLITE REALM

The BBC began plans for a satellite TV service in the 1980s. Earlier in the decade someone at BBC World Service suggested there should be a television version of their radio service but the proposal got nowhere. The idea resurfaced in 1986 when a brave soul pitched the idea for a TV station to the Foreign Office (since they already supported the radio service). This time it got the support of the BBC (and the Foreign Office) but it became apparent that the Prime Minister, Margaret Thatcher, was not inclined to finance the operation. The plan was kept alive by the Foreign Office but the BBC never received a penny from Whitehall. It later emerged that ITN's Chief Executive, David Nicholas, went to see Thatcher to complain that the BBC project would damage his own plans for an international news service (which materialized as Super Channel's international news bulletin, Chapter 2). Thereafter, although the proposal remained on Geoffrey Howe's Foreign Office desk, he always pushed it to the bottom of his tray because he was not prepared to go to Downing Street and have a row with Thatcher about it. Her lack of support for the BBC might appear surprising considering that ITN had no track record in international news, but her government was seeking ways to reform the financing of public service broadcasting and she was not inclined to fund the BBC's foreign adventures.[13]

Since the BBC refused to get involved in Europa and stayed at arm's length from Super, the corporation nearly passed the 1980s without getting involved in satellite television. Salvation came from Denmark where two telephone companies, KTAS and JTAS, approached BBC Enterprises (as the corporation's commercial arm was called) with a view to retransmitting BBC1 and BBC2 in Scandinavia. These channels were already relayed terrestrially to the continent (Chapter 1) but Denmark was too far away for terrestrial retransmission and offered to pay for satellite capacity. BBC Enterprises looked into it and realized that it was impossible to secure the rights to deliberately exploit BBC1 and BBC2 in that manner. Thus the corporation created a new channel for the Danes in 1987, BBC TV Europe, which was the live relay of BBC1 except for those programmes that the BBC had bought from third parties and for which it was unable to secure international rights. Copyright-sensitive programmes, notably American TV series, were replaced by BBC2 documentaries. The Danish companies, who paid for the transmission costs and the rights for Scandinavia, marketed

BBC TV Europe to cable operators in Sweden and Norway but were never able to make money out of the venture. In April 1989 BBC Enterprises assumed the satellite costs and began signing deals with a few other cable operators.[14]

As BBC TV Europe was building up its distribution and developing a profile on the continent, the corporation realized that its satellite offering remained fairly crude. Neither the schedule (programmed for UK time) nor the BBC2 fillers were entirely satisfactory. Above all, the BBC had not given up its dream of launching an international news channel. The corporation was pressed into action by the Gulf War in 1990–1, when CNN sprung to the world's attention. As elsewhere in Europe the BBC Director General, Michael Checkland, was frustrated to see CNN sweep the floor but his hands were tied financially. It was he who came up with the idea of using the revenue from BBC cable operations to revamp BBC TV Europe. On 15 April 1991 the corporation launched a channel specially created for Europe, BBC World Service Television. Its schedule remained similar to BBC1 but with the benefit of two continuity announcers and two news programmes specifically produced for the channel. These were a 15-minute *World Business Report* and a daily half-hour international news bulletin.[15] The BBC then looked for a partner to develop its fledgling international news business and Richard Li, Star TV's owner, stepped forward. The two companies created a dedicated 24-hour news channel for Asia, also called BBC World Service Television. This station originally broadcast from an old store cupboard that had been converted into a makeshift studio on the seventh floor of a building in White City (the BBC Television Centre in West London). Mirrors were installed to make the studio look bigger and roller blinds with different colours were pulled down for *The World Today*, the business news and the weather. The editorial side of the channel was controlled by Bush House and the editor came from the World Service radio newsroom.

As the two channels developed the situation gradually became clearer for the BBC. The corporation realized that BBC World Service Television was a difficult channel to sell and promote in Europe. In addition to its long name the public did not really understand what the channel was about. The marketplace was also increasingly crowded with stations that were more focused and better defined in terms of what they were offering. By way of contrast the corporation's news channel was doing well in Asia. The BBC decided to expand its news channel worldwide and rename it BBC World. It then launched an entertainment station called BBC Prime.

The corporation financed its project by entering into a joint venture with Pearson and Cox Communications.[16]

The launch of BBC World

The BBC achieved an old ambition when it launched BBC World, a global 24-hour news channel, on 26 January 1995. It invested heavily in the new channel that was based on the low-cost Asian version of BBC World Service Television. Staff was doubled, new presenters and journalists with television experience were brought in and editorial control was wrested from Bush House. Because BBC World News – as the channel was renamed in April 2008 – is a commercial property controlled by BBC Worldwide, it contracts the provision of news content to the corporation. From an editorial perspective, the channel is part of the Global News Division that brings together the World Service, BBC Monitoring and the international online news service (the other three divisions are News, Nation & Regions and Sport). BBC World News has its own newsroom, team of producers, presenters and directors, and has access to the unparalleled international newsgathering resources of the BBC (Chapter 9).

The journalistic and commercial sides of BBC World News occasionally collide, as when the sales team was keen to place advertising for Zimbabwe tourism, a country from which the BBC is banned. In addition, the BBC is protective of its own brand and refuses advertising and sponsorship deals from companies with less than impeccable credentials.

The schedule of BBC World News has been imitated countless times. It is based on a news bulletin at the start of every hour followed by the 'back half-hour' devoted to current affairs, business and lifestyle programming. Current affairs programming encompasses news specials, documentaries, talk shows, debates and interviews. Much of it is dedicated to the reporting and analysis of global issues. International affairs and the planet's social and cultural diversity come alive in specially commissioned documentaries and interviews with a wide array of personalities and power brokers.

No one at the BBC denies that the news network reflects European values.[17] This admission is no reason to accuse the corporation of cultural imperialism, a charge that some scholars aim at Western news organizations with a prominent role in the international news flow. While the channel comes with a worldview, it is well equipped to deal with the complexities of our global order. The World Service heritage has made it attentive to local sensitivities and its long-established network of experienced field correspondents gives it unique insight into local cultures. Evidence shows that BBC World News is appreciated by audiences around the globe (Chapter 9). Ratings have steadily increased ever since it began broadcasting and the station reaches about 80 million households in Europe and over 300 million homes worldwide (Tables 5.5 and 7.1).[18]

From BBC Prime to BBC Global Channels

BBC Prime was launched in 1995 and inherited the distribution base of BBC World Service Television, around 2.2 million European subscribers. The news and factual were thrown overboard in favour of general entertainment, financed exclusively by subscription revenue. The station became popular in Scandinavia and Switzerland, where there is a taste for British comedy programmes, and in Central and Western Europe, where the channel was positioned as an educational tool to aid English language learning. At its peak in the mid-2000s, BBC Prime reached over 20 million subscribers in Europe and was subtitled in more than ten languages.

In 2006 John Smith, BBC Worldwide's CEO since 2004, devised a new strategy for the commercial arm of the corporation. The company's old priority was to programme and format sales and BBC Prime was only an add-on line of business. The channel controller had to liaise continuously with the sales department in order to check that the rights of a particular programme had not already been sold to a third party, which was usually the case. BBC Prime was a brand with a confused identity and was not a particularly good showcase for the BBC's vast library of programmes. Smith's strategy was based on what other media conglomerates had grasped a while ago: selling programmes is good for the financial spreadsheet but only television channels allow a company to build assets at international level (Chapter 8). Accordingly, BBC Worldwide has changed focus from programme sales to development of international channel brands and businesses. A new division was created, Global Channels, and a team headed by Darren Childs was recruited from the best international broadcasters.

BBC Prime is being replaced by five channels: BBC Entertainment is a premium destination offering a mix of contemporary dramas (*Life on Mars*, *Doctor Who*), comedy (*Extras*, *Little Britain*), old classics and light entertainment (*Strictly Come Dancing*). BBC Lifestyle has six key programming strands: food, home, fashion and style, health and body, parenting and personal development. BBC Knowledge showcases the corporation's factual and documentary programming and its schedule is organized around five broad themes: the world, the past, business, science and technology, and people. CBeebies targets pre-schoolers with programmes like *Tweenies*, *Little Robots* and *Underground Ernie*, and BBC HD offers a mix of programmes in high definition.

Unlike BBC Prime, these channels are properly resourced with priority access to BBC programming. The modus operandi has been completely revised: instead of one pan-regional feed covering Europe, the new channels are all locally managed and fully adapted to each local market (Chapter 10). BBC Worldwide has started deploying its teams across the world. In Europe it launched its first-ever non-English channels in Poland in December 2007, managed by a 30-strong local team. Their impact has been dramatic, multiplying the corporation's Polish audience reach by ten. Similar plans have been drawn up for Scandinavia, Spain, Italy and France. The BBC has converted relatively late to transnational TV networks, but because of its formidable programming assets the new strategy should rapidly turn it into a global powerhouse in television entertainment.[19]

PUBLIC BROADCASTERS AND TRANSFRONTIER TELEVISION: ADAPTING TO THE NEW MEDIA ORDER

Transnational publicly-funded TV channels contribute to the diversity of international television and extend viewers' choice. Public funding can be justified in order to address gaps in channel provision and to reach audiences that may be overlooked by commercial broadcasters. However, these stations face a tough challenge in the emerging media order. They were designed for the 20-channel environment of the analogue cable platforms that prevailed in Europe in the 1990s. In an era when new TV channels are launched every month and satellite platforms carry hundreds of channels, a new strategy might be required.

Many commercial broadcasters, such as MTV or Discovery, have adapted to the extra competition by multiplying the number of channels (Chapters 7 and 11). Where once one station represented 5 per cent of a 20-channel cable platform, now ten are needed on a digital satellite platform in order to achieve the same presence and combat audience fragmentation. Public broadcasters' stand-alone international channels struggle to keep an audience because they lack visibility and are slipping out of viewers' sight. In the case of general-interest channels, such as Arte and TV5Monde, their offerings might be too broad in an era when cable and satellite viewers are getting accustomed to niche stations. The BBC alone among public broadcasters has come to terms with this problem by launching its own portfolio of channels. For the other public broadcasters a solution might be to discuss distribution agreements and bundle their channels together in order to break their isolation on satellite platforms and increase brand awareness.

Too many public broadcasters are still locked in a national mindset. They need to engage more in transnational production and distribution arrangements. Cross-border thematic channels offer a solid ground for constructive collaborations. In the past, public broadcasters' collaborative efforts under the aegis of the EBU have not always been crowned with success. Although Arte itself should have thought about enlarging its ownership structure, as a transnational organization it can provide a model for future joint ventures set up by two or more public corporations. Public broadcasters should pay particular attention to genres in which they could make an original contribution, such as factual entertainment and children's television.

CONCLUSION TO PART TWO

The pioneers of transnational television began the 1990s in an inhospitable environment. They faced entrenched monopolies, protectionist governments, obstructive politicians, an advertising industry unimpressed with their distribution figures and advertisers not equipped to deal with international television. But their situation changed dramatically in the course of the decade.

The legal framework became more accommodating with a series of EU directives that first legalized transnational broadcasting (the 1989 TVWF Directive) and then facilitated the international transmission of cultural works (the 1993 SatCab Directive). The rapid increase in homes with access to cable and satellite television services expanded the reception universe of transnational channels, alongside the collapse of the Berlin Wall which opened up new markets eastwards. The formation of satellite broadcast neighbourhoods through satellite co-location and the digitization of global communications networks facilitated the international transmission of TV channels and images. DTH broadcasting unlocked whole new markets for satellite channels in countries that were poorly cabled and increased choice for viewers in cabled areas (Chapter 4). The evolution of the advertising industry favoured cross-border TV channels with the emergence of international media buying agencies embedded in global communications groups. Their clients began to need international media to communicate with their stakeholders and expand their brand in a consistent fashion across the continent (Chapter 5). Public broadcasters launched several channels and continued to make their mark in the PETV industry (Chapter 6). During the 1990s conditions for cross-border television changed radically, announcing a transnational shift in European broadcasting.

PART THREE

TRANSNATIONAL TELEVISION IN EUROPE

CHAPTER 7

KEY ENTERTAINMENT GENRES AND CHANNELS IN TRANSNATIONAL TELEVISION

In some parts of the world cross-border TV channels have acquired an immense reputation. Al Jazeera is now an integral part of Arab identity and satellite channels are perceived to be at the heart of media and cultural changes in South East Asia.[1] So far the progress of European TV networks has been more inconspicuous because cross-border stations do not have the same cultural impact in Europe as elsewhere. Many European markets are very competitive and broadcasters must respond to viewers' tastes and advertisers' needs. It is a particularly arduous task for international broadcasters who must surmount the continent's cultural and linguistic diversity. Although growth remains strong in pay television, Europe is a fairly mature market and the inertia created by entrenched positions makes shifts harder to take place.

Despite these obstacles, European cross-border TV channels have developed rapidly since the late 1990s' transnational shift. International TV brands and channels have outperformed national television in recent times and their presence has grown considerably in the European cable and satellite universe. This chapter examines the expansion of cross-border TV networks in the last few years and provides an overview of the key international players in television entertainment.

PETV EXPANSION

The international distribution of transnational TV networks has expanded rapidly over the last decade or so. Table 7.1 shows the *full-time* European distribution of leading channels in the PETV industry. The number of connections to TV households is a technical figure that has no implication for ratings other than that people need to access a channel before they can decide to watch it. As indicated in Table 7.1, the average distribution has more than doubled and cumulative distribution has multiplied threefold since 1997. The current leaders have a European distribution that is marginally below the *total* number of TV households in Europe's five key markets (Germany, France, Italy, Spain and the UK). This figure even underestimates real PETV growth since many prominent transnational TV networks are not represented in Table 7. 1 for lack of continuous data since 1997 (their distribution is indicated on a case-by-case basis).

Distribution expands faster when channels are distributed for free or do not demand carriage fees (which is frequently the case with news networks). Either these stations do not have the pulling power with viewers to require payment from pay-TV operators or they operate exclusively on an advertising-funded business model. Most children's and factual entertainment stations function on a dual revenue stream basis (advertising plus carriage fees) and tend *not* to give their channels away for free. As Table 7.1 shows, the distribution of PETV channels varies greatly. MTV tops the table because the strength of this brand was such that, until recently, a pay-TV operator which did not include it in its bouquet had an awful lot of explaining to do to its customers.

Gross distribution includes partial distribution achieved through programming blocks or windows on third-party channels. For many networks partial distribution does not add much to their full-time connections but it makes a big difference for seven channels (Table 7.2). For instance, EuroNews is relayed at night by the public service broadcasters that are part of its consortium, and the children's channels have branded blocks (i.e. branded programming windows) on terrestrial stations across Europe. These windows often enable cross-border TV channels to sound out a market before launching a local feed. A particularity of the PETV industry is a strong out-of-home distribution, and these channels can be watched in millions of hotel rooms and other public places (Chapter 12).

A station's ratings cannot be deduced from its distribution range. Networks with a fairly similar number of connections may have quite different viewing figures. For instance, while MTV and TV5Monde have a comparable distribution, the former's weekly reach is nearly four times that of the latter (Table 5.5).

Assessing the overall ratings of transnational TV channels in Europe is fraught with difficulty. As explained in Chapter 5, the people meter methodology is still not standardized across Europe and the EMS survey only covers upmarket viewers in a selection of countries. People meters are not always suited to the needs of the PETV industry and not all cross-

Table 7.1: Full-time distribution of the leading pan-European television channels, 1997–2007 (in millions of TV households)

	1997	1998	1999	2000	2001	2002	2003	2004	2005	2006	2007
Arte	27.4	78.9	61.9	61.9	65.0	65.0	65.0	62.9	60.7	64.9	81.7
BBC Prime	4.9	6.3	7.2	8.2	10.5	10.8	10.6	17.3	22.0	22.5	22.5
BBC World News	25.1	33.1	39.3	45.5	49.4	56.4	57.5	66.0	72.6	82.2	78.5
Bloomberg	-	27.7	10.3	24.6	30.1	37.6	39.8	48.5	46.7	47.2	58.8
Cartoon Network[a]	31.2	36.0	49.7	21.0	28.6	26.9	28.4	31.5	34.9	40.0	43.1
CNBC Europe	12.6	21.0	26.7	32.9	40.2	41.9	54.3	55.5	63.5	61.6	57.0
CNN International	58.9	67.8	68.8	73.2	81.0	84.7	90.0	95.8	98.2	101.6	104.2
Discovery	7.0	16.3	20.4	26.7	31.4	32.9	34.3	39.6	42.5	55.7	88.2
ESPN Classic	/	/	/	/	/	4.5	4.5	6.5	8.0	20.0	22.0
EuroNews	30.4	34.3	34.9	34.0	44.0	48.9	55.5	56.0	62.8	75.9	86.0
Eurosport	71.9	75.6	80.6	88.3	93.0	95.3	94.4	95.6	101.2	104.5	109.9
Extreme Sports	-	-	-	-	-	-	11.8	17.8	19.5	20.8	24.3
Fashion TV	-	-	27.5	29.0	31.5	32.0	34.0	34.6	35.7	66.6	104.2
Hallmark	-	6.2	10.0	14.0	15.0	17.5	18.2	20.9	19.8	28.0	31.6
The History Channel	-	-	-	8.0	10.0	11.5	14.5	15.0	16.2	18.1	20.8
Jetix[b]	/	-	15.4	23.1	25.0	31.0	33.0	36.5	39.6	44.8	49.4
Motors TV	-	/	/	2.8	3.7	9.5	10.8	12.1	14.1	15.0	16.0
MTV	44.1	58.8	79.1	83.6	94.2	92.8	99.2	103.6	107.8	112.2	128.1
North American Sports Network	/	/	/	/	/	/	0.1	0.1	0.4	6.6	6.4
National Geographic Channel	4.0	14.9	15.3	19.2	22.9	26.9	31.4	34.4	37.2	43.9	48.2
NBC Universal Global Networks[c]	2.3	7.0	4.5	9.8	15.2	15.2	18.9	20.2	21.0	31.1	30.9
Nickelodeon	14.3	14.5	14.8	15.1	15.5	19.0	19.7	20.0	58.3	65.3	69.6
Sky News	2.4	-	38.9	18.6	22.7	24.0	24.0	29.7	34.9	40.3	49.8
Travel Channel	2.8	3.9	-	-	-	18.0	19.0	22.0	23.5	30.8	38.4
TV5Monde	45.5	55.7	57.6	65.1	68.0	71.4	83.7	87.4	94.6	99.3	110.0
VH1	12.9	15.0	20.4	23.1	19.2	18.5	17.7	20.0	22.3	27.3	18.6
Average distribution	23.4	33.3	35.4	33.1	37.1	37.2	37.3	40.4	44.5	51.0	57.6
Year-on-year growth (%)	/	+ 29.7	+ 6.0	- 6.6	+ 10.8	+ 0.3	+ 0.3	+ 7.7	+ 9.2	+ 12.8	+ 11.5
Cumulative distribution	397.7	566.8	673.3	727.7	816.1	892.2	970.3	1049.5	1158.0	1326.2	1498.2
Year-on-year growth (%)	/	+ 29.8	+ 15.8	+ 7.5	+ 10.8	+ 8.5	+ 8.0	+ 7.5	+ 9.4	+ 12.7	+ 11.5

Sources: company sources, *C&SE* and *M&M Guide.*

Data conventions: '/': not applicable; '-': not available.

[a] The figures from 1997 to 1999 include classic movies channel TNT.

[b] Formerly Fox Kids.

[c] Formerly Universal Studios Networks, comprising SciFi, 13th Street and Studio Universal.

border TV networks subscribe to them. In addition, these mass audience measurement systems can only monitor the channels that are registered in their country of reception and would ignore the French or English viewers of channels like Al Jazeera English or Deutsche Welle-TV.

However, an estimate can be made based on the figures published by the national audience measurement institutes. In Europe's most competitive markets (France, Germany, Italy and the UK), transnational TV brands' and channels' share of weekly viewing time is at least 10 per cent of the total viewing time. Within the cable and satellite universe, this share can climb up to about 25 per cent.[2] In the newer markets (Central Europe) and smaller countries (e.g. Austria, the Baltic states, Belgium, Cyprus, Ireland, Luxembourg, the Nordic nations, Switzerland), transnational channels' share of viewing time can exceed 50 per cent of total viewing time.[3]

Table 7.2: PETV channels with the largest partial distribution, 2007 (in millions of TV households)

	Full-time distribution	Gross distribution
Bloomberg	58.8	83.7
CNBC Europe	57.0	114.0
CNN	104.2	125.3
EuroNews	86.0	207.0
The History Channel	20.8	57.9
Jetix	49.4	180.1
Nickelodeon	69.6	114.6

Source: M&M Guide 2007.

KEY ENTERTAINMENT GENRES AND CHANNELS

The number of transnational TV channels in Europe has been growing exponentially for a number of years. Today they have diversified into many genres and have become particularly dominant in international and business news, children's television and factual entertainment. This section reviews the leading channels and analyses the specificities of the key entertainment genres listed in Table 7.3.

Table 7.3: Cross-border TV channels in Europe according to genre, 2008

Genre	Channel
News	Al Jazeera English; BBC World News; CCTV 9; CNN International; Deutsche Welle-TV; EuroNews; Fox News; France 24; NDTV 24x7; Russia Today; Sky News
Business news	Bloomberg Television; CNBC Europe
Children	BabyFirst; BabyTV; Boomerang, Cartoon Network, Cartoonito, Toonami; CBeebies; Cinemagic, Disney Channel, Playhouse Disney, Toon Disney; Jetix; JimJam; Nickelodeon, Nick Jr., Nicktoons
Music television	C Music, Trace; Mezzo; MTV, TMF, VH1, VIVA; Viasat Music
Factual entertainment	Animal Planet; BBC Knowledge, BBC Lifestyle; The Biography Channel, Crime & Investigation, The History Channel, Military History; Discovery suite of channels; E! International Network, The Style Network; Fashion TV; National Geographic suite of channels; Spektrum; Travel Channel; Viasat Crime, Viasat Explorer, Viasat History, Viasat Nature; Zone Reality
Entertainment	13th Street, Sci Fi; Animax; AXN; BBC Entertainment; Fox Channel, Fox Crime, Fox Life, FX; Hallmark; HBO; Paramount Comedy; Zone Club, Zone Fantasy, Zone Horror, Zone Romantica, Zone Thriller
Movies	Cinemax; MGM Channel; Studio Universal; Turner Classic Movies; TV1000 suite of channels; Zone Europa
Sports	ESPN Classic; Eurosport, Eurosport 2; Extreme Sports Channel; Motors TV; North American Sports Network; Viasat Golf, Viasat Sport
General interest	Arte; TV5Monde
Adult entertainment	The Adult Channel; Playboy TV; Private suite of channels
Religion	Daystar; The God Channel; Islam Channel; Revelation TV; TBN Europe
Migrant television	All channels that target an audience with a common linguistic and cultural background

CHILDREN'S TELEVISION

The Children's Channel

The Children's Channel, launched in September 1984, was one of the very first UK cable stations to seek cable distribution in Europe (Chapter 1). In the early 1990s the channel went through a period of change initiated by the management team installed by Flextech. They reoriented some programming strands towards early teenagers, renaming the channel TCC after discovering that children do not like the word 'children' in their television channels. When Flextech bought the station in 1991 it inherited a distribution of about two million homes spread between the UK, Ireland, the Netherlands and Scandinavia. Nonetheless it was still a UK-centric company and seemed hesitant to pursue its internationalization strategy. Once the big American children's TV brands arrived in Europe, TCC suddenly faced rivals who combined large libraries, marketing savvy and deep pockets. A hesitant management, its half-baked internationalization strategy and the competition all took their toll on TCC. In April 1998 one of the longest-running satellite channels was closed down and replaced by Trouble, a station targeting UK teenagers.[4]

Turner Broadcasting System Europe's kids' channels

Ted Turner launched numerous cable stations in his home market. Following WTBS, CNN and Headline News, he started Turner Network Television (TNT) in 1988, Cartoon Network in 1992 and Turner Classic Movies (TCM) in 1994. CNN arrived in Europe in 1985 (Chapter 2) and was followed by Cartoon Network and TNT in the autumn of 1993. In the beginning they shared a channel on cable and satellite platforms, alternating between daytime and evening.

Cartoon Network started as a library channel of animation. In 1991 Turner acquired the Hanna-Barbera library for US$200 million. With the addition of the MGM and Warner Bros libraries, Turner Broadcasting System (TBS) amassed some 8,500 animated shows. Properties include *The Flintstones*, *Scooby Doo*, *Tom and Jerry*, *Yogi Bear* and *Looney Tunes* (Road Runner, Bugs Bunny, etc.).

In the late 1990s, TNT and Cartoon Network were split to become two stand-alone channels and the latter carried on as a library-based channel until the launch of Boomerang in May 2000. Boomerang was established as the classic animation channel and Cartoon Network became more contemporary, the most popular shows including *The Powerpuff Girls*, *Dexter's Laboratory*, *Foster's Home for Imaginary Friends*, *Ed, Edd n Eddy* and *The Cramp Twins*. A third animation channel, Toonami, was a spin-off from Cartoon Network in October 2003. Its schedule is action-oriented and it targets six to 12 years old with shows like *Batman, Teen Titans, Pokémon* and *Star Wars*.

TBS Europe has made a series of more recent changes to its portfolio of channels. It launched Cartoon Network Too, scheduling classic animated shows, in the UK in April 2006. It confirmed its interest in the pre-school market by upgrading Cartoonito from a branded block on Cartoon Network into a stand-alone channel, also for the British market, in May 2007. Toonami has become a branded block on Cartoon Network Too in Britain and is now distributed in Italy. The two brands with the widest distribution are Boomerang and Cartoon Network, both of which have a pan-European feed and a large network of fully localized stations (Tables 7.1 and 11.1).[5]

Nickelodeon

Nickelodeon started in the USA in 1979 and arrived in Europe in September 1993. Its parent company, Viacom, was already present in Europe with MTV, and Nickelodeon came to the UK as a 50:50 joint venture with BSkyB. It launched in Germany in July 1995, with Ravensburg Film und TV as a minority partner, and reached Scandinavia in February 1997. A pan-European feed went on air in November 1998, followed by localized channels in Spain (March 1999), the Netherlands (February 2002), Italy (November 2004), Turkey (March 2005), Portugal (June 2005), France (November 2005), Austria (July 2006) and Poland (June 2008).

The channel's early days in Europe were not plain sailing. Nickelodeon had to pull out of Germany in May 1998 following a decision by the media authorities to grant a 'must-carry' status to a rival children's channel operated by ARD and ZDF. The ruling forced cable operators to drop Nickelodeon in favour of KinderKanal (now Kika).[6] Nickelodeon did not try to relaunch there until September 2005. Further, Viacom's non-music properties such as Nickelodeon only became a priority for the company in the early 2000s. There were issues with the brand – in Europe people did not know what it meant – and with the programming, which was too American in character.

Only progressively did Nickelodeon invest in local programming and replace its pan-European feed with fully localized stations.

By 2008 Nickelodeon was present in most European territories, which it covers with a pan-European feed and 11 localized versions (Tables 7.1 and 11.1). Distribution is particularly strong in the UK, Ireland, Benelux, Germany and Austria.[7] Nick Jr., Europe's first dedicated pre-school channel, was initially launched in the UK in September 1999 and has been in the Netherlands since February 2005. Nicktoons, an animation channel, went on air in the UK in July 2002 and in Benelux in August 2007.

The Nickelodeon suite of channels covers the entire genre of pre-school and children's programming from animation to live action. They schedule country-specific shows as well as global franchises that have proven cross-border appeal such as *Dora the Explorer*, *Rugrats* and *SpongeBob SquarePants*.[8]

Disney

Disney was meant to launch its first European channel on Sky's fledgling platform in 1989. It was supposed to be a joint venture between the two businesses but Murdoch and Disney parted company acrimoniously within months, accusing each other of seeking control over the venture.[9] Next Disney acquired a stake in GMTV, a contractor supplying morning television programming to ITV, and formed a joint venture with CLT in order to start Super RTL.[10] Disney eventually launched its own branded channel in Britain in October 1995, this time with BSkyB holding a 20 per cent stake. David Hulbert, then president of Walt Disney Television International, exclaimed that 'no one ever chooses to hand over equity in their channels', implying that Murdoch was able to leverage Sky's reach in Britain in order to force his way into the venture's capital.[11] Disney then launched local versions of its channel in France (March 1997), Spain (April 1998), Italy (October 1998), Germany (1999) and Scandinavia (early 2000s). By the mid-2000s Disney Channel was in 14 territories across Western Europe, where it reached about 14 million homes. Its first foray in Central Europe came in December 2006 with a channel launch in Poland, adding 1.3 million subscribers. Disney Channel did not have a particularly large distribution because it was initially a premium service but it has been moved in to basic packages. In most territories Disney Channel is accompanied by Toon Disney, an animation channel, and Playhouse Disney for pre-schoolers. This portfolio is completed by Cinemagic, launched in Britain in March 2006 and France in September 2007. It is a premium service that screens movies from the Disney and Pixar libraries. Taking into account every local station, there are in excess of 50 Disney-branded channels in Europe today.[12]

Over recent years Disney has enjoyed great success in Europe, performing strongly in most markets. The company has never had a pan-European satellite feed and has always been careful to offer fully localized versions of its lead channel that span live action, animation, movies, TV series and game shows. The Disney-branded channels air acquired programming but the emphasis has always been on original content. The company can rely on its vast library of movie titles, animated shows and steady stream of international TV hits including *Hannah Montana*, *High School Musical*, *That's So Raven* and *Wizards of Waverly Place*. Disney is also able to produce strong local content such as the high school sitcom *Quelli dell'Intervallo*, which has been a formidable success for Disney Channel Italy and has been adapted for other territories. In April 2007 Disney opened its Global Original Programming hub in London, which handles the development of live action and animated series for worldwide distribution outside the United States. Disney's objective is to collaborate with 'the best creative talent in Europe' and several co-productions have been announced with British companies.[13] For the 2008/9 season, the Disney channels, together with Jetix, have access to an excess of 445 hours of new programming.[14]

Jetix

Jetix was the fourth network to enter the pan-European children's television market in the 1990s. Its majority shareholder was Fox Family Worldwide, a joint venture formed in the United States in 1995 between Haim Saban's Saban Entertainment and Rupert Murdoch's Fox Broadcasting. The group's main assets were two Fox Kids channels in the USA and Latin America, and the Saban library, containing some 6,000 half-hours of animated shows. Fox Kids arrived in Europe in 1996, launching on the Sky platform in October. This was followed by channels in the Netherlands and France in 1997, Poland, Spain and Scandinavia in 1998, Belgium in 1999, Italy, Turkey, Germany and Hungary in 2000, the Czech Republic and Slovakia in 2001 (through an extension of the Hungarian feed), and Greece in 2001.[15]

That same year a chain of events led to a change of ownership. Saban made known his intention of selling his stake in Fox Family Worldwide to News Corp. Murdoch considered his options and, ultimately deciding that he needed the cash to finance his acquisition of DirecTV, sold the operation to Disney for US$5.3 billion. Disney set about rebranding its new property as it did not own all the rights associated with the Fox brand. Fox Kids became Jetix in 2004 and the integration with Disney began in earnest. Today, Jetix Europe is a public company registered in the Netherlands that is 76 per cent owned by Disney. Synergies were created at multiple levels and a series of agreements was concluded between Jetix and various sales, distribution and licensing subsidiaries at Disney. Above all, Jetix has entered into a global programming alliance with its majority shareholder, enabling both companies to mutually reinforce their programming.

Jetix fits well in Disney's portfolio of channels because it is geared towards boys aged six to 14, while the Disney Channel and Playhouse Disney are family oriented and remain close to the traditional Disney values. Jetix is an all-animation proposition that concentrates on action and adventure series. Key shows comprise the hit properties *Power Rangers*, *Shaman King*, *Sonic X* and Emmy-winning *Tutenstein*. As an all-animation channel, Jetix is easier to deploy internationally than a full service network and by the end of 2007 Jetix was reaching about 50 million European homes with 15 feeds and 19 languages (Tables 7.1 and 11.1).[16]

JimJam

The latest arrival in children's transnational television is JimJam. The network was launched in 2006 and became a joint venture between Chellomedia and HIT Entertainment, a leading producer of children's programming, in September 2007. It was rolled out across Central and Eastern Europe two months later and had reached Switzerland and the Netherlands by May 2008. JimJam is aimed at pre-schoolers, and benefits from HIT Entertainment's library of classic titles that includes *Angelina Ballerina*, *Bob the Builder*, *Fireman Sam*, *Kipper*, *Thomas & Friends* and *Pingu*.[17]

The babies and toddlers market: BabyTV and BabyFirst

Television channels that are intended for an audience even younger than pre-schoolers have emerged over recent years. They are dedicated to babies, toddlers and their parents. They sometimes produce or commission country-specific content but this is a genre that fits easily within the transnational since programming is driven by visuals and a good amount of these shows are non-verbal. All these stations claim to consult experts and state educational benefits, alleging that they develop babies' learning and enrich the interaction between children and parents.

The market leader is BabyTV, which went on air for the first time in Israel in December 2003. It began to internationalize in 2004 with the help of François Thiellet, managing director of Thema and one of Fashion TV's founders. As its distribution reached 30 territories worldwide it was acquired by Fox International Channels (FIC), the News Corp division, in October 2007. BabyTV covers Europe with one video feed in three languages (English, French and German). It is available on about 50 cable or satellite platforms across 22 European territories.[18]

BabyFirst is an independently owned ad-free US network that started in May 2006. It crossed the Atlantic to launch on Sky in the UK in February 2007 and has since signed major carriage deals in Europe, notably with Canalsat in France. It is already a player with global reach that is able to broadcast a considerable amount of original content.[19]

Channels for the under-threes have expanded rapidly in recent years and still have plenty of potential. One of the genre's advantages is that although the audience is limited it is constantly renewed and the same shows can be aired again and again to a new public.

DIVERSIFIED ENTERTAINMENT CONGLOMERATES AND PAN-EUROPEAN CHILDREN'S CHANNELS

It is no coincidence that three of the world's leading media conglomerates, Time Warner, Disney and Viacom, crossed the Atlantic at about the same time to establish transnational children's networks in Europe.[20] The advantages of running these channels rise well above the risks. First, a television network offers a controlled branded environment. Cartoon Network or the Disney Channel are branded 24 hours a day, seven days a week, and it is a place where Time Warner or Disney can nurture and control their brand to a far greater extent than when they license their programmes. When programming is licensed to third-party broadcasters it is placed alongside different types of programmes and brand awareness of the property is weakened. Conglomerates and their subsidiaries have control over the scheduling of their own channels, helping them to build *franchises* such as *Batman*, *Power Rangers*, *Pirates of the Caribbean* or *Winnie the Pooh*. Franchises are usually driven by movies and TV shows and become multiple revenue sources once they have been expanded into the consumer product market. Control over a transnational TV network greatly facilitates this process, and contributes to overall growth by helping build brands that can be exploited across a range of platforms and businesses.

Furthermore, running a channel is far more lucrative than simply selling content to third-party broadcasters. A station owned by a conglomerate will often pay the full market value for content purchased from another affiliate in the same group. When Cartoon Network buys a show from the Warner Bros studios, there is no 'sweetheart deal' between the two Time Warner subsidiaries because otherwise they would raid the bottom line of their parent company. In addition to the money received for purchased material, pan-European children's channels make substantial profits and are thus able to contribute to the overall company revenue. On average, the contribution from a channel in children's television is more than three times what the conglomerate would get from simply selling content to third-party broadcasters. Another advantage is that *channels represent long-term investment that helps a company build up its asset value*. By way of contrast, the sale of a television programme to a broadcaster is a mere cash transaction: once the sale is concluded there is no asset left.

Conversely, a channel can greatly benefit from being owned by a conglomerate. In an environment that can count hundreds of stations, channels need to be precise about the public they target. Channels operated by a media group can be part of a *portfolio strategy* and avoid the positioning problems that beset The Children's Channel when trying to target a too disparate audience. They can also have access to unique content. Historic libraries (e.g. TBS's Hanna-Barbera catalogue) help establish a network and build its brand. After a few years, when the schedule needs to be renewed and expanded, the new material can be acquired from third parties but can also be sourced from within the conglomerate or associated companies.

Among divisions of the same conglomerate, say an animation studio and an international channel subsidiary, much of the content is acquired at market rate. For instance, when Disney Channel in the UK wanted to show *Eight Simple Rules*, a successful sitcom that ran on the ABC Network in the USA, it had to outbid third-party television channels to win the right to air it. Crucially, however, there exist priority agreements and first refusal rights for certain material. In the Disney group, Disney-branded movies, animated and pre-school series are usually covered by such arrangements.

Similar agreements prevail between Warner Bros and TBS's children's channels. Since TBS became a Time Warner affiliate in 1996 the group has merged the home video and TV syndication departments of the two companies. Time Warner focused Warner Bros on production and syndication and specialized TBS in running their cable and satellite stations. Both affiliates are closely coordinated and not all the material produced by Warner Bros is available on the open market. Agreements are in place that stipulate that TBS can buy what Warner Bros produce, and because it is produced in the group the terms and conditions are slightly better than they would be for outside parties. The Disney and Warner Bros studios are leaders in their industry and TV channels that belong to the same conglomerates hold a decisive advantage over the competition by having these content acquisition deals in place.

In addition, stations owned by a conglomerate have the opportunity to co-produce shows with other affiliates. Jetix co-produces *Power Rangers*, *W.I.T.C.H.*, *Super Robot Monkey Team Hyperforce Go!* and *Yin Yang Yo!* with Disney. While Disney exploits these properties in Latin America, North America and Asia, Jetix uses them in Europe. The advantage for the European channel is access to world-class programming at a fraction of the price.[21]

Channels run by media groups have the freedom to acquire and co-produce material with third parties. These networks sign co-production agreements with partners ranging from small independent production companies to terrestrial broadcasters. For instance, one of Cartoon Network's current hits, *Cramp Twins*, is a co-production between the station and TV-Loonland in Germany. Besides the fact that independent producers have fresh ideas, they may have content that might help a channel do well in some significant market even though the show might not be relevant everywhere. An added benefit is that the acquisitions and co-productions made in European territories help channels to fulfil their quota of European content (Chapter 4). Conglomerate-owned channels have the best of both worlds: they have access to exclusive content and always have the ability to complement it with third-party material acquired in the marketplace.

MUSIC AND YOUTH TELEVISION

Viacom's music properties

As seen in Chapter 2, in 1987 MTV was the second American cable network to arrive in Europe. Since then it has grown into one of Europe's most successful TV brands. As a pace-setter in the practice of localization, MTV's development is narrated in Chapter 11. Suffice to say here that full-time distribution was in excess of 128 million households in Europe alone in 2007 (Table 7.1). It is a transnational network of about 40 localized stations that spread from Portugal to the Baltic states (Table 7.4). Every channel broadcasts a mix of local and global shows and music that is set according to local demand. MTV was also the first music TV channel to expand to youth programming and not to rely solely on video clips. In the process it pioneered reality television and established itself as a leading youth brand.

Table 7.4: MTVNE's music channels in Europe, 2008

MTV		**VH1**
Adria (incl. separate	Romania	European
feeds for Bosnia, Croatia,	Russia	Poland
Macedonia, Serbia &	Sweden	Russia
Montenegro, and	Turkey	UK
Slovenia)	UK/Ireland	**VH1 Classic** (European)
Baltic (incl. separate	Ukraine	**VH2** (European)
feeds for Estonia, Latvia	**MTV2** (multi-territory)	**The Music Factory**
and Lithuania)	**MTV Base** (multi-	Belgium
Denmark	territory)	Flanders
Spain	**MTV Brand New** (Italy)	Netherlands
European	**MTV Classic** (Poland)	UK
Finland	**MTV Dance**	**TMF Party** (Netherlands)
France	(UK/Ireland)	**TMF Pure** (Netherlands)
Germany	**MTV Entertainment**	
Hungary	(Germany)	**VIVA**
Italy	**MTV Flux** (Italy,	Austria
Netherlands	UK/Ireland)	Germany
Norway	**MTV Hits** (multi-territory)	Hungary
Poland	**MTV Idol** (France)	Poland
Portugal	**MTV Pulse** (France)	Switzerland

VH1 (Video Hits One) started life in the USA in 1985 and first aired the clips that were not hip enough to make it on to MTV. It progressively acquired its own identity, targeting a more mature audience and offering a distinctive rock- and jazz-based playlist. VH1's European journey was tortuous. It first launched as two separate feeds in the UK and Germany in spring 1995. A pan-European channel was manufactured out of the British feed and in June 1999 VH1 Export started broadcasting across 20 territories. The channel had a short life-span and was pulled from Europe within two years. Unlike MTV, where videos have a promotional purpose, rights to VH1 tracks usually have to be paid for. Plus, many songs aired on VH1 Export had UK clearance only. The channel broadcast a lot of UK-centric shows containing cultural references that made no sense outside Britain. In 2001 VH1 Export and VH1 Germany were replaced by VH1 Europe. While VH1 UK carried on as a local station, the schedule of VH1 Europe was made as clear and consistent as possible: a horizontal stripped schedule was introduced across the week alongside vertical scheduling at the weekend. Over the years VH1 has remained a pan-European channel and only Britain, Poland and Russia have their own VH1 station. Two pan-European sister channels were introduced at a later stage: VH1 Classic and VH2 (Table 7.4).

As a pan-European network VH1 prioritizes the cultural commonalities of its audience in core markets and pushes big international acts such as ABBA, the Bee Gees, Queen or Aretha Franklin for VH1 Classic and Coldplay, Bon Jovi or Céline Dion for VH1. The European feed has aired its own weekly international *Album Chart* show since September 2005, and on 1 July 2007 the network broadcast live from Wembley in London the concert that commemorated the life of Princess Diana. The VH1 channels schedule a growing amount of original programming, moving away from music videos and their declining ratings. Although music and music-related content remain VH1's backbone and unifying theme, the network has branched out into celebrity culture. VH1 Europe has aired *Love-Crazed Celebrity Couples*, *Shortest Celebrity Marriages*, *Celebrity Tattoos*, *Celebrity Swag*, *Celebrity Baby Names*, and also *Celebrity Fit Club*, *Celebrity Eye Candy* and *Celebrity Paranormal*. VH1's progression in Europe has been steady (Table 7.1) but the network has yet to acquire the pulling power of the MTV brand.[22]

Viacom has acquired two other music networks in Europe over the years. TMF (The Music Factory) was launched by a Dutch DJ, Lex Harding, in 1995. TMF shunned the international music acts to concentrate on the local music scene and became immensely popular in Holland and Flanders at a time when MTV insisted on a pan-European approach. When Viacom acquired the station in 2001 it expanded programming to youth- and music-related content, and although it internationalized the playlists it kept the focus on local culture. TMF was launched in the UK in October 2002 but it has little connection to its Dutch sister channel. Viacom's other brands having signed an exclusivity agreement with Sky, TMF was chosen to get on digital terrestrial television in Britain.

VIVA was launched in December 1993 in Germany by major record labels (Warner Music, EMI and Sony) and local partners who felt that MTV was neglecting a key territory. The local VJs and music worked wonders with the audience and the channel soon dominated the music television market in German-speaking countries. A second channel went live in March 1995, VIVA Zwei, which focused on indie music but became more mainstream when it relaunched as VIVA Plus in 2002. Viacom got hold of the network in 2004 and turned it into a 14-to-24-year-old female-oriented channel. Today VIVA focuses on the German top 30 chart and schedules popular dating and singalong shows specifically aimed at this demographic (e.g. *Shibuya*, *Are U Hot?*, *Date oder Fake?*) alongside local versions of MTV formats such as the *Virgin Diaries*. The year's highlight remains the music awards ceremony, Comet, which has been shown since 1995. MTV Germany has more of an international playlist and targets an older audience. VIVA broadcasts slightly different versions in Austria and German-speaking Switzerland and separate channels cover Poland and Hungary (Table 7.4). It is now a single-channel network since VIVA Plus was turned into Comedy Central in January 2007 (see below).[23]

Lagardère Networks International's MCM and Mezzo

MCM-Euromusique, a francophone music video channel, was launched by François Thiellet in July 1989 with the backing of nine shareholders who controlled between eight and 15 per cent of the shares. The members of the consortium, nearly all French, involved the Générale d'Images, the cable and media interests of Compagnie Générale des Eaux (the future Vivendi), NRJ, a private radio station, and Radio Monte Carlo, which at the time was partially state-owned.

MCM (Monte Carlo Musique) was primarily designed for the French market, but being transmitted on the high-power satellite TDF 1 it found cable relays across Eastern Europe. A proper transborder feed, MCM

International was launched in 1993 and the station's coverage continued to expand, reaching Asia, Latin America and Africa. Towards the end of 1996, two new international stations were created, MCM Africa, featuring world music, and Muzzik, concentrating on classical fare. The MCM international network reached its apex in the late 1990s when its worldwide distribution attained 150 million homes and included local feeds in Romania, Belgium, Thailand and India. MCM was geared to become the world bearer of francophone music and rival MTV on the world stage but it was no match for the American network. The French station was never able to get distribution in three of Europe's core markets: the UK, Germany and Italy. Early in 2001 MCM was sold to Lagardère Networks International, a division of the Lagardère media group.[24]

Lagardère centred its efforts on the francophone feed, which was relayed in France and the French-speaking parts of Belgium and Switzerland. To this day, MCM is market leader in France, which is one of the few remaining territories where MTV is beaten by a local rival. Everywhere else, Lagardère has pretty much given up and the network's international distribution has plummeted. Late in 2003, the French group pulled up its international feeds and relaunched two cheaper all-clip stations, MCM Top (music charts) and MCM Pop. MCM Top is distributed in about 30 countries but the connections do not exceed a few million homes. Question marks hang over the future of these stations because their programming is not distinct enough from the plethora of local stations that transmit back-to-back clips for free.

Lagardère's most significant international property is Mezzo. The French public broadcaster launched a classical music station of the same name in 1996, which merged with MCM's Muzzik five years later. Today Mezzo is an international station with an excess of ten million paying connections in about 40 European territories. It is a fairly high-profile channel in the cable and satellite universe that covers all the performing arts and specializes in the retransmission of performances taking place in Europe's leading venues.[25]

Thema's Trace and C Music

When Lagardère rejigged MCM's international feeds, MCM Africa was sold to Thema, Thiellet's company, who relaunched it as Trace. Trace is about urban music and cultural trends (Hip Hop, R&B, Groove, Electro, Dance, Reggae, etc.) and urban sports such as free running and skateboarding. Its outlook is cosmopolitan and its documentaries embrace a great variety of cities around the world. Trace has about 12 million connections in Europe which it covers with two feeds, one in English and one in French. The station's programming is sufficiently cutting edge to attract teenagers but not scary enough to frighten away investment bankers. Thiellet secured financial backing from a leading investment bank, Goldman Sachs, which helped the channel progress in Europe.

Thiellet began internationalizing the UK's Classic FM TV in 2007. The station is marketed as 'C Music' in Europe and is present in Germany and most of Central Europe. It defines itself as a classical music station for a broad audience (unlike Mezzo which demands a higher cultural capital from its viewers). C Music takes a 'pop-style approach' to classical music and covers 'cross-over' (Il Divo, G4, Vanessa Mae, etc.) and 'chillout' (e.g. William Orbit, Craig Armstrong).[26]

FACTUAL ENTERTAINMENT

Discovery: from factual entertainment to entertainment that is factual

Following its European debut in the UK and Scandinavia in 1989 (Chapter 2), Discovery launched in the Netherlands a few months later, in Spain and Portugal in 1994, and in Germany, Austria and Switzerland two years later. Over the years, feeds were added for Central and Eastern Europe, Poland, Denmark, Italy, France (2004), Hungary (2005), Romania (2006) and Russia (2007). Discovery's European distribution has progressed rapidly in recent years and is particularly strong in the UK and Ireland, Scandinavia and Central Europe, although it remains weak in Spain, France, Italy and Germany. Today the network has access to 88 million homes in 45 European countries which it covers with 15 feeds and 22 languages (Tables 7.1, 7.5 and 11.1). It is a remarkable feat considering that it receives a carriage fee for every subscriber.

Few broadcasters have more brands in their portfolio than Discovery Networks International (DNI). It has 13 brands in Europe alone: Discovery Channel, Animal Planet, Discovery HD, Discovery Home & Health, Discovery Travel & Living, Discovery Real Time, Discovery Science, Discovery World (that replaced Civilisation in April 2008), Discovery Geschichte, Discovery Historia, Discovery Turbo, People + Arts, and DMAX. The number of brands per market varies and in all Discovery broadcasts 47 channels in Europe.

Table 7.5: Discovery Networks Europe's suite of channels, 2008

Europe

Discovery Channel Europe[a]
Discovery Channel Benelux
Discovery Channel Poland
Discovery Channel Nordic
Discovery Channel Sweden
Discovery Channel Denmark
Discovery Channel Italy
Discovery Channel France
Discovery Channel Germany
Discovery Channel Hungary
Discovery Channel Spain/Portugal
Discovery Channel Finland
Discovery Channel Russia

Animal Planet Europe[b]
Aninal Planet Benelux
Animal Planet Nordic
Animal Planet Poland
Animal Planet Germany
Animal Planet Italy

Travel & Living Europe[c]
Travel & Living Italy
Science Europe/Middle East[d]
Science Italy
Science Poland

World Europe[e]
World Italy
World Poland
Real Time France
Real Time Italy
HD Germany/Austria/Switzerland/South Tyrol
Geschichte (Germany)
DMAX (Germany)
HD Europe
Discovery Historia (Poland)
People + Arts Portugal & Spain

UK

Discovery Channel
Home & Health
Animal Planet
Real Time
Real Time Extra
Science
Knowledge
Travel & Living
Turbo
Discovery HD
DMAX

[a-e] Pan-regional feeds for markets without dedicated channel.

DNI is in the process of change. The network is moving away from the single show to series such as *American Chopper, Dangerous Jobs* (including *Deadliest Catch*), *Dirty Jobs* and *Mythbusters*. In the cable and satellite universe, while shows can sink without trace, series are easier to publicize. They are a safer bet as the broadcaster knows what works with viewers and they are easier to develop because of the ongoing relationship with the producer.

DNI is gradually shifting its positioning from factual entertainment to entertainment that is factual. The broadcaster has noticed that the audience for documentaries has not gained a single share point since 1998 and is getting older by the day. Thus it is replacing 'classic documentary' with entertainment that is based on facts. Series such as *American Chopper* contain information but are personality-driven and told in an entertaining way. Discovery is also producing more lifestyle-style shows and adding brands to its portfolio that have a stronger entertainment component. DMAX, which launched in Germany as a free-to-air channel in September 2006 and in the UK in January 2008, mixes documentaries, dramas and lifestyle programming.

For DNI, Europe is part of a global jigsaw: it reaches 241 million households in 172 territories with 102 feeds and 18 brands. It produces about 850 hours of original content every year outside the United States alone and has co-production agreements with leading broadcasters. Its partnership with the BBC has led to *Blue Planet* in the early 2000s, *Walking with Dinosaurs* and, more recently, *Planet Earth*. *Nefertiti Resurrected*, *Hatshepsut: Secrets of Egypt's Lost Queen*, and *The Flight That Fought Back*, a reconstruction of Flight 93 on 9/11, are among other global hits.[27]

The National Geographic suite of channels

The National Geographic Channel, although an American franchise, was first launched outside the USA. It went on air in the UK (Sky) and Australia (Foxtel) on 1 September 1997 and was available in Scandinavia a few weeks later. A few months into its life, the station's distribution received a massive boost from NBC, one of its shareholders.

In October 1993, NBC and Crédit Lyonnais took control of Super Channel, which was languishing in the hands of the Marcucci family, and relaunched it as NBC Super (Chapter 2). Two experienced executives were hired to run the station: Ruud Hendriks, managing director, came from RTL, and Patrick Cox, chairman, was a veteran from Sky Channel. They attempted to establish a pan-European general entertainment channel based on NBC's schedule in America. NBC Super mixed news, documentaries and talk shows such as Jay Leno's *Tonight Show*.[28] The project did not develop according to plan. Cable systems were at full capacity and keeping NBC Super on the networks was a running battle for its management. The programming, lifted from the sister network in the USA, failed to catch European viewers' attention. The management then tried to strike distribution deals with Hollywood studios which were not interested in signing anything pan-European.

In the first half of 1998 it was decided to fold NBC Super into the new CNBC (Chapter 9), and on 1 July 1998 NBC Super's distribution in Europe, which stretched back to Music Box (through Super Channel), was handed over to National Geographic. The conversion affected the UK, Ireland, Scandinavia and Benelux, adding at a stroke about 11 million homes to National Geographic's distribution. By the end of the year the network had made its first foray into Central Europe and launched a dedicated feed in Belgium and the Netherlands. At the turn of the century, the station was reaching about 20 million homes in 35 countries. For many years, Germany remained a big gap in the channel's distribution until the launch of a local feed in November 2004. Today National Geographic Channel has 48 million connections throughout Europe, which it serves with 13 feeds and 26 languages (Tables 7.1 and 11.1). Globally, the network reaches 250 million homes (including part-time distribution) across 166 countries. Nat Geo's main channel has a broad remit and schedules infotainment series such as *Megastructures*, *How it Works*, *Seconds From Disaster* and *Air Crash Investigation*.

Unlike DNI, National Geographic has long refrained from creating new ventures for fear of diluting an iconic brand. For many years the only spin-off was Adventure One, a channel targeted at younger viewers and available in Italy and the UK. It was replaced by National Geographic Adventure in May 2007, a station also aiming at a young audience and one that revolves around the theme of the journey. Its first commissioned programme was *Chasing Che*, a series of shows written and presented by two travellers who retraced the route Ernesto Guevara described in his *Motorcycle Diaries*. Nat Geo Wild, a channel dedicated to wildlife programming (exploration and conservation), was launched in the UK in December 2006, followed by Italy, Ireland, Scandinavia and Central Europe (Czech Republic, Slovakia, Croatia, Serbia, Hungary and Romania) in 2007, and Portugal in 2008. Nat Geo Music, a station dedicated to world music, started on Sky Italia in October 2007 and expanded to Portugal in March 2008.

In the UK and Northern Europe, the network is owned by BSkyB (50 per cent) NBC (25 per cent) and National Geographic Ventures, the commercial arm of the not-for-profit society behind the magazine. In France and Southern Europe, BSkyB is replaced by FIC, the News Corp division. Global programming is overseen by Washington-based National Geographic Global Media group, the consumer media unit of National Geographic.[29]

AETN International's portfolio: The History Channel, Military History, The Biography Channel and Crime & Investigation Network

New York-based Arts & Entertainment Television Networks' international division, AETN International (Chapter 8), oversees the global development of four brands: The History Channel, Military History, The Biography Channel and Crime & Investigation Network. Once The History Channel was launched in the USA in January 1995, the station was quickly taken abroad. Britain was the first destination, where the channel started on the Sky platform in November 1995, followed by Spain and Portugal in January 1999, France in May 2003 and Italy in July of the same year, Germany in December 2004, Greece in September 2005, Scandinavia in February 2007 and Benelux three months later. It was launched in Poland and Hungary in April 2008 and the Czech Republic, Slovakia, Slovenia and Romania later in the year. Central Europe, Scandinavia, Benelux and Greece receive a rescheduled subtitled extension from The History Channel UK, itself a joint venture between AETN and BSkyB, while the rest are local channels. History is structured in eight programming strands, which span ancient history, modern history, conflict, religion, technology, mysteries, current affairs and worldwide events. Popular series aired in 2008 include *Battle 360*, *Cities of the Underworld*, *The Crusades*, *Engineering an Empire*, *Digging for the Truth*, *Ice Road Truckers* and *Modern Marvels*. Military History, a spin-off channel, launched in the UK in July 2008.

The Biography Channel delves into the lives of past and present figures from the worlds of the arts, music, cinema, fashion, business, politics and sport. A more recent creation than History, its launch in the USA in 1998 was followed by the UK (2000), Italy (2005), Spain and Portugal (2005) and Germany (2007). Biography is a fast-growing proposition but its worldwide presence remains below that of History: Biography had 80 million subscribers in eight territories (including the USA) in 2007, while History reached over 230 million homes in about 130 territories.

AETN's fourth international brand is Crime & Investigation Network. It started its internationalization programme in 2005, first launching in Australia, followed by the UK at the end of 2006. Documentary series look at the judicial system, the work of police forces and law enforcement agencies (e.g. *Crime & Punishment, Parole Board, SWAT*) and criminal investigations (e.g. *Crime Scene, The First 48* [hours of homicide investigation]), probe unsolved mysteries (*Cold Case Files, The Unexplained*) and examine the lives of high-profile criminals and murderers (e.g. *Unusual Suspects, The Making of a Monster*).

AETN International's modus operandi is to work with local partners. Channels are either set up as joint ventures (e.g. BSkyB, Multicanal TPS in Spain or FIC in Italy) or the content is licensed to a third party which becomes the 'affiliate'. In the latter case companies like Kabel Deutschland in Germany or Histoire in France have the responsibility of putting the channel together. Local partners ensure that all channels are perfectly adapted to a local audience. Stations share a fair amount of shows but they source up to about 30 per cent of their material locally. People enjoy watching documentaries that are locally relevant and since history can be a controversial subject not all shows are appropriate for all territories. Even in Britain, all American programmes are revoiced with an English accent.[30]

Chello Zone's Zone Reality

Zonevision was first renamed Zonemedia when it became part of Chellomedia, the content division of Liberty Global, in 2005, and is now called Chello Zone (Chapter 8). Zonevision started as a syndication business when the TV market opened up in Poland and moved into local representation for clients like Discovery and MTV. The company became a one-stop shop for cross-border channels in Central and Eastern Europe, negotiating with hundreds of cable operators on their behalf, dealing with administration (e.g. invoicing) and offering a full range of localization services. Zonevision founder and chairman, Chris Wronski, decided to move into programming and his company launched its first channel, Romantica, in Poland in 1998 (see below), and started its future flagship brand the following year.

Reality TV grew out of Central and Eastern Europe towards Western Europe, Scandinavia and then Southern Europe, reaching Portugal in mid-2004. Zone Reality – as the channel was renamed in 2006 – covers much of Europe with one video feed and is transmitted in 16 different languages using a mix of voice-over, subtitles and dubbing (Table 10.1). The UK has had its own localized station since October 2002 thanks to the strength of its advertising market. 'Reality television' has come to be defined by entertainment producers and today loosely designates game show formats. But Zone Reality remains faithful to the origins of the genre and sticks to factual programming: traditional fly-on-the-wall documentaries on law enforcement agencies and emergency services (e.g. *Cops*, *Rescue 911*, *High Speed Pursuits*) are supplemented by series like *Cheaters* and *Animal Miracles*. Zone Reality Extra, started in 2006, has been designed to stretch the brand's original concept and schedules shows such as real-life re-enactment programmes and dramas inspired by true stories.[31]

Fashion TV

Fashion TV is the brainchild of Michel Adam Lisowski, its president and main shareholder, who launched the station in 1997. He was supported by Marie-Paule Jensen, who had contacts in the fashion industry, and François Thiellet who brought the expertise in satellite television he had acquired with MCM. Based in Paris, the station became a global TV network in less then a decade. In Europe it currently has 104 million subscribers and covers the region with one feed and two languages (English and Russian) (Table 7.1). Out-of-home viewing is one of Fashion TV's strengths. It is seen in one million public places such as hairdressing salons, boutiques, bars (including Fashion TV's own franchise), clubs, gyms, hotels, restaurants and airports.

Fashion TV scheduling has two main strands. At the core of its programming philosophy is coverage of the fashion industry with the minimum of interference. The network presents the collections of hundreds of designers worldwide and broadcasts about 300 new catwalks each season, all produced in-house. All the world's fashion weeks are extensively covered, starting with the four big ones in Paris, New York, London and Milan. This strand is supplemented by magazines and series that revolve around the world of fashion and its players (photographers, designers, models and so on). Shows comprise *Designers Talk*, *Models Talk*, *Tendances*, *Hair and Make Up*, *Fashion & Music*, *Fashion & Film*, *Stars & Cars* and *Shoot Me*, which documents the working life of a supermodel. Fashion TV throws its own parties, broadcast on the network, and started the FTV Model Awards in 2003. Fashion TV is still a young brand but will soon have to make a choice: does it want to remain a trade channel for the fashion industry or become a destination for fashion on top of other genres such as reality TV shows? For the time being it remains an aspirational channel that is watched by a young audience and has excellent coverage in Eastern Europe.[32]

E! International Network and The Style Network

E! Networks is an entertainment broadcaster that owns several US cable networks, including E! Entertainment Television, The Style Network and G4. The Los Angeles-based company is solely owned by the Comcast Corporation who bought out Disney in November 2006 for US$1.23 billion. E! Entertainment Television is marketed as the E! International Network (E! for short) outside the USA and is managed by the Comcast International Media Group, a company division. E! was first launched in the USA in June 1990, then across Latin America in 1997 and in Europe in 2002. It started in Western and Southern Europe and expanded into the Central and Eastern parts of the continent in 2006. Today it reaches about 22 million households in Europe. E! began localizing in summer 2006, dividing its pan-European feed in order to launch fully localized channels in France, Italy and the UK. It was followed in Europe by The Style Network, a fashion and design channel, which debuted in the UK in summer 2008.

The four pillars of E!'s programming mix are Hollywood, entertainment, pop culture and celebrity. It features A-List Hollywood stars, music and fashion icons, local reality TV players and sports people. The network is investing in local shows, which represent up to 20 per cent of localized feed schedules. E! offers local coverage of the BAFTA Awards in the UK, the Venice Film Festival in Italy and the Cannes Film Festival in France. For the Oscar ceremony, E! produces a 12-hour show broadcast across its network and translated live by a team of UN translators hired for the occasion. The network also adapts international shows, such as its countdown series (e.g. *101 Most Embarrassing Moments in Entertainment*), by re-producing them locally. The American commentators are taken out and replaced by local comedians. Comcast's international division has its own production division which adopts a global perspective on all the shows it creates. When this division produced the *25 Sexiest . . .* series (movie stars, rock stars, etc.), it took about ten people from Hollywood and 15 from the rest of the world. Europe got Audrey Tautou and Monica Bellucci and Latin America a selection of telenovelas stars. But E!'s unique selling point is the fact that its main subject matter, Hollywood, represents the apex of global culture. Hollywood A-listers are famous around the world because of US dominance in the world film market.[33] Thus E!'s signature shows such as *E! True Hollywood Story* and the countdown series have universal appeal and are ensured widespread distribution.[34]

The Travel Channel

The Travel Channel was among the first wave of satellite services in the USA, where it began in 1982. It launched in the UK and Scandinavia in February 1994, in the Netherlands the following year, and progressively expanded across Europe. Today Travel Channel reaches about 38 million homes across Europe in 14 languages (Table 7.1). The station was first owned by a publishing company based in Atlanta, Landmark Communications, which sold its American operations in 1997 but hung on to its international channel until spring 2004, when it was acquired by Richard Wolfe, the station's chief executive. It is the largest pan-European travel broadcaster and its programming mixes entertainment with practical advice. Hit series include *Angry Planet* (extreme weather), *Beyond Borders* (adventure) and *Global Nomad* (exploration).[35]

ENTERTAINMENT

Comedy Central/Paramount Comedy

Comedy Central was launched in the USA in April 1991 following the merger of two competing services owned by Viacom and Time Warner. In April 2003 Viacom bought out Time Warner for US$1.2 billion. Although the channel is well established in its home market, it has the lowest international distribution among Viacom international networks. Comedy is difficult to export and the conglomerate concentrated on developing its music properties until the early 2000s.

The channel launched as Paramount Comedy in the UK in November 1995, in Spain in March 1999 and in Italy in 2005. It reverted to its original name when it launched in Germany in January 2007. In the USA, Comedy Central came to public notice with *South Park*, which was premiered on the station in 1997. *Reno 911!* (a police comedy that went into its fifth season in 2007), the discontinued *Chappelle's Show* and two satirical news shows, *The Daily Show with Jon Stewart* and *The Colbert Report*, are among the station's other successful original series. These American hit shows are exported to Europe but since humour does not always travel well, each channel is put together locally. They produce their own comedies, develop shows with local comedians, and mix this material with American and British content. The network claims that these local shows have helped launch the careers of several comedians in Europe and mentions Sacha Baron Cohen (of Ali G and Borat fame) in Britain and Joaquín Reyes in Spain.[36]

Hallmark

Hallmark Cards, the American greeting card company, decided to diversify into television in the early 1990s, acquiring RHI Entertainment, an independent producer of TV dramas and movies. It then created Crown Media and launched its first-ever cable channel outside the United States, in the Benelux countries, in June 1995. The Hallmark Channel launched in the USA in August 2001, following Crown Media's acquisition of the Odyssey Network, which had been set up by the National Interfaith Cable Coalition, an alliance of faith groups dedicated to media production and distribution.

Crown Media International was placed in charge of development outside the USA, and by the mid-2000s the European network reached about 20 million homes across 28 countries with ten localized feeds. Despite a few ratings successes the business was making substantial losses (£11 million in 2003 alone) and was put up for sale. In 2005 the Hallmark channels outside the USA and associated library rights were acquired for US$242 million by a private equity consortium headed by David Elstein, Five's former CEO. The Hallmark international network was controlled by Sparrowhawk Media Group and the executive team was headed by CEO David Hulbert, who joined from Disney. The number of European feeds was reduced in order to cut costs and two new channels were launched in the UK, Movies 24 and Diva TV.

When Sparrowhawk acquired Hallmark, NBC Universal became a key supplier of programmes for the network. The media conglomerate was seeking to expand its international interests and when given the opportunity it bought the company in October 2007 for US$350 million. Hallmark has now joined NBC Universal's Global Networks Division, which comprises some 30 channels (see below). Hallmark's distribution in Europe reached about 32 million households in 2007 but there is a notable lack of progress in France, Germany and Spain, where the network has yet to sign a single carriage deal.

The Hallmark Channel broadcasts made-for-television movies and mini-series, most of which are produced for the company, giving the network a distinct identity. The channel's own library consists of some 4,000 hours of programming. There may be some truth to the perception that Hallmark is about B movies packed with out-of-work B-listers, but the network deals with the leading studios and the high standard of some of its programming has been recognized with industry awards. Hallmark's four-pronged programming strategy revolves around drama (e.g. *Blue Murder*), adventure (*McLeod's Daughters*), romance (*Family Plan*) and mystery (*Murder 101*).[37]

Chello Zone's entertainment channels

Over the past ten years Zonevision (now Chello Zone) has launched a host of transnational channels, many in the entertainment genre. Chris Wronski's first channel, Romantica, started in Poland and originally broadcast back-to-back telenovelas. It progressively added lifestyle programming to its diet of soap operas. Now called Zone Romantica, the channel has expanded across Central and Eastern Europe and is also available on Sky in the UK, reaching a total of 15.8 million subscribers by early 2008. Also targeting a female audience, Club started in 1999 as a lifestyle channel combining chat shows, dramas and documentaries. Rebranded Zone Club, it has about 7.4 million subscribers across 24 territories in Europe. It runs distinct channels in Poland and Hungary, with the remainder showing pan-European feed, available in several languages.

A few other channels were subsequently added but they have a smaller geographical spread for the time being because they target the more saturated markets of Western Europe. Zone Horror started in 2004 and is available in the UK and Ireland and the Netherlands (two separate feeds) to about 13.9 million viewers. Zone Fantasy, which offers a blend of horror, sci-fi and supernatural, launched in Italy in 2006, and the same year Zone Thriller went on air on Sky in Britain.[38]

From Universal Studios Networks to Universal Television Networks to NBC Universal Global Networks

The ownership history of what is now known as NBC Universal Global Networks (UGN) and which comprises a suite of three brands, Sci Fi, Studio Universal and 13th Street, is a convoluted one. It starts in 1992 when the Sci Fi Channel was launched by Mitch Rubenstein in the United States.

The channel was subsequently bought by USA Networks, a cable operator controlled at the time by two Hollywood majors, Paramount and MCA. In the second half of the 1990s, Sci Fi became part of Universal Studios Networks (USN), an outfit controlled by another major, Universal Studios. When Vivendi acquired Universal Studios in 2000, USN became Universal Television Networks and was managed, briefly, from Paris. The objective of Jean-Marie Messier, Vivendi's CEO at the time, was to integrate the channels that had since been added to Sci Fi with the ensemble of stations that Vivendi already owned, most notably those operating under the Canal Plus brand. Following Vivendi's collapse (Chapter 8), NBC bought Universal from the French company and its network of channels became part of the new conglomerate in May 2004.

It is the international division of USA Networks that brought Sci Fi to the UK in November 1995, with the channel grabbing a few connections across Benelux and Scandinavia. USN subsequently launched a movie channel in Italy, Studio Universal, which began on a satellite platform called Stream (now Sky Italia) in May 1998. Vivendi took the channel to Germany and Spain in 2000 and launched in the UK as The Studio in February the following year. 13th Street (action and suspense) was launched in France in 1998, Germany in 1999 and Spain the following year.

The network developed slowly under Vivendi. Sci Fi was launched in Germany in 2003 and was doing well in the UK but the management had given up on the multi-territory feed. They had difficulties securing multi-territory rights and had problems with local quotas. Studio Universal only operated as a stand-alone station in Italy. It became a branded block scheduled into local Sci Fi stations in Spain and Germany, and in the UK The Studio closed down in December 2002.

Today NBC Universal has ambitious plans for the network. It has invested in high-profile series for Sci Fi, and although *Nip/Tuck* did not perform as well as was hoped, *Heroes* (an NBC property) has been a great ratings success and brought the channel to a new level. Truly local Sci Fi channels were started in the Netherlands and Flanders in 2007 and in Romania and Scandinavia in 2008. 13th Street began in the Netherlands in 2007 and many other launches are planned across Europe for the near future.[39]

HBO Central Europe

Since HBO launched in 1972 (Chapter 2), the pay-TV service has expanded to the four corners of the world. Its first foray outside the USA was in

Hungary, where it launched in September 1991, followed by the Czech Republic in November 1994 (HBO Czech expanding to Slovakia in April 1997), Poland in September 1996, Romania in January the following year (from where it expanded to Moldova in December 1999) and Bulgaria in April 2002. HBO Adria – the industry code for ex-Yugoslavia territory – started in September 2004. It initially covered Slovenia and Croatia, the Serbian version being added in March 2006. Following the separation of Montenegro from Serbia in June 2006, HBO reached the Montenegrin cable networks in July 2007. The countries of the 'Adria' region share the same video feed but receive three different audio and subtitles packages: Serbian, Slovene and Croatian. Subscribers in Montenegro can choose which audio feed they prefer. All in all, HBO Central Europe has about 1.2 million subscribers across eleven countries. In most territories, HBO is supplemented by HBO2 and HBO Comedy.

HBO Central Europe is a joint venture between Home Box Office, the Time Warner division, Sony Pictures Television International and Buena Vista International Television, Disney's distribution arm. Content is broadly similar across the network, although local channels occasionally acquire shows for themselves. Hungary, the Czech Republic and Poland produce a certain amount of local content. HBO is a premium service that offers a mix of Hollywood blockbusters, acclaimed original series produced or co-produced by the Time Warner division, as well as concerts and special events.[40]

Sony's AXN and Animax

Sony Pictures Television International (SPTI) is rolling out two global brands in Europe. AXN, which first went on air in Asia in 1995, arrived in Spain in 1998. It launched in Israel in 2000, in Portugal in 2002 (as an extension of the Spanish feed) and across six markets in Central Europe in 2003 (Poland, Hungary, the Czech Republic, Slovakia, Romania and Bulgaria). The following year the channel started in Germany, Switzerland and Austria, and AXN Italy was launched in October 2005. In 2006, two sub-brands, AXN Crime and AXN Sci-Fi, were created for Central Europe. In 2008, AXN Sci-Fi was introduced into several countries of the Commonwealth of Independent States (CIS) region, including Russia, Ukraine and Belarus.

AXN started as a male-skewed brand focusing on action and adventure but it is now labelled 'high energy' entertainment. The channel airs global

TV series (e.g *The Shield*, *ER*, *Lost*, the *CSI* franchise), local drama produced by the Sony studios, feature films and reality shows such as *Survivor* and Sony's own *The Amazing Race* and *Ultimate Escape*. AXN does particularly well in Spain and Portugal, where it is the leading thematic channel in terms of ratings, and in Central Europe, where the AXN suite of channels reached twelve million subscribers in August 2008.

Sony's second international brand that is coming to Europe is Animax, a channel entirely dedicated to Japanese animé, a fast-growing genre. It launched in Hungary, Romania, the Czech Republic and Slovakia in April 2007, in Germany two months later and in Spain in April 2008.[41]

MOVIES

A few transnational networks are exclusively dedicated to films, although movies are scheduled by channels across many genres (including factual entertainment sometimes). The film genre is underdeveloped in transnational television because movies are difficult to exploit at pan-European level, rights being rarely available on a multi-territory basis (Chapter 11). It is a genre that is politically sensitive and local quotas set up by the AVMS Directive need to be adhered to (Chapter 4). Film channels are also affected by new technology: DVD players, personal video recorders and piracy are taking many viewers away from them. Movie channels are not difficult to put together and international broadcasters face stiff competition from stations set up by pay-TV operators. Thus it is a genre where it is difficult to find synergies at international level and brands are few and far between.

Turner Classic Movies (TCM)

When Ted Turner brought TNT to Europe in 1993, he turned it into a classic movie channel. It was rebranded Turner Classic Movies (TCM), like its American sister channel, when TNT and Cartoon Network were split to become two stand-alone channels in the late 1990s (see above). In 1985 Turner bought the Metro-Goldwyn-Mayer Studios but, being unable to service the debt he had contracted, he sold it back to Kirk Kerkorian while keeping the studio's film library. TBS continued to exploit the MGM rights through syndication and created TCM in order to showcase the MGM catalogue. Together with the Warner Bros library, the MGM catalogue gave TCM access to thousands of titles, including classics such as *Dr Zhivago*, *Casablanca* and *Gone with the Wind*.[42]

MGM Channel

The Metro-Goldwyn-Mayer Studios' international TV division, MGM Networks, has been rolling out its own network around the world since 2001. When MGM Channel arrived in Europe it first launched in the German-speaking countries and small markets like Greece, Portugal, Cyprus, Malta and Iceland. It went on air in Spain in 2004, Ireland the following year, and formed a joint venture with Chellomedia in Central and Eastern Europe (Poland, Hungary, the Czech Republic, Slovakia and Romania) in 2006. The following year, it launched in Bulgaria and replaced its English-language multi-territory feed with a fully localized channel in the Netherlands and Flanders. In June 2008, a local-language version was launched on Sky Italia, and in September new channels appeared in Serbia, Albania and Macedonia.

For the Hollywood major, the MGM Channel is an opportunity to integrate vertically and exploit internationally a catalogue of some 4,000 movies and 10,000 TV episodes. The content used on this TV network is different from the MGM material that is still owned by TCM, as the major held on to the titles dating from the 1960s onwards. This, however, excludes the studios' 'crown jewels': the Bond franchise.[43]

Zone Europa

Europa Europa was launched by Zonevision in 1999. Now called Zone Europa, it reached 8.1 million subscribers in Central and Eastern Europe in 2007. The channel is marketed as the home of European cinema and showcases movies that range from classics to avant-garde productions.

Cinemax

Cinemax was launched by HBO Central Europe in Hungary, the Czech Republic, Poland, Romania and Bulgaria in February 2005. Cinemax 2 was added in October of the same year and is also available in different language versions. Cinemax is designed to complement the HBO network and is a premium pay movie channel. Its schedule includes international hits and movies that had limited theatrical releases. It has adopted a themed approach and focuses on a different genre each day of the week.[44]

SPORTS

Eurosport in the 1990s and 2000s

A few international sports TV channels have started broadcasting in recent years but Eurosport remains the market leader. The network's European distribution is the third-largest in the PETV industry with nearly 110 million connections across 54 territories (Table 7.1). Eurosport broadcasts in 20 languages and with a few exceptions covers the whole of the continent with the same video feed (Table 10.1). It has distinct channels in France and the UK: Eurosport France is a Screensport legacy (Chapter 2) and British Eurosport was launched in January 1999. Eurosport's local channels used to be more localized than they currently are. Today, British Eurosport airs the occasional live event, such as rugby, and complements the coverage of international events with reporting from its own presenters and correspondents, but the difference resides more in the scheduling and packaging than the programming.

At the end of 2000 Eurosport launched a second network, Eurosport News, as a rolling 15-minute sports news service. In January 2005 it was relaunched as Eurosport 2 and changed to live events. Having two complementary channels allows the network to avoid scheduling clashes and enables it to broadcast two different sports events concurrently. It is being positioned as the channel for 'next generation' sports and its schedule offers niche activities such as freestyle football, three-cushion billiards, carom and extreme sports.

Eurosport's philosophy is to be a pan-European channel and show sports events across the continent. For the sports federations whose events are broadcast this way this strategy provides them with two benefits: it gives their sports wide exposure and grants them access to markets where they would not usually be seen. When Eurosport acquires the pan-European transmission rights of winter sports such as alpine skiing, ski jumping or biathlon, it is not primarily for the Swiss or Austrians but for the purpose of showing them in Italy, Spain or Britain, where there is a viewer base, albeit tiny, for these sports. When the network transmits Roland Garros, the French Open tennis tournament, live for two weeks, or Le Tour de France, it is not for the benefit of the French, who get saturation coverage on France Télévisions's local stations, but for the rest of Europe where these events are not consistently covered.

Today less than 10 per cent of Eurosport's rights come from the EBU;

the rest is acquired by a ten-strong acquisitions team. The network is in continuous discussions with the numerous sports federations from which it buys rights. They also meet at Sportel, the biannual sports rights and marketing fair, and at global sports events. Eurosport owns a large array of pan-European rights which enables it to broadcast some 800 hours of live events every year. The portfolio embraces all the winter sports (with the exception of ice hockey), the ATP Tennis Tour, Pro-tour cycling, the FIA World Rally Championship (among other motorsports), all major athletics competitions, the European and world championships of sports like volleyball and table tennis, the Olympic Games and Le Tour de France. In football, the network has managed to obtain the live rights of the African Cup of Nations (2008) and some UEFA Cup games.

Acquiring sports rights can be an expensive business and Eurosport is sometimes pushed to the limits of its budget by domestic satellite sports channels and terrestrial stations. The European network targets sports that are not popular enough to be on terrestrial television and/or generate the fees charged by domestic satellite operators for their premium sports channels. Fortunately for Eurosport, only a very small proportion of sports federations can cash in on their television rights. Most sports do not pass the audience threshold to justify their presence on terrestrial television and be financed by advertising. The overwhelming majority of sports are desperate for exposure, without which they are unable to generate increased TV audiences, sponsors, new adherents to the sport, lucrative TV rights contracts and sometimes Olympic status. This desperation is such that sports federations have recently adapted their rules for biathlon, volleyball and the World Touring Car Championship, among others, in order to accommodate television. In this context, Eurosport's trump card is that it provides exposure for sports that need it more than money or, more exactly, that need visibility before they can monetize their rights (see also Chapter 11).[45]

Extreme Sports Channel

Extreme Sports Channel started in the late 1990s as a joint venture between UPC, formerly an independent multi-territory cable operator in Europe, and Extreme Group, a consortium of companies involved in the extreme sport arena. UPC was subsequently acquired by United Globacom (UGC), a company that at the time was partly owned by Liberty Media and which has since become fully owned by Liberty Global. In 2005 Liberty Global took control of the station when it acquired Extreme Group's interest. It has since transferred management to Chello Zone, a company subsidiary.

Extreme Sports Channel was rolled out across Europe from the Netherlands, where it went on air in 1999. A separate feed was launched in the UK in 2000, Poland in January 2006 and France later in the year. Together with the pan-European feed, Extreme Sports reached 25.6 million subscribers in over 50 countries in 2008 (Table 7.1). The network spread rapidly across Europe because the management wanted to get first-mover advantage and make it difficult for competitors to launch in these markets. The rush stems from advertisers' keen interest in the channel's core audience, which consists of males aged between 16 and 34, a demographic that is notoriously difficult to pin down.

Extreme Sports Channel covers a wide array of sports including snowboarding, mountain biking, watersports (surfing, kite surfing, windsurfing, etc.) and urban sports (BMX and skateboarding). It has acquired the rights to several notable extreme sports events (the Gravity Games and the X Games) and world championships (the ASP Surf Tour and the FIM World Motocross Championship). The channel pays great attention to the lifestyle associated with extreme sports and its programming illustrates this with related music and fashion slots. Like other fledgling stations, Extreme Sports needs to develop its schedule over and above acquisitions and start creating its own intellectual property. It has begun commissioning shows and investing in productions in order to create its own unique content for viewers exclusive to the station.[46]

Motors TV

Motors TV was founded by Jean-Luc Roy, a motoring journalist who had set up his own TV production company, Motor Production. The station launched in France in 2000 and spread to 30 European territories within five years. It reached about 16 million subscribers early in 2008, the bulk of them in Britain and France (Table 7.1). The fledgling network has three feeds covering the UK, Germany and France. The French feed is exported to about 32 countries and all channels are available in French, German or English. Feeds air the same material except when rights for a competition are not available at pan-European level.

Philippe Deleplace, Motors TV's deputy CEO, calls his station a 'tiny Eurosport dedicated to motorsport', and indeed both networks share similarities.[47] Motors TV combines a pan-European approach with a programming philosophy based on live events. It holds the rights to numerous races and championships in the world of motorsport, including the World Enduro Championship, the Junior World Rally Championship, the Formula 3 Euro Series, Germany's touring car championship and Australia's V8 Supercars. The channel's main annual event is the French endurance race, the 24 Hours of Le Mans, which it broadcasts live.[48]

ESPN Classic

ESPN has had a long-term interest in pan-European broadcasting. The American sports cable network first invested in Bob Kennedy's Screensport in 1984 and took a stake in WH Smith Television's The European Sports Network five years later (Chapter 1). When TESN merged with Eurosport in the early 1990s, ESPN became a shareholder of the pan-European sport channel (Chapter 2), which prevented the American network from launching an ESPN-branded channel in Europe. ESPN, by now part of Disney, sold its stake in Eurosport in 2000 to come back to Europe two years later. It returned with a channel first launched in the USA in May 1995 which was acquired by ESPN in October 1997 and was branded ESPN Classic Sport (today shortened to ESPN Classic).

ESPN Classic began in Europe with a channel for the francophone territories that went on air in March 2002, closely followed by another for the Italian market. Both stations are fully localized and scheduled independently from one another. In December 2003 ESPN launched a multi-territory feed for Scandinavia and Central, Eastern and Southern Europe. All these territories receive the same base feed that is versioned in different languages (English, Dutch, German, Polish and Portuguese). ESPN's fourth European channel was launched in March 2006 in Ireland and the UK. Altogether, ESPN Classic reached 22 million homes in Europe at the beginning of 2008 (Table 7.1).

ESPN Classic is a channel dedicated to non-live events that features vintage sporting moments, profiles of sport legends, interviews, documentaries and sport movies. ESPN is the USA's leading sports network but it arrived too late in Europe to be involved in live sports rights, where it faces competition from well-established players. ESPN Classic is not simply an archive service and its schedule closely follows the sporting calendar in each nation where it broadcasts. For example, during a rugby competition where France meets New Zealand and England plays South Africa, the French feed will show past games between France and New

Zealand, and the British feed will do the same with matches between England and South Africa. The same strategy is adopted for all major sports events and championships. ESPN Classic places emphasis on its territories' most popular sports, its national heroes and teams. Thus, while cricket is shown in Britain, rugby can be scheduled in France and cycling in Italy. Rights holders vary from event to event but quite a few rights remain with national broadcasters with whom ESPN Classic has agreements to use their archive.[49]

North American Sports Network

The North American Sports Network (NASN) was launched in Ireland and the UK in December 2002, and a second feed was subsequently added to cover mainland Europe. NASN provides live and pan-European coverage of all the major professional and college leagues, including American football (NFL, NCAA), baseball (MLB), basketball (NBA, NCAA) and ice hockey (NHL, NCAA). In addition to about 800 live games broadcast annually, NASN also schedules talk shows and news shows. Although American sports have failed to attract widespread interest in Europe, some sports are increasingly popular in certain countries, giving NASN considerable growth potential as a niche channel. The distribution of the pay service has considerably expanded over the past few years, reaching more than 13 million subscribers across 43 countries in 2008 (Table 7.1).

NASN started life as a joint venture between Setanta Sports, the sports broadcaster and rights holder operating from Dublin, and Vulcan European Media. Vulcan eventually sold its interest to Setanta, which formed a new joint venture with Benchmark Capital, a private equity firm, in 2005. In December 2006 the network was acquired by ESPN in a transaction estimated at €90 million. The deal presented two advantages for ESPN: it gave the American sports network access to the coveted European live sports market and it can take advantage of synergies between ESPN Classic and its new acquisition, which will be renamed ESPN America in February 2009.[50]

ADULT ENTERTAINMENT

The first erotic service to seek European distribution was The Adult Channel, launched in the UK in 1992. The station was placed on the Astra system and by the second half of the decade it had more subscribers in Europe than in Britain. Playboy originally established its presence in this region through syndication and then launched its first channel on the Sky platform in October 1995. The UK channel was a joint venture between Flextech, the majority shareholder, BSkyB and Playboy.

Then, a chain of events occurred towards the end of the 1990s that changed the face of the adult entertainment market in Europe. In 1998 the Playboy Entertainment Group, a division of Playboy Enterprises, acquired Spice Entertainment and took control of the Spice TV network in America and the Adult Channel in Europe. The following year Playboy Entertainment and the Cisneros Television Group, the Venezuela-based conglomerate, formed a joint venture, Playboy TV International, with the intent of developing Spice- and Playboy-branded TV networks worldwide. Playboy TV International bought out Flextech and BSkyB from the UK channel and began a drive for European expansion. In 2000 services were launched in Benelux and Scandinavia and four years later in Germany. Playboy subsequently gained distribution in France and Poland and is today available in 17 territories. The group launched Spice Platinum in 2001, today replaced by Private Spice, a joint venture with another adult entertainment group that is distributed in 23 countries (see below). Playboy TV International's assortment of brands enables the company to adopt a portfolio approach and differentiates its services. The Adult Channel is a pan-European feed while Playboy is a more localized brand that is marketed as a premium service.

Private is the only other player in the European adult entertainment TV industry that is international in scope. The company started in the 1960s as a publishing concern based in Sweden and progressively expanded to other media sectors. Now located in Barcelona, Private distributes three pay-per-view networks in selected European markets: Private Gold, Private Blue (glamour) and Private Girls.

For the adult entertainment industry local adaptation is not only a marketing necessity. The regulatory environment on decency and nudity varies a great deal from one market to another. Laws range from the particularly lax in Spain, where most hardcore semi-legal channels are today based, to the far more stringent in the UK, where European material cannot be aired without editing.[51]

CONCLUSION: THE TELEVISION INDUSTRY'S TRANSNATIONAL SHIFT

Cross-border TV channels were given up for dead no longer than a decade ago (Chapter 3). The need for local relevance and the surge of local TV stations would surely make them disappear before the end of the century. But as seen in Part Two, the legal, political, commercial and technological context considerably improved for cross-border TV networks in the 1990s. International broadcasters held on and ten years later transnational TV networks are thriving in Europe.

The dynamic of the television industry has changed so much that anyone launching a TV brand today does so on a transnational basis. It would be erroneous to predict the demise of national television, even though terrestrial stations are continuously losing audiences. Europe still presents innumerable challenges for broadcasters operating across frontiers and transnational TV networks are better adapted to some genres than others (Chapter 11). But it is apparent that the situation of cross-border TV channels is vastly better today than it was ten years ago, and it looks certain that they will continue to prosper and affirm their presence in European broadcasting.

CHAPTER 8

POWERING TOMORROW'S EUROPEAN TELEVISION: AMERICAN TV BRANDS AND DIVERSIFIED ENTERTAINMENT CONGLOMERATES

As became apparent in Chapter 7, diversified entertainment conglomerates occupy a prominent place in the PETV industry. They have the resources, expertise and determination to develop an international TV business. These media owners have invested for the long term and progressively implement the corporate strategies and managerial practices that have ensured success at transcultural level.

The vast majority of these companies have crossed the Atlantic to seek their fortunes away from the home market. The three precursors to arrive in the 1980s (CNN, MTV and Discovery) were joined over the next decade by a host of American cable programmers who grew bigger as the years passed. Today American-based conglomerates and their brands are the dominant force in PETV. This chapter examines how these media companies have achieved this position. It then argues that conglomeration in the media industry is a necessary process that responds to a given commercial and industrial environment (the need for scale) and brings several advantages (the benefit of scope). The last section analyses the involvement of each entertainment conglomerate in transnational television.

THE FRENCH CRASH

American media conglomerates owe their success in Europe to several factors: the advantages derived from a large domestic market, the experience of operating in a crowded and competitive cable environment, a willingness to take risks and plan for the long term, ownership of large libraries and the capacity to produce and commission attractive programming, early adoption of a viable pan-European strategy, ability to cut costs in multi-territory operations and finding synergies among each company's divisions. They also faced meek opposition. Many broadcasters in Europe had difficulty looking beyond their national borders. They rarely placed the public at the heart of their concerns and were lured into a false sense of security by protectionist measures. Their attitude was often complacent and conservative, when not downright paternalistic. In particular, American conglomerates benefited from the decline of France's transnational television interests, the sole nation apart from Britain that had managed to shine in international broadcasting.

France does keep a foothold in the PETV industry: French companies – Thema in particular – have launched their fair share of cross-border channels over recent years, and France Télévisions remains very much involved in international broadcasting (Chapters 6, 7 and 9). But the fact remains that France has lost a lot of ground since the 1990s. For a country that is anxious to see its culture flourish across the world and to offer an alternative to Anglo-American cultural fare, its media companies are performing spectacularly poorly on the European stage. In recent years many of these companies have experienced such setbacks that they have had to retreat to their home market.

Canal Plus: no longer Europe's conqueror

Canal Plus started as a pay-TV channel in France in November 1984. The station was a domestic success and the company rapidly expanded abroad, unleashing a series of Canal Plus-branded channels with local partners in Belgium, Spain and Scandinavia. It launched Premiere with Bertelsmann in February 1991. The French company was progressively turning these stations into multi-channel satellite platforms when it acquired Nethold late in 1996, which was a joint venture between Richemont, a Swiss holding company with investments in luxury brands, and MultiChoice, the South African satellite platform. With Nethold, Canal Plus acquired satellite bouquets in Benelux, the Nordic countries, Central Europe, Italy and Greece, and added 1.7 million subscribers to its own operations. The largest acquisition in European broadcasting at the time created the region's dominant player in the fledgling European DTH market. In 1997 Canal Plus withdrew from Germany but remained active in France, Belgium, the Netherlands, Italy, Spain, Poland and Scandinavia.[1]

The same year Canal Plus's controlling company, Havas, was acquired by the Compagnie Générale des Eaux (CGE). CGE's CEO, Jean-Marie

Messier, who was in a rush to transform a utility company into a media conglomerate, embarked on an acquisition spree, notably buying Universal Studios (Chapter 7). When the synergies failed to materialize in the early 2000s, Vivendi Universal – the company's new name – very nearly collapsed under the weight of its debt. The international operations of Canal Plus were sold off. Jean-Marie Messier's successor, Jean-René Fourtou, who was at the helm of the company between 2002 and 2005, also disposed of the company's American media assets, Universal.

At its peak, Canal Plus was Europe's largest pay-TV operator with 15 million subscribers across Europe. Once Vivendi had acquired Universal the group controlled some 60 channels across Europe, which ranged from its own-branded stations to Universal Studios Networks' properties. Today, Canal Plus is France's most successful pay-TV operation but it is confined to the domestic market. As for Vivendi, it still holds a 65 per cent stake in Canal Plus and has started to expand overseas again, notably in the telecom and games industries, but its only significant international media asset is its 20 per cent stake in NBC Universal.

Multithématiques and Lagardère Group

Multithématiques is another case. This Paris-based company was created in 1995 by three partners involving Canal Plus, Générale d'Images and TCI. Its objective was to develop channels in Europe, Japan and Latin America. Six networks were created in the course of the 1990s, which were Cinecinemas, Cineclassics, Planète and Planète Future (documentaries), Seasons (outdoor activities) and Canal Jimmy (youth/fiction/TV series). They were all launched in France first before being exported abroad. Planète was their strongest international brand, Cinecinemas had the widest distribution (France, Italy, Benelux and Scandinavia), while Canal Jimmy France had one sister channel in Italy. Until about 2002 Multithématiques retained strong backing from its shareholders, which at the time were Canal Plus (27 per cent), Lagardère Media (27 per cent), Liberty Media (27 per cent) and Havas Images (9 per cent).[2] Since then most have left and today Multithématiques is simply a division of Canal Plus. The international network has been dismantled and the company only operates these stations in France. Some of these brands can still be found on platforms across Europe but they have all been sold to local operators.

The trajectory of Lagardère Group's audiovisual division (called Lagardère Active today) is less dramatic but it is not a success story either.

While the company is one of the most powerful players in the French media market – CEO Arnaud Lagardère is a close chum of President Sarkozy – its international performance has been disappointing. Mezzo is still going strong but the group has failed to establish all its other channels as international brands, including MCM. Lagardère's other thematic channels (e.g. Canal J, Paris Première, Match TV) are designed for the French market and have no significant international distribution outside francophone territories.

In May 2007 the group merged Lagardère Networks International with another division to form Lagardère Television International (LTI). LTI does manage the group's international brands and assets but its main function is to act as a management and consulting group for third-party broadcasters. It helped Al Jazeera launch its children's channel in 2005 and has managed the international distribution of LuxeTV on behalf of NonStop Television since January 2007.

Why French companies struggle in transnational television

The first reason behind France's decline in transfrontier television is cultural in scope. While English has become the world's lingua franca, knowledge of French has fallen off.[3] The lack of a vast French-speaking market is not necessarily an obstacle – several French companies are well versed in the art of localization – but it remains a disadvantage. English-speaking channels have a much bigger natural constituency than their French counterparts; when they expand to non-English-speaking territories they can get away with broadcasting in English for several years before starting to localize their feed. And should a channel broadcast in just one language that crosses several linguistic communities it can only be in English. The difficulty of overcoming linguistic boundaries is reflected in the international distribution of many French TV channels. For every station that is distributed across Europe, many more remain confined to the francophone territories in Europe and Africa.[4] Many stations that can be seen across the remains of the French colonial empire in places as far apart as Guadeloupe and Martinique in the West Indies, La Réunion in the Indian Ocean or New Caledonia in the Pacific Ocean never even cross the Channel.

As fewer people learn French, worldwide exposure to French culture is in rapid decline. As Lagardère realized not long ago, it makes the exportation of French TV channels far more complicated. In the early 2000s the company began exporting Match TV, a station modelled on the popular weekly magazine *Paris Match*, which features French film stars and entertainment celebrities. It quickly dawned on the Lagardère management that with a few exceptions these people were absolutely unknown outside France and they took Match TV back home. This is a fate that stands in contrast to that of E! International Network, a channel that is growing on the back of Hollywood stars' global aura (Chapter 7).

The French companies' worst enemy is not American cultural imperialism, as some observers would have us believe, but the French government itself. The majority of French politicians and high-ranking civil servants have been nurtured in the traditions of statism and dirigisme and have imposed their views on the industry for decades. When they do not take measures to frustrate market mechanisms, their favourite pastime is to second-guess the market, and they invariably fall flat on their faces. In the late 1980s, when the French government was trying to fill its beloved high-power satellite TDF 1 – a white elephant that cost the taxpayers billions of francs – it offered transponder space in very generous terms to Maxwell, Berlusconi (the French thought he was a Socialist!) and Kirch.[5] A few years later, Maxwell was dead, Berlusconi was a full-time politician and Kirch was bankrupt. In October 1992 Canal Plus and News Corporation announced a partnership to exploit the nascent digital technology and launch digital channels.[6] The collaboration made strategic sense as it would have brought together Europe's biggest pay-TV operators. It never came to fruition, in part because the French government did everything it could to make it collapse: it saw the partnership as a Trojan horse to bring Murdoch to France. Had it let it happen, Canal Plus would be sharing the European pay-TV market with Murdoch today.

The French government's interventionism has crippled its own television industry. In the late 1980s it became a leading advocate in the botched attempt to impose a European transmission standard, MAC. In essence this was a protectionist measure designed to shield Philips and Thomson (a French state-owned company at the time) from Asian electronics manufacturers. The 'standard' was pushed by the European Commission through the 1986 EC Directive on MAC, which it eventually had to withdraw in the face of concerted opposition from SES and many European programmers. The point is, while SES and Sky were left to choose their own transmission standard, the French government unsettled its own programmers – and Canal Plus once again – by insisting that they adopt MAC. The only reason why Canal Plus was not forced to transmit in a 'standard' that nobody could receive is because France's very own TDF system collapsed under the weight of its own technical deficiencies.[7]

In addition to having to deal with a government that took a wrong turn at just about every crossroads (for good measure they also supported cable, thought easier to control than DTH), French cable and satellite channels also had to contend with an overzealous regulatory agency. In the early 1990s the Conseil supérieur de l'audiovisuel (CSA), as well as forbidding commercials and making sponsorship all but impossible on children's channels, stipulated the number of hours per day, per month and per year that these stations had to devote to different types of programming.[8] Only recently, Fashion TV got into trouble with the CSA for broadcasting in English. As a result the channel is no longer French: it is registered in Austria and uplinks to European satellites from Israel.

Protectionist measures allow the government to please certain lobbies and sections of the public but the long-term effects on local industry are devastating. Protectionism slows down foreign investment and isolates local companies from global capital flows. It makes home very cosy for a few players and thus acts as a disincentive to invest abroad. It also turns these companies into clients of the state: once erected, protectionist barriers can in theory be dismantled, thus giving governments leverage on any industry artificially sheltered by them. Protected companies further lose their way trying to please government officials rather than serve the people who pay for their services.

The damage is now irreversible. France has lost too many industrial and cultural battles not to have lost the war, and spending taxpayers' money on channels like TV5Monde and France 24 will make no difference. It is an edifying tale for those who like to dabble with interventionism and protectionism.

THE NEED FOR SCALE: ENTERTAINMENT CONGLOMERATES AND THE GLOBALIZATION OF ADVERTISING

The entertainment conglomerates that dominate the PETV industry are a regular target for criticism. It is alleged that they accentuate 'American cultural imperialism' in Europe. Their size is also a matter of concern and some observers accuse them of threatening pluralism.[9] Media groups may not be liked by everyone but they respond to a necessity in the age of globalization and current business climate.

First, diversification and vertical integration are a logical answer to the *risks* that are inherent in the entertainment industry. The popularity of a cultural product can never be predicted. For every TV series that makes it into production many pilots are never developed and countless projects do not even see the light of day. About eight out of ten movies never regain capital on expenditure. Being involved in different segments enables diversified entertainment companies to spread risks and soften the blow of loss-making ventures.

The need for scale arises above all from the commercial environment in which these conglomerates operate. Media owners face an advertising industry that has been through a long period of worldwide mergers and acquisitions to become dominated by four holding companies: Omnicom, WPP, Interpublic and Publicis. These groups incorporate the full range of marketing and advertising services, including branding, design, public relations and direct marketing. They bring creative and media buying agencies under one roof, many of them global networks in their own right (Table 8.1).

Table 8.1: World's top advertising holding companies by revenue, 2006

Holding company	2006 revenues (US$ billion)	Country of origin	Key creative agencies	Key media buying agencies
Omnicom	11.4	USA	BBDO Worldwide; DDB Worldwide; TBWA Worldwide	OMD; PHD
WPP	10.8	UK	Grey Global Group; J. Walter Thompson; Ogilvy & Mather; Young & Rubicam	MediaCom; Mediaedge:cia; MindShare
Interpublic	6.2	USA	Draftfcb; Lowe Worldwide; McCann Erickson	Initiative; Universal McCann
Publicis	5.9	France	Leo Burnett; Publicis; Saatchi & Saatchi	Starcom; ZenithOptimedia

Source: www.mind-advertising.com/agencies_index.htm.

Of the media space that is booked worldwide, a vast chunk is purchased by these holding companies' media agencies (Table 8.2). Among the world's top, only London-based Carat remains independently owned by Aegis. It is the same agencies that dominate billings in the PETV industry (Table 5.3).

Table 8.2: World's leading media buying agencies by worldwide billings, 2006

Media buying agency	Worldwide billings (in US$ billion)
Starcom	25.6
OMD	24.9
MindShare	23.8
Carat	20.7
ZenithOptimedia	19.3
Mediaedge:cia	18.8
MediaCom	17.9
Universal McCann	13.6
Initiative	12.3

Source: www.mind-advertising.com/agencies_index_media.htm.

Like all conglomerates, media buying agencies seek economies of scale and in this case find them in volume deals and multi-market opportunities. Supposing a media agency, say MindShare, is handling the media account of a multinational like Unilever. MindShare will take advantage of its vast network of local offices across Europe and local staff will negotiate their own media deals for Unilever's numerous brands. However, the regional or global account director will note how much the network spends across different territories with one particular media owner, say Time Warner, and then will hold a conversation centrally with them in order to see what benefits can be accrued by improving on the aggregated volume. They negotiate what are called *volume-linked triggers* that deliver discounts above a certain level of purchasing. These economies of scale have encouraged multinationals to consolidate their media accounts at regional and global levels. Companies like Adidas, HP, HSBC, Motorola, Unilever, Samsung, Toyota and Vodafone have now placed their global media accounts under one, sometimes two, media buying networks.

Media buying networks are holding increasingly sophisticated discussions with multi-market conglomerates. They try to get closer to media owners and develop a symbiotic relationship with them. Agreements that aim to form closer marketing partnerships may involve cross-division, cross-media and cross-territory deals, and content development. Large-scale media conglomerates can respond favourably to these requests and have formed ad-hoc structures like MTV Networks' International Marketing Partnerships and Time Warner's Global Marketing division. The remit of these divisions is to form integrated partnerships with their advertising clients and develop brand-driven marketing solutions with them that cut across media businesses, distribution platforms and territories. These integrated partnerships entangle media owners' and advertisers' initiatives that involve programming, promotions, events, co-branded content or online marketing.[10]

Given such an environment, it is perhaps absurd to accuse media conglomerates of gigantism. Media corporations respond to an environment that dictates certain organizational choices and corporate strategies. The system in which they operate presents them with risks and opportunities that can best be handled by organizations of a certain scale. They face global media buying networks that derive considerable power from their ability to buy advertising space in bulk. They, in turn, must be able to engage in partnership with multinationals that depend on their international reach to develop global brands. In the present context, a global network can best engage in a meaningful dialogue with a network of similar powers and this partly explains why media conglomerates have reached a certain size.

THE BENEFIT OF SCOPE: ENTERTAINMENT CONGLOMERATES AND TRANSNATIONAL TELEVISION

Conglomeration in the media industry is a response to commercial pressures but it also presents several advantages that are clearly visible in the context of cross-border TV channels. Media groups with a large international TV channel business can pursue *economies of scale*. A company that runs a host of channels can centralize different departments such as accounts, acquisitions, ad sales, marketing and the press office. These cost-saving arrangements enable them to set up and run channels with a minimum of personnel. Larger economies of scale can be pursued across a conglomerate's divisions, as a transnational company can leverage its global scale in research, technology and procurement activities.

Synergies can be achieved between the international TV channel business and the conglomerate's other divisions. When Disney and Jetix join forces to produce an animated series, Disney can develop the property in different formats across its business lines, from motion pictures to theme parks.

They might also decide to split the rights geographically for Disney to take the property where Jetix is not established. It is also easier for a conglomerate the size of Disney to license or enforce the intellectual property rights associated with media properties.

International companies can acquire talent and expertise across markets, finding the best managers and identifying the best practices and implementing them across the board. They can also leverage their understanding of local markets: the knowledge that a division acquires of a territory can be transferred to other parts of the conglomerate. For instance, the first channel to arrive in Poland will act as an outpost for all the incoming stations and Poland itself can act as a Central European base.

Conglomerates are more likely to have the resources to produce and distribute TV networks that can thrive in a competitive marketplace. Channels that are owned by diversified media companies benefit from unparalleled in-house expertise and resources. Marketing is increasingly important to ensure product visibility. Disney and Viacom, for instance, were able to spend US$2.6 billion and US$1.6 billion respectively on advertising in 2007 alone.[11] These channels also have the opportunity of generating attractive content either by way of co-productions or priority purchase agreements with the group's other divisions.

Without the advantages that media groups can derive from scale and scope, many cross-border TV channels would simply not exist. On the other hand, these channels help conglomerates increase their revenue and build franchises (notably in children's television, Chapter 7). This mutually beneficial relationship becomes apparent when considering the conglomerates' extensive investments in transitional television in Europe, as listed in Table 8.3. The remainder of this section analyses their involvement in PETV.

Viacom

MTV Networks International, the Viacom division that runs the company's TV and multimedia properties (including non-music brands), has an unparalleled global reach: its 141 channels were seen in 507 million households across 160 territories in 2007. In Europe, MTV Networks Europe (MTVNE) is the undisputed star performer of the PETV industry. In 2008 it was running in excess of 80 channels, making it the region's largest broadcaster in terms of quantity and distribution scope. Most growth has been organic although MTVNE acquired two local television companies

Table 8.3: Diversified entertainment companies' main interests in cross-border TV channels in Europe, 2008

Channel	Type of distribution	Genre	Key owners
AXN suite of channels	Large distribution	Entertainment	Sony Pictures Television International
BabyTV	Pan-European	Children	News Corporation
The Biography Channel	Selected European markets	Factual entertainment	AETN International: Disney (37.5%), The Hearst Corporation (37.5%), NBC Universal (25%)
Cartoon Network suite of channels, Boomerang	Pan-European	Children	Time Warner
CNBC Europe	Pan-European	Business news	NBC Universal
CNN	Pan-European	News	Time Warner
Discovery suite of channels	Pan-European	Factual entertainment	Discovery Holdings (66%), Advance/Newhouse (33%), John Hendricks
Disney suite of channels, Cinemagic	Large distribution	Children	Disney
EI International Network	Large distribution	Entertainment	Comcast International Media Group
ESPN Classic	Large distribution	Sports	Disney
Extreme Sports	Pan-European	Sports/lifestyle	Liberty Global (through subsidiary Chello Zone)
Fox-branded channels	Selected European markets	Entertainment	News Corporation
Hallmark	Large distribution	Entertainment	NBC Universal
HBO Central Europe, Cinemax	Selected European markets	Entertainment	Time Warner; Disney; Sony
The History Channel	Large distribution	Factual entertainment	AETN International: Disney (37.5%), The Hearst Corporation (37.5%), NBC Universal (25%)
Jetix	Pan-European	Children	Disney (76%), public share (24%)
MGM Channel	Large distribution	Movies	MGM Studios
MTV suite of channels	Pan-European	Music	Viacom
NASN	Pan-European	Sports	Disney
National Geographic suite of channels	Pan-European	Factual entertainment	BSkyB/Fox International Channels (50%), NBC Universal (25%), National Geographic Ventures (25%)
Nickelodeon suite of channels	Large distribution	Children	Viacom
Paramount Comedy/ Comedy Central	Selected European markets	Entertainment	Viacom
Sky News	Pan-European	News	News Corporation (controlling interest)
Turner Classic Movies	Large distribution	Movies	Time Warner
Universal Global Networks	Selected European markets	Entertainment/movies	NBC Universal
VH1 suite of channels	Pan-European	Music	Viacom
VIVA	Selected European market	Music	Viacom
Zone-branded channels	Selected European markets/ large distribution/pan-European	Entertainment, factual and movies	Liberty Global (through subsidiary Chello Zone)

Sources: company sources; *C&SE; M&M Guide.*

'Selected European markets' designates distribution in up to six territories of any size;

'Large distribution' means presence in at least ten territories without pan-European feed.

along the way: TMF in 2001 and VIVA in 2005 (Chapter 7). The company dominates music television but runs well-established brands in entertainment and children's television (Table 8.3). The channels come in all shapes and sizes and cover pan-European feeds (VH1), networks of local channels (MTV, Nickelodeon), multi-territory stations (Comedy Central/Paramount Comedy, MTV2, TMF, VIVA), and single-territory ones such as Game One in France (see Table 7.4 for music channels). The emphasis on content coupled with apparent disinclination to own or control distribution platforms reflects the philosophy of Sumner Redstone, Viacom's chairman and founder, who once talked of transforming the conglomerate into the 'number-one software-driven media company in the world'.[12]

In the course of its history MTVNE has broken new ground several times. It was the first broadcaster to adopt a *network-centric organizational structure* and pioneer the practice of localization, a strategy that is now an industry standard (Chapter 11). However, some of the Viacom brands have lost their shine in recent years. MTV, in particular, is losing its audience to gaming, video-sharing and social-networking websites. Tom Freston, Viacom's former chief operating officer and the architect of MTV's international development, left the company in September 2006. In 2007 MTV Networks International went through a period of restructuring and about 250 jobs were axed. Viacom now aims to deepen the multimedia integration of its brands and further the delivery of its content across as many platforms as possible. Given the likelihood that the music television ride is over, a new emphasis is being given to non-music channels and content. As for MTV, the channel will probably never regain its past glory but it is being revived through investment in new programming and local productions.

Disney

The Walt Disney Company has always had a low profile in the international television industry despite controlling one of Europe's largest networks of TV channels. It is partly because the company has eschewed pan-European feeds in favour of country-specific stations. Disney's television strategy is two-pronged. It develops its own-branded channels, of which there are more than 50 in Europe taking into account all the local versions. In addition, the company has a hand in other major international TV brands: it owns ESPN Classic (which controls NASN), it has a majority interest in Jetix and holds a 37.5 per cent stake in AETN (Table 8.3).

Disney's strategy reveals astute choices and a well-executed game plan. It is a leader in family entertainment and it has successfully branched out into other lucrative genres in international television. Disney's networks are highly profitable and the company is a master in the art of using them as brand-building vehicles. These channels play the role of *brand drivers* for the company's franchises, which are then used and monetized on a variety of platforms. Disney's ability to integrate TV content and move it around the company is second to none. This can be seen again with *High School Musical*, a TV-led franchise that has become a global phenomenon and which the company exploits in all its guises, such as licensed shows in schools, interschool dance competitions (called *My School Rocks* in India), a Bollywood adaptation, and a reality show called *High School Musical: La Selección* in Mexico and Argentina.[13]

Time Warner

Time Warner's global TV networks are operated by TBS, brought in by Ted Turner when he joined Time Warner in 1996. More than any other media company, TBS has long favoured the pan-European approach for its television business in the region. Its strategy reflects Gerald Levin's and Turner's legacy in satellite distribution in the USA (Chapter 1). Once in Europe pan-regional feeds seemed to be the natural way of developing TV networks. Today all TBS entertainment properties are fully localized, including TCM, Boomerang and Cartoon Network (Table 11.1).

TBS operates some of the best-established transnational TV networks in Europe. CNN remains the world's leading brand in international news (Chapter 9) and their entertainment networks are leaders of their genre. TBS is also reintroducing TNT (Turner Network Television) in Europe: following launches in Spain and Turkey, a German version debuted in summer 2008. The Time Warner division is investing heavily in content and has set up a development hub for its children's channels, predominantly in Europe. US$100 million has been spent on the London-based International Cartoon Network Original unit and the first animated series will come to air in 2009.[14]

News Corporation

Rupert Murdoch was a forerunner in satellite television in Europe with good knowledge of the European media market, at a time when many

American media executives were still struggling to locate Paris on the map (Chapter 1). Sky Channel taught Murdoch two facts: the pan-European advertising market is puny and cable operators are a nuisance who stand between a business and its customers. From this premise Murdoch sought to establish a TV business in a territory with a sizeable advertising market and searched for a technology that would allow him to sell his content directly to customers. The result was Sky in Britain (Europe's largest DTH platform and pay-TV business), followed by Sky Italia.

News Corp's core strategy consists of integrating its content and distribution assets, which in pay-TV terms involves the distribution of the company's own channels on its satellite platforms.[15] Thus both Sky and Sky Italia offer a large selection of channels that are either wholly owned or majority owned by News Corp. The Sky- and Fox-branded channels tend to be country-specific but News Corp is increasingly involved in cross-border TV networks such as Sky News, National Geographic and BabyTV (Table 8.3). The company also broadcasts Fox News in Europe and India's Star suite of channels in the UK.

Fox International Channels (FIC) – 'a relatively unheralded part of our global group', according to Rupert Murdoch – is the global channels division of News Corporation.[16] Los Angeles-based FIC is responsible for developing and distributing News Corp's channels in Europe and across the world. It controls BabyTV and National Geographic in Southern Europe, and three Fox-branded channels (Fox Channel, Fox Crime and Fox Life) that are present in Italy, Portugal and several Central European territories. There is also FX, an entertainment channel slanted towards men (UK, Italy, Portugal), Voyage, a station dedicated to travel and culture distributed in the francophone territories, and another Fox Channel, which was launched in Germany in May 2008. FIC's objective is to build a global portfolio of channels managed under the same umbrella. Economies of scale are realized by grouping human resources, finance and marketing under one roof.

News Corp's strength in Europe rests on its unique access to millions of consumers in two key European markets. Its reach has expanded with the 20 per cent acquisition of Premiere, Germany's satellite platform, in February 2008. Murdoch is now able to leverage his powerful position in distribution as his satellite business eases the expansion of his own country-specific and cross-border channels in Europe.

NBC Universal

NBC Universal remains the most US-centric of the world's leading media conglomerates. For many years CNBC Europe was NBC's only significant international property. The 2004 acquisition of Universal and its international network of channels was the company's first significant step at international level. Following a review conducted in 2007 by Jeff Zucker, NBC Universal president and chief executive, international growth has been placed at the top of the agenda and the company aims to double revenue from its Global Networks division. It is in this context that the 2007 acquisition of Hallmark must be placed (Chapter 7), but much of this growth will be organic and NBC Universal is aiming to launch 20 additional channels in 23 territories across the world within the next two years.[17]

Liberty Global

Liberty Global was born out of the merger of Liberty Media International and United GlobalCom (UGC) in June 2005. Historically it is an American cable company that has grown internationally and progressively diversified into other distribution platforms (broadband and DTH) and content provision. It is smaller than the other conglomerates but it is growing fast and its revenue stood at US$9 billion in 2007, up from US$6.5 billion in 2006 and US$4.5 billion the year before.[18] The company operates in Europe through LG Europe, a wholly owned subsidiary, which is organized in two divisions: UPC Broadband (distribution, Chapter 4) and Chellomedia (content provision). The latter operates both country-specific and cross-border thematic channels. It moved into acquisitions in the mid-2000s when it bought Extreme Sports Channel and 87.5 per cent of Zonevision (now Chello Zone, Chapter 7). In September 2008 it acquired Spektrum, a multi-territory documentary channel that reaches 3.6 million homes in Hungary, the Czech Republic and Slovakia.[19]

Today, through its subsidiary Chello Zone, Liberty Global counts among PETV industry's leading players. However, John Malone, the company chairman, and Michael Fries, CEO, have long focused on distribution platforms at the expense of content, and thus the company's channels still rely overwhelmingly on acquired programming. Liberty Global does not control a Hollywood studio or a major TV production unit, which is a handicap when its channels compete with those of larger conglomerates. Nonetheless, the channel business potential is great and is ably supported by the company's distribution platforms.

A&E Television Networks

The Arts & Entertainment Television Networks (AETN) is an American cable company set up in 1983 that has progressively diversified into content provision. AETN was founded by Nickolas Davatzes, a Greek American, who remained at the helm of the company until April 2005, when Abbe Raven succeeded him. The shareholders are The Hearst Corporation and Disney (37.5 per cent each) and NBC Universal (25 per cent). The launch of the company's flagship channel in the USA, A&E Network, was followed by a stream of cable stations such as The History Channel, Military History and History International.

AETN International is developing four networks at global level (The History Channel, Military History, The Biography Channel and Crime & Investigation Network) that have gained significant international footprint in a short period of time (Chapter 7). Although it is a relatively small company, it has played its cards well. AETN localizes its channels with care and always collaborates with local partners. It sticks to factual entertainment, a genre in which it excels and that crosses borders well. It owns an extensive content library that includes over 8,500 hours of original programming, to which it adds about 1000 hours every year. AETN channels have a clear identity and contain first-rate content that can cut through the competition.[20]

Sony Pictures Television International (SPTI)

Sony Pictures Television International, based in Culver City (California), is the division responsible for the worldwide development of Sony Pictures Entertainment's channel business. Sony entered the sector far later than the other conglomerates as it began building its international TV network in the mid-1990s only. Europe came third in the pecking order, after Asia and Latin America. The company has argued that entering the industry so late enabled it to avoid the mistakes made by the early international broadcasters as it immediately adopted a country-by-country approach. On the other hand, SPTI has had to wriggle its way through crowded markets and find a niche for its channels among well-established brands. To this day it arguably does best in the region's newer markets and 'soft' territories such as Spain and Central Europe.

Despite considerable progress in recent years Sony remains the entertainment corporation with the fewest assets in transnational television.[21] SPTI's core multi-territory brand is AXN, today followed by Animax

(Chapter 7). The company is also involved in digital terrestrial television in Spain through Sony Entertainment Television (SET) and serves the South Asian diaspora in the UK with a local feed of SET Asia.

Sony's strength lies in the corporation's huge production facilities, which range from local studios to Hollywood majors Columbia Pictures and TriStar Pictures. The Sony Pictures Entertainment library is among the world's largest, including 'more than 3,500 feature films, [. . .] 35,000 television episodes, 275 television series and more than 22,000 episodes of game-show programming from 50 years of television history'.[22] A fair amount of this content ends up in the schedules of AXN channels, giving these stations a distinct flavour and allowing Sony to build assets in the region.[23]

CONCLUSION: PAN-EUROPEAN TELEVISION IN EUROPE REMAINS A STRATEGIC PRIORITY

Entertainment conglomerates that operate transnational TV networks in Europe have adopted different approaches because of distinct assets and heritage. But their European TV business has acquired a crucial significance for all. International television is among media corporations' main growth drivers. In Europe, revenue from TV channels has increased many times faster than syndication income. While ten years ago a conglomerate would seek to balance its channel and syndication business, today it invariably prioritizes the former. In addition, TV networks help expand international reach and build franchises, they constitute an asset and offer a steadier stream of revenue than filmed entertainment.

Europe may neither have the cachet of the Middle East nor the lure of the Chinese market but it remains a far better commercial proposition and offers a more stable policy environment in which to do business. The senior executives of diversified entertainment conglomerates may gloat about the global span of their companies but Europe is still the place from where most of their international revenue is derived.

CHAPTER 9

THE SUN ALWAYS SHINES ON GLOBAL NEWS TV NETWORKS

This chapter surveys international news TV networks in Europe, building on the book's numerous passages on the subject (notably in Chapters 2, 6 and 12). Making sense of the diversity of these channels is a challenge, and the purpose of this chapter is to offer a typology based on their degree of transnationality. It distinguishes between the 'Big Three' that tell stories *beyond* their borders (CNN International, BBC World News and Al Jazeera English), the 'mid-level' networks that tell stories *within* their borders (EuroNews and Sky News) and those that tell stories *about* their borders (e.g. Deutsche Welle-TV, France 24 or Russia Today). It argues that although the number of global news TV stations has steadily increased over recent years, only those with connections to the transnational power elite can claim to be influential. The last section examines the two global business and financial news networks, CNBC Europe and Bloomberg Television.

TELLING STORIES BEYOND BORDERS: HOW THE 'BIG THREE' REPORT THE WORLD TO THE WORLD

CNN International

CNN Worldwide, as the news group is called, has developed extensive newsgathering facilities over the years. Until 2007 its operations consisted of 36 bureaux: 11 in the USA, seven in Europe (Berlin, Frankfurt, Istanbul, London, Madrid, Moscow and Rome), five in the Middle East, two in Africa, eight in Asia Pacific and three in Latin America. Late that year the news group embarked on a major investment in newsgathering, adding correspondents to existing bureaux, planning new operations in nine countries (Afghanistan, Belgium, India, Kenya, Malaysia, Nigeria, the Philippines, Poland and Vietnam), and opening a regional newsgathering hub in the United Arab Emirates.

There are a few cities in Europe where CNN should arguably have a permanent presence but these places are covered by a mobile network of correspondents and stringers. London is CNN's European headquarters and their biggest facility outside the USA. It has become a hub of production and broadcast, and sends out correspondents across the region. CNN Worldwide has nearly 4,000 staff with more than 120 field correspondents, not including CNN's anchors who often work as correspondents themselves. It has agreements with about 1,000 affiliates with whom the network exchanges news feeds. CNN implemented a regionalization programme in 1997 when it broke its global feed into a worldwide network of five separately scheduled channels: Europe/Middle East/Africa, Asia Pacific, South Asia, Latin America and North America. London, Hong Kong, Mexico City and, since 2009, Abu Dhabi have been turned into major production centres and fully integrated digital newsrooms.

TBS, CNN Worldwide's parent division in the Time Warner group, runs two joint ventures in Europe. In Spain, TBS and Sogecable, owner of Canal Plus España, operate CNN+, a local-language 24-hour news channel staffed with 150 journalists that went live in January 1999. TBS's second local partnership is CNN Türk, which it owns jointly with Turkey's Dogan Media Group. Both CNN+ and CNN Türk are entirely produced locally from studios in Madrid and Istanbul and have extensive newsgathering facilities. Both stations benefit from the resources of CNN Worldwide and contribute to its news network. Several times in recent years, CNN's local partners have delivered news to the network that it would not have obtained without them, notably for the Madrid trains bombing in 2004 and the parliamentary and presidential elections in Turkey during the summer of 2007.

All CNN programming is tailored to deliver international news and current affairs. *International Hour,* which went live in March 1984, was American television's first news show to be exclusively devoted to foreign news. *World Report,* launched in October 1987, was a global newscast that consisted of unedited news reports from affiliates in about 100 countries. CNN's contemporary delivery of international news is among the most extensive in the industry. The London bureau alone, staffed with 130 people and capable of producing some 50 hours of programming every week, broadcasts the following daily shows: *CNN Today* (morning world news), *Business International* (European and global business news headlines), *World Business Today* (European and global business news evening round-up), *World News Europe* (world news from a European perspective) and *World Sport* (also with a European focus). CNN International also airs *Inside the Middle East* and *Inside Africa,* two weekly current affairs programmes, and shows like *Global Office* (international management issues) and *International Correspondents*, a roundtable discussion bringing together international journalists and correspondents debating items on the news agenda.[1]

CNN International remains the world's leading brand in international news, although its position is being seriously challenged. EuroNews has become Europe's most-watched international channel and BBC World News is the most trusted brand among elite audiences (Tables 5.5 and 9.1). CNN's main strength is also its Achilles heel. It covers the United States very well, which is a great advantage when US presidential elections take place. Its home market also gives the network the lucrative opportunity of selling foreign news feeds to local TV stations that would never send reporters farther than two miles from the newsroom. CNN is the world's only news channel that makes a profit. However, its reporting is sometimes perceived as West-centric. It is an opinion not entirely fair and based on false impressions: being of American origin and having kept the look and feel of a US cable channel, the news network is often perceived as more American than is perhaps the case. It remains true that CNN recently felt the need to bolster its presence in the Global South, adding to its two bureaux in Sub-Saharan Africa (Johannesburg and Lagos). The network's fresh expansion of international newsgathering resources is an admission that it has had to raise its game at a time of increased competition from both new and established players in the field.

BBC World News

BBC World News is a commercial channel with an operating budget of about £45 million. It has yet to turn a profit but with 20 per cent revenue growth year-on-year for the last three years it should break even in the near future. As mentioned in Chapter 6, operationally the network is part of the BBC Global News Division that incorporates the World Service, its international online service and BBC Monitoring. About 80 people work in BBC World News's newsroom, which is staffed 24/7. These are the people who put together the channel's output but this is a fraction of the staff who can work for the station at any given time. The network commissions services from BBC Television News, giving it permanent access to the vast news resources of the corporation. This amounts to some 2,000 journalists, excluding producers, technicians and people working in newsgathering. Overseas, the BBC has about 43 television-capable bureaux, which range from one-person operations to the Washington bureau that employs about 30 people. When needed, BBC World News also has access to World Service radio correspondents, so there are few places left in the world that are beyond its reach. All in all, BBC World News has at its fingertips the world's best-trained news personnel and most expansive newsgathering facilities.

BBC World News is split into five feeds covering Europe, the Americas, Africa, South Asia and the Middle East, and Asia Pacific and Australasia. The schedule format is an international news bulletin broadcast on the hour, followed by the back half-hour of current affairs shows, documentaries and lifestyle programming.

Producing a single bulletin for a worldwide audience presents a few challenges. The first difficulty is picking stories that have significance around the world. The global news agenda may be determined by world events but, as with any other news outlet, BBC World News's editorial staff make selections based on their professional judgement and expertise. Those stories often require a fair amount of effort to make them work across boundaries. A news item from a particular country may need additional background explanation if its importance is not to be lost on audiences on the other side of the world. Stories are also made more relevant to international viewers by focusing on themes that resonate across borders. For this reason, BBC World News avoids producing a news agenda that is too dry and restricted to diplomacy and the global economy. BBC journalists strive to establish a connection between people's lives and global issues in order 'to make [them] feel that they are part of a global conversation that is going on all over the world'.[2] Thus the news bulletin covers a broad range of issues which are reported as engagingly and vividly as possible.

BBC World News must also juggle with differences in taste and decency. In Europe viewers have a low sensitivity threshold when it comes to images of death and devastation from war zones, while audiences are accustomed to more explicit pictures in India and the Middle East. Conversely, some audiences find it difficult to watch an item about a fashion show with acres of naked flesh on display.

Finally, there is the issue of time. On terrestrial channels news bulletins follow a natural cycle throughout the day that is recognized both by TV presenters and the audience. For BBC World News, however, it is always the morning or the evening somewhere on the planet. Thus presenters never say 'today' or 'tomorrow' but 'Monday' or 'Tuesday', because 'today' is a bit of an issue since it can be a different day in some parts of the world. Not knowing what the time is can make presenters feel lost and sometimes not terribly connected to their audience. BBC World News's way of dealing with this problem is to indicate the time from whichever location it airs a live feed.[3]

Broadcasting the same material across cultures generates dilemmas but the task is not as difficult as it sounds. International news channels like BBC World News communicate to a fairly homogeneous audience. Their viewers speak English, usually as a second language, they have a good level of education and a cosmopolitan outlook. By definition, they are interested in what is happening beyond their own borders and tend to hold positions in government or business that have an international dimension. Thus, these viewers may have different cultural backgrounds but their commonalities help news broadcasters find international benchmarks that work.

Similarities among international news audiences are an illustration of global news networks' complex relationship with globalization. These channels may well contribute to globalizing processes but they also feed off them. After 9/11 people recognize more easily that events occurring on the other side of the globe can affect their lives. The growing number of workers who are building their careers on the back of globalization are also developing an appetite for international news. These stations may have all sorts of effects – or maybe none – but they are also the manifestation of an increasingly interdependent world.

BBC World News's bulletin is broadcast worldwide but the back half-hour is regionalized. Daily shows include *World News Today* (comprehensive round-up), *BBC News Extra* (behind-the-headline analysis), *World Business Report*, *Asia Today* and *Sport Today*. *This Week* (a showcase for reports from BBC correspondents), *Reporters* (analytical pieces from around the world), *Middle East Business Report*, *Extra Time* (interviews with sports personalities) and *Talking Movies* are broadcast weekly. In addition to *Dateline London* – a roundtable of foreign correspondents posted in London discussing world events – interview shows such as *HARDtalk* and news specials feature power brokers on the international stage. The schedule is complemented by special series such as the *Earth Report* (environmental stories worldwide) and *Holidays in the Danger Zone*.

BBC World News acknowledges a European political heritage and its output reflects the values of free speech, fairness and democracy (Chapter 6). However, this, does not make it a 'perspective' channel that pushes a particular national agenda. The editorial staff make a conscious effort to give a platform to diverse arguments and not to project a British point of view. The channel benefits from the World Service tradition of international journalism and prolonged exposure to a variety of cultures. It has enabled

BBC World News to gain the trust of viewers in Europe and across the world.[4] Overall, the channel's output reveals a news organization that is remarkably aware of the globalized nature of the world and the cosmopolitan character of the human condition in the twenty-first century.

The Voice from the South: Al Jazeera English

The Qatari broadcaster Al Jazeera, which achieved fame with its Arabic network, launched a separate English service in November 2006. Al Jazeera English (AJE) is also based in Doha but has its own building and personnel. About 850 people work for AJE worldwide, of which there are 30 field correspondents spread across 18 bureaux. The Arabic and English services share technical resources, contacts and pictures, bringing the total number of bureaux to over 30.

AJE is notable for its network of broadcast centres in Doha, Kuala Lumpur, London and Washington, DC. Kuala Lumpur was preferred over Hong Kong for many reasons, not least because serious question marks hang over the status of press freedom in the Chinese city today. Kuala Lumpur is cheaper, has a good pool of labour and is conveniently placed midway between Beijing and Sydney. Further, Qatar and Malaysia are secular Muslim countries with cultural ties.

AJE's four television centres are connected by fibre optic cables and require constant attention to make sure that they all pull in same direction. The advantages that such a network brings far outweigh the difficulties of running it. It is an elegant solution to the issue of time frame. AJE can follow the sun round the globe by broadcasting its news bulletin from where the world is awake: starting the day in Kuala Lumpur, followed by Doha, then London and finally Washington. These newsrooms may also broadcast together and look at major stories from different regional perspectives. For the big events the network enables AJE to move its resources and base its operations where it is most appropriate.

Part of AJE's mission is to bring understanding through others' perspectives for audiences around the world. Nigel Parsons, managing director, sees AJE as a 'bridge between communities' that is furthering the cause of peace.[5] Another objective is to redress the balance of the information flow and bring the political South to the North. Thanks to its parent company AJE enjoys unparalleled access in the Middle East. The network also has 12 bureaux in Africa alone. AJE is in a good position to offer news from under-reported parts of the world but it does not want to be boxed in as the channel for the Middle East. It aims to be a market leader and is not 'setting out just to compete with other channels so that they do A and we do B'.[6] Although the channel faces strong competition, Al Jazeera is an experienced news provider with solid journalistic foundations. It has shown its willingness to take the necessary steps to ensure a successful international expansion. The network is well funded and has hired executives and high-profile journalists from leading news organizations. Nonetheless, its target of setting the global news agenda is ambitious and although AJE can be a success in the long term it has yet to make the impact it hoped for when it set out to conquer the West in 2006.

AJE is a news and current affairs channel that broadcasts a great number of magazines. It has adopted the BBC's back half-hour in order to offer in-depth analysis (e.g. *Inside Iraq, Inside Story, Frost Over the World*), interviews (Riz Khan's *One on One*) and explore a wide range of cultural and social issues (e.g. *Everywoman, The Fabulous Picture Show*). These magazines are essential in differentiating AJE from the rest in the field and contribute to the channel's distinct identity.

TELLING STORIES WITHIN THEIR BORDERS: THE 'MID-LEVEL TWO'

EuroNews: an embryonic European public sphere

As a network controlled by a consortium of public broadcasters, EuroNews' development is documented in Chapter 6. Today there are 160 journalists working in Lyon and a bureau in Brussels is staffed with three correspondents. News footage is provided by the participating public broadcasters and commercial television news agencies that reach the station through the EBU's Eurovision News Exchange (EVN). The absence of field correspondents can be seen as a shortcoming compared with the leading networks that derive a large part of their credibility from their expansive newsgathering resources. Commenting on images that may not be exclusive, it has taken a long time for EuroNews to develop its own editorial line and establish its reportorial authority. Although EuroNews occasionally sends its own team to cover key events, a foreign correspondent reporting from Baghdad via his or her satellite phone has more gravitas than a journalist in Lyon voicing over images received from APTN or Reuters Television.

However, this has not prevented EuroNews from becoming Europe's most popular international news channel in 2007 (Table 5.5), notably because of its multi-lingual prowess. It began broadcasting in five languages (French, German, English, Italian and Spanish), adding Portuguese, Russian and Arabic along the way. A drawback of multi-lingualism is that interviews need to be translated into eight languages, a costly enterprise. It is also difficult to hold debates. Politics is an elite-driven activity, which explains why interviews and discussions constitute the bedrock of public affairs television. The relative absence of talking heads on EuroNews may add to the perception that the station is a bit remote from events but two programmes partially remedy this issue: *Agora* stages small-scale debates (up to four participants) and *Europinion* is an interview-based magazine. Journalists, guests and experts express themselves in their own tongue and are then voiced over in the other languages.

EuroNews's unique selling point is its European perspective. Its newscasts blend European news from the EU member states and institutions, and world news from a European angle. The station airs a range of current affairs programmes that explore European subjects and debates: *Pass*, *Europa* and *Europeans*. *Parlamento* gives much-needed coverage to the European Parliament, which is either ignored or maligned by national media.[7]

Europe might be the world's most advanced transnational democracy but the evolution of European television has not matched its ground-breaking developments.[8] More than a quarter of a century after the first satellite TV channel, there is still no European public sphere to accompany and support an array of transnational institutions that encompass all the branches of power.[9] There is no shortage of transnational players in the media industry but they have learned to adapt closely to local audiences (Chapter 11). Thus EuroNews addresses a market failure and fulfils an important mandate for European democracy by trying to communicate the same news across borders and informing citizens about European institutions.

Sky News: the British prism

There are some ambiguities about the international status of Sky News. International news providers do not recognize it as a competitor and a channel source insists that it is a 'British-based service available internationally'.[10] Many years ago internal discussions took place to turn the station into a global news network but Rupert Murdoch, Sky's major shareholder through News Corp, had doubts – and rightly so – about the financial wisdom behind such a project.

However, no investment was spared to establish Sky News as a leading news channel. The station's coming of age was the death of Princess Diana in August 1997 when it had sufficient resources to provide non-stop coverage for nearly two weeks. It repeated the performance with the trial of a British au pair in Boston (USA) two months later and reached another journalistic landmark when it received a BAFTA Award for its coverage of 9/11.[11] Today, Sky News has substantial newsgathering capabilities with 600 dedicated staff, 300 journalists and ten well-staffed news bureaux outside the UK (Dubai, Dublin, Brussels, Belgrade, Moscow, Jerusalem, Johannesburg, Delhi, Beijing and Washington, DC). It has formed alliances with major broadcasters worldwide and has a supply deal with Reuters. It also receives news from Enex, the commercial broadcasters' news exchange based in Luxembourg.

John Ryley, head of Sky News, recognizes that 'the way we think is a British mentality' but this has not prevented the station from acquiring a sizeable international following.[12] It has about 50 million connections in Europe alone and the third-highest reach among upscale viewers (Tables 5.5 and 7.1). The network operates three separate feeds (Ireland, the UK and international), which share the same editorial output but have different commercial breaks. At night, the channel's international audience outweighs domestic viewers and thus news editors select stories that are relevant. The emphasis is on African news between 4:00 am and 6:00 am GMT in order to catch people getting up in Southern Africa where the station is attracting a sizeable audience. There are plans to further internationalize the output between 1:00 am and 4:00 am GMT, this time with views on the Asian market.

Sky News is relevant to a European-wide audience because opinion formers are interested in watching world news 'through the prism of the British mindset'.[13] Viewers also appreciate the station's informality and liberal tone – it is not a national broadcaster – its impartiality and speed of coverage. The all-news channel is flexible and always prepared to deliver breaking news.

TELLING STORIES ABOUT THEIR BORDERS: TELEVISION AND ELECTRONIC NATIONALISM

Deutsche Welle

Deutsche Welle's television channel, DW-TV, started broadcasting in April 1992. The station rotates between German and English and broadcasts a news bulletin on the hour, which is followed by magazines (Chapter 6). DW-TV compares favourably in terms of distribution with the other international news and current affairs channels but lags behind in terms of reach (Table 5.5). The German station has limited newsgathering resources, with only three news bureaux outside Germany, in Brussels, Moscow and Washington, DC. Unlike the BBC's integrated international operations, DW-TV's relationship with the German public broadcasters is not symbiotic and the station must request and pay for each news story it gets from ARD or ZDF. But the station's purpose is not to become a leader in the international news market, rather to ensure a German presence in the satellite realm.[14]

Russia Today: the Empire strikes back

Russia Today went on air in December 2005, broadcasting from Moscow and employing about 700 staff. It is funded by the government, which gives the channel US$30 million per year. It has bureaux in Kiev, Tbilisi, Vladikavkaz, Jerusalem, Cairo, Paris, London, New York and Washington, DC. The Kremlin's view is that there is not enough coverage of Russia in the Western media and the little that exists is too negative. Thus Russia Today's mission is to spearhead a counter-propaganda offensive, 'balance the negativity' and tell the world about Russia.[15] Although the station focuses on Russia and the CIS countries, it also covers world news.

France 24: 'CNN à la française' or 'La voix de la France'?

France's voice in the global TV news arena, France 24, went live in December 2006. It was a project initiated by former President Jacques Chirac in 2002. As a long-standing Gaullist, Chirac always thought that television should be made to serve state interests. He was particularly frustrated to see two of the other four permanent members of the UN Security Council (Britain and the United States) dominate the global news agenda through well-established news agencies and TV networks. In fact, by the time France 24 launched, France was the only permanent member without an English global news channel: Russia Today was already on air and China's CCTV 9 had been broadcasting since 2000. Restoring 'la voix de la France' was Chirac's objective when he called for the creation of a French international news network. His views were widely shared among the French political elite. Dominique de Villepin, France's then Foreign Minister (and subsequent

Prime Minister until Spring 2007), referred to the news network as an 'instrument of power' at the National Assembly in 2003, adding that the project was crucial for 'France's image in the world, the defence of French interests and France's capacity to influence world events'.[16]

The preparations for France 24 were beset by problems and the launch was delayed for about two years. An issue that needed to be resolved was the network's ownership structure. After months of hesitation the government opted for a 50/50 joint venture between France Télévisions, the public broadcaster, and TF1, a commercial TV network. It was a poor decision considering that public/private partnerships suited neither Eurosport nor EuroNews (Chapters 2 and 6). Unsurprisingly, TF1 was already trying to sell its shares by 2008. France 24 broadcasts three feeds, in French, English and Arabic, and can also be watched on the Internet. Since the news network is generously subsidized by French taxpayers and does not claim carriage fees, full-time distribution has already reached 50 million homes in Europe.

France 24, headed by Alain de Pouzilhac, employs 180 journalists and 160 technicians. It claims 36 correspondents and has access to the images produced by TF1's and France Télévisions' foreign bureaux. It has signed cooperation agreements with Agence France Presse (AFP), the news agency, Radio France Internationale (RFI), the international radio network, and Réseau France Outre-mer (RFO). Since 2008, France 24 has been part of umbrella company France Monde, which also includes TV5Monde and RFI (Chapter 6).

France 24 mixes news bulletins with magazines, privileging short formats. The first half-hour is dedicated to headline news and five- to ten-minute-long news bulletins devoted to financial markets, business or culture. This is completed by special news reports, background analysis, sport and world weather. The back half-hour is devoted to magazines (health, the environment, politics, science, people, fashion, etc.), talk shows and interviews with French personalities.

France 24 claims to be the French CNN but the truth is that it cannot be compared to the field's leading brands, not least because it is a 'perspective' channel (see below). In addition, its resources do not match those of market leaders. Its annual budget of €80 million is only slightly higher than that of Sky News, a channel that does not make fanciful claims about being a global news network. France 24's parent broadcasters have fewer field correspondents than the BBC and only a minority can express themselves in English. Finally, the channel is handicapped in the world market because it is not anglophone: talk shows and interviews on the English feed are often voiced over from the French, which is less desirable for a non-francophone audience.

One world, too many voices?

The number of cross-border 24-hour news channels has expanded rapidly in recent years. It is a field that has attracted all kinds of broadcasters (in addition to those already mentioned). State organizations include China Central Television, which operates CCTV 9, and the Islamic Republic of Iran Broadcasting (IRIB), which launched Press TV in July 2007. Japan's public broadcaster has inherited the onerous task of launching an international news network. The Japanese government, having failed to sell the project to commercial players, has assigned it to NHK, who have gained valuable international experience with NHK World (Chapter 10). The channel is scheduled to come on air in January 2009 and aims to promote the understanding of Japanese culture. It also coincides with the country's diplomatic campaign to become a permanent member of the UN Security Council.[17]

New Delhi Television, the commercial broadcaster, launched two international news channels in April 2003: NDTV India broadcasts in Hindi and is aimed at the Indian diaspora, while NDTV 24x7 is in English and targets an international audience. Both channels concentrate on domestic news. Fox News, the Washington-based News Corp property, is available on several platforms in Europe. Viewers get the US channel's international feed which displays local inserts carrying commercials, world weather and information screens. Fox News is a domestic channel and is relevant to European audiences in so far as it gives them a glimpse of the United States and lets them see the world from an American perspective.

INTERNATIONAL NEWS NETWORKS AND TRANSNATIONALISM

It is apparent that international news channels differ from one another, but how does one make sense of this diversity? The first possible criterion is the status conferred upon the image. Sky News has adopted an approach based on the power of the picture. Likewise, EuroNews places greater emphasis on images since ITN's involvement in the station (e.g. the signature programme *No Comment*). By way of contrast, AJE and France 24 are more discursive in character. These channels' controllers adhere to a more analytical brand of journalism than the Anglo-American school of reporting. It is a choice that is reflected in the back half-hour of these two stations, which comprises language-driven programmes such as interviews and talk shows.

Another difference is the level of priority attached to breaking news. The issue is not so much about who breaks news first but how much airtime networks devote to what is considered breaking news at any given time. Sky News has no pre-set bespoke programming: it is a rolling news service that reports what happens at any moment. Most other networks are news and current affairs channels that mix bulletins with magazines. It is a format that is favoured by the networks' commercial managers since it is far easier to raise advertising and sponsorship revenue from magazines than news.[18] Thus a related matter for news and current affairs stations is: at which point does news become breaking news and warrant a programme interruption? Although CNN has moved away from a rolling news model over the years, it still has no qualms about introducing programme interruptions if it sees fit. BBC World News also reacts swiftly, while Deutsche Welle-TV and France 24 will disrupt their programming only in exceptional circumstances.

The degree of political independence these channels enjoy varies greatly. All the leading brands must be considered independent. Doubts are sometimes voiced about Al Jazeera because the broadcaster receives most of its funding from the Qatari government, but the output of AJE is clear evidence that it does not represent the views of any particular authority. On the contrary, the Qatari government has shielded the broadcaster from threats raised by autocratic regimes in the region. While Deutsche Welle-TV is fiercely independent, France 24's output often betrays the channel's close ties to its paymaster. The network's senior executives have occasionally received phone calls from the president's office dictating terms about presidential coverage.[19]

At the other end of the scale, CCTV 9, Russia Today and Press TV are the mouthpiece of regimes with a poor democratic record. Russia Today is professionally put together and run by the news agency RIA-Novosti but it is an instrument of public diplomacy sponsored by the state and controlled by the Federal Security Service, the successor of the KGB. Similarly, the Chinese state broadcaster is controlled by the State Council Information Office, which itself reports to the all-powerful Communist

Party's Propaganda Department.[20] These stations are driven by propaganda imperatives and their journalistic standards are corroded by lack of independence. The image of a country that these stations project is not only distorted but fashioned to suit the needs of a political elite: CCTV 9 does not merely try to promote a fictitious image of China, but the image that the Communist Party wants to sell abroad.

The key differentiating factor among these networks is their degree of transnationality. Since these channels are intended to cross borders, transnationalism should be a core feature. It also enables us to comprehend the nature of their contribution to the global public sphere. The three criteria to measure transnationality comprise the extent of operational integration at global level, geographical spread of newsgathering facilities and character of the news agenda. It is on this basis that this chapter's distinction between the three classes of channels has been set.

CNN and AJE have both built a worldwide network of interconnected newsrooms. Their interdependent and deterritorialized operational structures do not only deliver cost efficiencies but confer scope and flexibility on their news coverage. BBC World News has seven regional hubs (Washington, Brussels, Moscow, Jerusalem, Delhi, Johannesburg and Singapore) and the best geographical spread of news bureaux. The newsgathering facilities of these networks give them the ability to break international news and deliver round-the-clock coverage of world events in real time. The other channels' newsgathering capabilities are not in the global range and tend to concentrate on one region. For instance, Russia Today has only a few foreign correspondents and occasionally calls on CNN for help.

The 'Big Three' report the world to the world and although they sometimes articulate different regional perspectives, they do not follow a national agenda. Newsrooms might well reflect some of the assumptions and traditions common to the culture in which their networks are headquartered, but their staffing is purposely multinational and their journalists operate under strict – and public – guidelines. Similarly, EuroNews reports Europe to Europeans, and while Sky News is primarily aimed at a domestic market it is not set to articulate a national outlook.

By way of contrast, the news agenda of the networks in the third category remains nation-centric in scope. Their *raison d'être* is to project a nation onto the international stage and give it a voice in the global news arena. These networks cover key national events to give them international resonance, and report on the international activities of the nation's heroes: politicians, business leaders, artists, scientists and sportsmen and women.

Their coverage of the world comes with a national slant. For instance, when they report on global get-togethers such as UN conferences or G8 summits, they invariably focus on their respective head of state.

There have never been so many voices in the international public sphere. News networks contribute to its diversity by participating in a global conversation and exchanging perspectives. However, it should be recognized that not all viewpoints are equal: some channels have more scope, capability and integrity than others. Not all sources are equally trusted and not all voices speak with the same authority. And not all networks are transnational in character: some aim to report the world to the world while others remain wedded to the nation-state.

MANY VOICES, ONE CURRENCY

The currency of international news is influence: advertising agencies that book airtime on these channels do so because they are deemed prestigious and influential brands, not because of their ratings. Thus it is not surprising that many 24-hour news networks aspire to the influence of BBC World News and CNN International and have vowed not to let them set the global news agenda alone. How successful can they be? The answer depends on how well they connect to the transnational power elite.

BBC World News and CNN are considered influential because they know how to speak to influential people: they command the attention of an elite audience that is elusive, exclusive and difficult to impress. Both broadcasters research and target these viewers and spend considerable resources trying to match their demands. This blue-chip audience like their news fresh, accurate, impartial and first-hand. They want *credible* and *trusted* sources of information that have unmatched newsgathering resources and access to places and people other broadcasters cannot reach. They need a great amount of business and financial news. They look for networks that abide by their values and remain within the broad ideological agenda discussed and developed at global get-togethers such as the World Economic Forum in Davos. It is difficult to imagine a public of high-powered and high net-worth individuals turning away from trusted sources of information and tuning into channels that pursue their own agenda and try to cover world news with inadequate resources.

The latest edition of the European Opinion Leaders Survey, which measures Europe's most influential audience (Chapter 5), shows that channels such as AJE and France 24 face an uphill struggle to win the trust of these viewers. As Table 9.1 shows, only 4.3 per cent and 1.9 per cent of this select universe of 31,731 individuals (sample: 2,021 respondents) think that France 24 and AJE are authoritative.

Table 9.1: Leading news networks' weekly reach and brand values in EOLS universe, 2007 (in percentages)

	Weekly reach	Authoritative	Relevant	Impartial and unbiased
BBC World News	26.9	27.1	29.9	17.5
CNN International	31.3	15.7	24.0	7.2
EuroNews	19.4	10.0	15.9	6.6
France 24	8.8	4.3	7.8	2.9
AJE	3.5	1.9	4.0	2.9

Source: EOLS 2007.

News channels target a larger audience than the very select EOLS universe but these figures show how difficult it is to break into the elite club of global TV news providers. Despite poor EOLS results – and well-publicized teething problems – the network with most potential to join this group is AJE.[21] This channel is produced by a news organization that has established credentials for independent journalism, has a transnational outlook, is adequately funded and offers unrivalled expertise on the Global South. Even though there is still uncertainty about the positioning of the Qatari network and the level of 'Islamic slant' in its news coverage,[22] AJE does not push a national perspective. This is a crucial advantage when aiming at a cosmopolitan elite who conduct their business in an interdependent world and for whom nation-centrism is an occupational hazard.

CONNECTING THE WORLD'S FINANCIAL MARKETS: PAN-REGIONAL BUSINESS NEWS CHANNELS

For many opinion leaders who constitute the core audience of international news channels, finance and business rank as high as politics in their list of interests. Bloomberg Television and CNBC, the two international networks that provide specialist coverage in this field, have been in Europe since the mid-1990s.

An NBC Super offshoot: CNBC Europe

As NBC was struggling to establish its pan-European general entertainment channel (Chapters 2 and 7), rumours abounded about the imminent launch of business news channels in Europe and the NBC management decided to seize the moment. In 1995 NBC Super's flagship programming was the five-hour long European version of *The Money Wheel*, which was supplied by Financial Times Television. It was decided to create a fully fledged channel out of this programme, and CNBC Europe went on air in March 1996. While the European station built up its local programming, its American sister channel CNBC (Cable News and Business Channel) provided the remainder of the schedule. CNBC Europe also received footage from ANBC in Asia, which NBC had started in 1994. For the next two years CNBC Europe and NBC Super, which by now was going by the name of NBC Europe, broadcast concurrently on European cable networks.[23]

By the time NBC got CNBC under way, two other business news channels were operating in Europe: in addition to Bloomberg (see below), Dow Jones and minority partner Flextech (the London-based subsidiary of TCI) launched European Business News (EBN) in February 1995. EBN managing director, Michael Connor, decided to concentrate on local programming and provide 'news about European business to a European audience'.[24] He tried to broaden the appeal of the station by expanding coverage to technology and personal finance. Dow Jones had begun its television operations in the USA in 1987 and Asia in 1993, where ABN (Asia Business News) was the first pan-Asian news network. Together, these three regional channels produced the first global business news programme, *World Market Outlook*, broadcast live in Europe, Asia and America.[25]

Despite their prowess, both CNBC and EBN were losing money and it became apparent that the market was too small to sustain both. The two companies merged their non-US operations and the new pan-European channel started broadcasting under the CNBC brand in January 1998. CNBC Europe terminated its contract with Financial Times Television and built on the two partners' merged facilities, combining their extensive newsgathering resources. Dow Jones's *Wall Street Journal* and its news wire service supplied in excess of a thousand journalists while the CNBC channels brought in a few hundred.

In 2005 Dow Jones withdrew from the CNBC partnership and NBC Universal assumed sole ownership of the global network. Before going their separate ways the two companies signed a supply agreement giving CNBC access to Dow Jones's news output until 2012. In the summer of 2007 Dow Jones was acquired by Rupert Murdoch, who subsequently launched the Fox Business Network. The supply agreement was not revoked but the new Fox channel constitutes a clear threat for CNBC in the US market. In order to mitigate the risk, CNBC has agreed with *The New York Times* to share digital content and explore further cooperation.

CNBC serves Europe with one feed and there are local CNBC channels run as franchises by local partners in Italy and Poland. The CNBC management believes that its pan-regional channel is best adapted to the structure of the financial sector. In addition to the European currency, which has brought currencies together and created a European Central Bank, the leading European exchanges have gone through a round of consolidation. Most European derivatives exchanges have amalgamated into either London-based Euronext.Liffe or Eurex, the German-Swiss rival. In April 2007 Euronext merged with the NYSE Group, bringing under one roof six equities and six derivatives exchanges spanning five countries. Banks and brokerage firms have reorganized accordingly and no longer approach markets country by country but on a sector-by-sector basis.

In Europe, CNBC has correspondents in all the main stock exchanges from Amsterdam to Zurich and 150 static cameras installed in banks and trading floors. The London newsroom has one desk solely dedicated to the booking of occasional satellite capacity that requests tens of daily hits. When stories come out, CNBC has reporters on air within minutes, delivering information in real time.[26]

CNBC Europe begins its coverage of European markets early in the morning with *Before the Bell*, which previews the trading day. The network's signature show, *Worldwide Exchange*, kicks off at 9:00 am and is presented by three anchors in London, Singapore and New York. They review the world economy, discuss issues that affect international business and analyse the performance of stock and equity markets around the world. Then CNBC covers market openings across the continent and follows European trading until early afternoon. At 2:00 pm (GMT) *US Morning Call* covers the openings of various exchanges on the East Coast (NYSE, NASDAQ, the NY Mercantile Exchange, etc.), followed by *Squawk on the Street*. It comes back to Europe at 4:00 pm with *European Closing Bell* in order to catch the London close followed by the European exchanges. The coverage is Europe-wide – correspondents from all over the continent contribute to the show – and the anchor talks in front of a huge electronic map of Europe flashing up countries in red (down) or green (up). In early evening CNBC broadcasts *US Power Lunch* from New York, returning to London at 7:00 pm for some post-trading analysis with *Europe Tonight*. It returns to New York for *US Closing Bell* at 8:00 pm and stays there for some entertainment plugged from NBC network (*The Tonight Show with Jay Leno* and *Late Night with Conan O'Brien*), then broadcasts the Asian feed – where the markets are open – before coming back to London as the sun rises for another trading day.

Bloomberg Television

Bloomberg has delivered financial information to dealers' desks and market analysts since 1982 and added television to its services in the USA in February 1994. It started broadcasting in the UK in November 1995, then launched four channels in mainland Europe in the space of two years (France in July 1996, Italy, Spain and Germany in 1997).

Bloomberg is essentially a financial information company with one foot in the broadcasting industry. Its core business is the delivery of financial news, data and analytics on as many platforms as possible, including mobile devices, the Internet, radio and television. Bloomberg Television is also beamed directly to Bloomberg terminals on trading floors and is available on many cable and satellite networks in Europe. The company lays claim to the invention of the multi-screen format, displaying video and data including equity index quotes, bond prices, currencies and commodities, and a scrolling ticker delivered by Bloomberg Professional, which is the real-time data and analytics tool used by professional investors.

Bloomberg Television – named the 2008 International Television Channel of the Year by The Association of International Broadcasting – employs 2,500 journalists spread across 135 news bureaux, many equipped with broadcasting facilities. There are no trading floors, banks or stock exchanges beyond the reach of Bloomberg. Like CNBC, Bloomberg Television is committed to global reporting. Its channels benefit from formidable international newsgathering resources and they are capable of breaking or following stories whenever and wherever they develop. Daily programme plans cover European, emerging and international (mostly US) markets, asset allocation, money and politics. Daily shows, of which a good proportion are produced in Europe, include *Morning Call, Starting Bell, First Word on Money, Market Pulse, Money Tracker, Analyze This, Economic Essentials, European Market Report* and *Emerging Markets*.[27]

Bloomberg Television and CNBC have adopted slightly different approaches. Bloomberg's content is more localized than pan-European CNBC and its style is more sedate and conservative than its rival. Bloomberg's coverage places greater emphasis on data and analytics compared to CNBC because its TV channels are an integral part of the company's professional terminals. But both networks have similar EMS figures and their European distributions are markedly close to one another (Tables 5.5 and 7.1). They also have global capabilities and are able to follow markets around the world in real time (Chapter 12).

PART FOUR

INSIDE GLOBALIZATION:
THE TRANSNATIONAL SHIFT

CHAPTER 10

REASONS AND STRATEGIES FOR CROSSING BORDERS

The variety of transnational TV networks currently operating in Europe is striking and the question of how to make sense of this diversity arises. Faced with such a collection of channels, the first reflex is to classify them according to genre (Table 7.3). Albeit useful for descriptive purposes, such a categorization cannot shed light on the many differences between cross-border TV networks. The term 'transnational' hides myriad TV operations in terms of scope of distribution, audience, internationalization strategy and resources.

Does the channel address an international and multi-cultural audience, or a group of expatriates from the same cultural background? Is it distributed in a handful of countries, on a pan-regional basis or across the globe? Is the schedule made of recycled content from a terrestrial station or is it specifically produced for a multinational audience? Does the broadcaster try to adapt its transnational feed to local audiences or does it focus on international programming? Is the content produced in one place or does it come from a multinational network of production centres? Broadcasters have many ways and reasons for crossing borders and the purpose of the following typology is to comprehend these differences.

MIGRANT TELEVISION

Migrants' channels share two characteristics. Firstly, they address an audience with a common linguistic and cultural background. Migrant populations with access to transnational television services range from European expatriates established elsewhere on the continent, to American, South Korean and Japanese executives on three- to five-year stints in Europe. Among the biggest migrant markets are the Turks, predominantly established in Germany, Britain's South Asian population (approximately 1.5 million people), roughly the same number of Chinese speakers spread across the continent, East Europeans who have established themselves in Western Europe, and six to eight million Arabic speakers. Secondly, when migrants' channels use a specific feed to reach an audience overseas, the schedule is based on the recycling of existing programmes. A small number of shows can be added to these feeds but most of the programming is originally produced for the home market. Beyond this common ground these channels vary on the basis of cross-border strategy, amount of local input and type of ownership.[1]

Migrant television in Europe: an historical overview

The first European broadcaster to reach out to expatriates was RAI, the Italian public broadcaster, which was among the launch programmers of ECS 1 in 1984 (Chapter 4). Until 1986 the only cable operators who relayed the domestic channel were in Belgium before distribution extended to Switzerland and Luxembourg. In 1989 the public corporation uplinked RAI Due on a Hot Bird satellite followed by RAI Tre in 1991. Today European viewers can receive up to eight RAI channels. In 1995 a proper international feed was launched for audiences outside Europe, giving the broadcaster a global footprint. A European version of this channel began to air some twelve years later, in December 2007, mixing content from RAI national stations with a few shows produced by the broadcaster's international department. After a law passed in 2006, Italian expatriates can vote for candidates and get elected to the Italian parliament. This channel is meant to help them follow the political debates that are most relevant to them.[2]

The Spanish and Portuguese public broadcasters (RTVE and RTP) ventured abroad with purposely assembled international feeds from the start. TVE Internacional went on air in 1989 and RTP Internacional in June 1992. It was important for the Portuguese to get involved in international broadcasting: 4.5 million Portuguese people live outside their country of origin (nearly half of Portugal's total population) and there are 200 million Portuguese speakers around the world. RTP Internacional expanded its distribution and added regional schedules to acquire global coverage towards the end of the 1990s. Today, RTP Internacional mixes live news and talk shows with sport (essentially football) and factual and fictional material. All the programming comes from RTP's domestic stations, except for 10 per cent of the schedule that is bought from two commercial stations, SIC and TVI. In 2004 RTP Internacional began to produce its own magazine, *Contacto*, which is made by local Portuguese communities and has prompted some people and businesses from different communities to get in touch with each other. RTP, together with RAI, were among the founding members of the Bruges group, which brings together public broadcasters involved in satellite broadcasting (Chapter 4).[3]

The first non-European broadcaster to propose a service in Europe was probably Japan Satellite TV (JSTV), the satellite arm of the Japanese public broadcaster NHK. JSTV began broadcasting two hours each day in 1991, slowly building up to 24 hours a day by 2000. NHK World TV, as the channel was christened in 1995, is a free channel that broadcasts 24-hour news and information. In 1998 it was joined by NHK World Premium, a subscription-funded entertainment station. The small team based in London are involved in the marketing and distribution of the premium channel, which at present has 10,000 subscribers across Europe and the Middle East. They also produce the promos and pick the rest of the schedule from NHK's five home channels, mixed with Japanese commercial television's most popular programming.[4]

Throughout the 1990s, international dedicated satellite services have proliferated. These services enable broadcasters to adapt the scheduling according to the time zone, select the most popular programmes from their own terrestrial channels and – resources permitting – add some original programming. Today, such services come from all corners of the world, as illustrated by Brazil's TV Globo Internacional, Russia's RTR Planeta, Norway's NRK International or the Korean Arirang TV.

For the broadcasters that service Europe's largest migrant populations the key is to attract second- and third-generation transmigrants. To effect this they add as much original programming to the schedule as is economically feasible. It is the approach adopted by many broadcasters chasing Asian viewers in Europe. The first mover and current market leader, Zee Network, started its European operations back in 1995. Today Zee Network has about 150,000 subscribers across Europe who pay £15.99 per month each to receive a package of up to five channels: Alpha ETC Punjabi, Zee TV, Zee Cinema, Zee Music (UK only) and Zee Gujarati (UK only).

Ninety-five per cent of the schedule of the main channel, the family-oriented Zee TV, comes from India and the rest is locally produced. Zee TV's London facilities produce a local community programme, *Out and About*, and a few music shows. In Europe, the Indian network is positioned as an Asian channel and also targets Pakistani viewers. Indian movies and TV series are carefully selected and only those that are deemed to be inoffensive to Pakistani subscribers are scheduled. Zee TV also airs Pakistani shows and sports like the Pakistan test match series.[5]

Serving the market or in the 'market for loyalties'?

There is a division among migrants' channels that are either state-controlled or independently owned by commercial operators. State broadcasters launch satellite television channels with the intention of serving a political and national agenda, such as promoting the country abroad and helping the government to stay in touch with its expatriates, who are then reminded of where their loyalties should lie. These governments use satellite technology to electronically expand the boundaries of the nation.

Such channels proliferate in the Middle East where all the governments have launched satellite channels since the 1991 Gulf War. Egypt's state broadcaster, the Egyptian Radio and Television Union (ERTU), launched its first international satellite television service in the aftermath of the Iraqi invasion of Kuwait in December 1990. The Egyptian Space Channel was originally set up to counteract Iraqi propaganda and was aimed at Egyptian soldiers posted in the Gulf. Today, it is known as ESC 1 and reaches millions of Egyptians established overseas. In the early 1990s Safwat al-Sharif, Hosni Mubarak's minister of state for information, realized that satellite television could also be used to promote the country abroad and subsequently the ERTU launched Nile TV. This channel broadcasts in French and English with three target audiences: tourists and investors, foreign expatriates living in Egypt and second-generation Egyptian migrants with little or no knowledge of Arabic. In 1996 the ERTU formed the Egyptian Satellite Company (Nilesat) to coordinate its satellite activities. It launched several communications satellites (the Nilesat series) and a string of thematic channels (Nile News, Nile Drama, Nile Sports, etc.) with international distribution. All these stations are the carriers of an official ideology and viewpoint.[6]

Plans for state-sponsored channels might sound exciting in official circles across the Middle East but doubts remain about their success in the marketplace. Independent and commercial channels are grabbing the lion's share of viewers because they adapt more easily to local conditions and operate with higher broadcasting standards. The lies and half-truths of state-sponsored broadcasters do not fool many people in Europe. These organizations are constrained by their national agenda and the necessity of playing identity politics. Unlike independent broadcasters that seek to serve a market, they are in the market for national allegiances and loyalties.[7]

The principle of local adaptability is illustrated by Zee Network which, as noted above, is Indian at home and Asian abroad. Hong Kong-based network Phoenix follows a similar strategy. The pan-European feed, Phoenix CNI, mixes programming from four different Asian countries. Half the schedule is provided by the Phoenix network in Hong Kong, 25 per cent is given free of charge by various TV stations across China, 10 per cent is bought from Asian TV, a rival Hong Kong network, 5 per cent comes from Taiwan and 2 per cent from Singapore.[8] Phoenix's schedule mix makes the channel far more attractive to overseas Chinese viewers than CCTV 4, the Mandarin-speaking international satellite service of China's state broadcaster.

Transnational viewers inevitably compare satellite services from independent and state broadcasters and realize the latter are often not up to standard. Evidence shows they prefer independent television channels that can report openly on the day's issues and present an uncensored image of the country. A study cites young Turkish migrants in London who enjoy watching commercial channels that convey to them the vibrancy and cosmopolitan aspects of contemporary Turkish culture.[9] Arabic speakers in Europe have turned en masse to Al Jazeera, whose Arabic version has had a well-established international distribution for many years. The channel's ground-breaking talk shows and lively debates, which have now entered broadcasting history, contrast with the insipid programming of the state satellite channels hindered by convention and censorship.[10]

From transnational broadcasting to transnational viewing

The commercial provision of television to migrant audiences is bound to expand because it is a fast-growing market. An ever-increasing number of expatriates have access to international television services and the largest communities are spoilt for choice. A plethora of broadcasters compete for Asian viewers in Europe. Following Zee Network, B4U and Sony Entertainment Television Asia entered the field in 1998. India's state broadcaster relaunched two international feeds, DD News and DD India (a general entertainment channel) in 2007. There are also NDTV India, Star Network (Star Plus and Star News), Vectone (which offers channels in languages such as Urdu, Hindi and Tamil) and the Pakistani ARY and Prime TV. Arabic speakers have access to an even greater variety of channels covering all genres and provided by about every broadcaster in the Middle East and North Africa.

Europe's leading DTH providers offer several dozen migrants' channels, seeing the provision of these services as a way of promoting their mainstream services.[11] However, increased competition is coming from Internet distribution and satellite platforms that specialize in the transmigrant market. For instance, Arab Digital Distribution (ADD) markets several packages across Europe for Arabic and Asian audiences. Arabesque, one of its bouquets, aims to provide a 'complete viewing alternative for Arab-speaking families' and offers all the leading Arabic satellite channels.[12] SRG SSR, the Swiss public broadcaster, has created its own mini-satellite platform and placed all its seven TV channels and 16 radio stations on Hot Bird 3. The signal is encrypted in order to protect rights, and thousands of Swiss households across Europe have equipped themselves with a digital receiver and smart card.

GlobeCast offers a dedicated and specialist service to migrants' channels. In addition to contribution and distribution services (end-to-end delivery of the signal), the satellite service provider handles tasks such as programme management (standards conversion, ad insertion and replacement, subtitling, etc.), conditional access services (encryption, conditional access software and hardware), subscriber management (marketing, invoicing) and customer care such as a technical support help desk. These services not only considerably lower the costs of international transmission but many of them are well beyond the technical abilities of small broadcasters (see also Chapter 4).[13]

Today, technology opens up many options for transnational viewers. In addition to broadband distribution, viewers can directly access satellites packed with hundreds of TV and radio channels. Anyone equipped with a small dish, digital receiver and smart cards for those encrypted channels can downlink TV signals from Europe's main broadcast satellite neighbourhoods. And for those with further requirements there exist several possibilities to enhance their access to communications satellites:

- Satellite dishes equipped with dual-feed or multiple LNBs to downlink signals from different satellites, such as the Astra and Hot Bird positions (Chapter 4).
- Motorized dishes guided by remote control to catch signals from different orbital positions.
- Larger dishes (e.g. 90 or 120 cm diameter) to catch a clear satellite signal even when located at the margins of a satellite's footprint.

Latin Americans and Brazilians in Europe often equip themselves with motorized dishes so that they can reach the Hispasat position where many Latin American TV channels are located. Arabic speakers tend to buy large dishes in order to catch the signals from the Arabsat and Nilesat spacecraft. Transnational viewers can also subscribe to a pay-TV provider in their country of origin and then install the dish and decoder elsewhere in Europe. Many British and Portuguese expatriates choose this solution in order to follow their respective football leagues. It is also the option picked by many Poles and other Central Europeans who have recently settled across Western Europe.

The new technologies raise questions about the viability of broadcasters' international feeds. One may query the need to compress local programming into one channel when transnational viewers have the possibility of watching domestic stations abroad. These feeds serve a role in so far as they can adapt schedules and programming and make themselves relevant to migrants.

The contrast is stark between today's migrant television and the 1980s when videocassettes were the lead distribution platform in this market. Satellites have transformed the consumption of migrant media. Some governments use this technology to play identity politics and project an image abroad. But influencing the mindset of transmigrants is becoming an ever more elusive task because new technologies are giving them choice and freedom. Migrants are progressively taking control of and directing their cultural experience, and use their access to satellites and the Internet to construct their own transnational knowledge space.[14]

MULTI-TERRITORY CHANNELS

Multi-territory channels follow a country-by-country development plan. They do not beam a feed across the region but 'copy/paste' a station from territory to territory. Each local version is distributed on an indigenous platform and has its own schedule, budget, management team and marketing plan. Local teams are encouraged to respond to factors like competition and audience interests and thus their stations can evolve independently in terms of positioning, visual identity and programming priorities. Across territories, channels share a philosophy and concept, a brand and a certain amount of programming. Broadcasters who follow this plan carefully target the territories in which they operate and very frequently involve local partners.

This internationalization strategy was pioneered by European broadcasters because they were naturally sensitive about the region's diversity. European executives were particularly aware of the different market conditions that prevail in each country, as determined by broadcasting legislation and policy, the shape of the distribution platforms and the weight of public service broadcasting. The multi-territory strategy also enabled them to concentrate on key markets, offering them the possibility of expanding internationally on a limited budget.

Canal Plus used to be a major exponent of this strategy. Encouraged by the channel's success in France following its launch in 1984, André Rousselet and Pierre Lescure became interested in international expansion. They understood that success in Europe would take more than a pan-regional satellite feed, especially since the channel's scheduling mix (movies plus football) has a strong local element.[15] Viewers are primarily interested in domestic football games, necessitating the acquisition of local TV rights in each market. On this premise they decided to launch separate channels with local partners in each territory, exporting their brand and pay-TV expertise in several European countries. MultiThématiques followed a similar path. All the broadcaster's channels were launched in France before being exported abroad one by one (Chapter 8).

In the 1990s broadcasters rarely opted for the multi-territory strategy: they were still dazzled by satellite technology and could not resist the lure of a pan-European feed. Among the most notable exceptions were AETN International and Disney. Today, however, this international pathway is back in favour. Fox International Channels and NBC Universal operate on a country-by-country basis. MTVNE is developing Paramount Comedy/Comedy Central one market at a time. Another adept at this model is Sony: although AXN has a few multi-territory feeds, each one has been developed separately and is managed by a strong local team (Chapters 7 and 11).

The reasons for this revival are simple: European TV markets have become far too competitive for a one-size-fits-all feed to be beamed across Europe. Viewers – and cable and satellite operators – demand adaptation, and with the expansion of the European cable and satellite reception universe, national markets have enough depth for TV brands to be tailored to each territory. No one illustrates the strategy shift better than BBC Worldwide, which is in the process of replacing its pan-European feed, BBC Prime, with a portfolio of local channels. The broadcaster first identifies the markets in which it wants to operate, then hires and trains a local team, and finally launches its stations (Chapter 6).

PAN-REGIONAL CHANNELS

Pan-European channels are committed to the idea of a cross-border video feed servicing the region. While migrants' channels target a culturally homogenous audience spread across borders, pan-regional stations aim at an international and multi-cultural audience, and while the former are not necessarily based in Europe, the latter are usually broadcast from within.

All existing international news networks are pan-regional (Chapter 9). In the entertainment genre, these channels include E! International Network, ESPN Classic, Eurosport, Extreme Sports, Fashion TV, Mezzo, Motors TV, North American Sports Network, Travel Channel, Trace, TV5Monde, VH1, Zone Club and Zone Reality. Since European TV markets are so competitive, pan-European channels must make sure they remain relevant to local audiences. They can avoid direct competition with national channels provided they can build up the international side of their brand identity and turn it into a salient feature of their programming.

International entertainment channels

There are only a few cross-border TV channels in entertainment with an international outlook. A key attribute of VH1 European's identity is its international dimension (in contrast to its sister channel MTV, a localization champion, Chapter 11). VH1 concentrates on global music acts, the scheduling is kept clear and simple and the programming is based on the common denominators of the station's core markets. All shows are designed to cross frontiers easily: they avoid country-specific references and are either music-based or focused on global celebrities (Chapter 7).

Arte – although not present everywhere in Europe – and Trace have a cosmopolitan feel about them and both try to expand the cultural horizon of their viewers. Arte not only broadcasts documentaries about non-Western societies but schedules movies and series from the Global South. Trace defines itself as 'transcultural' and this is evident in its focus on worldwide urban cultures that evince a cosmopolitan outlook (Chapter 7).[16]

LOCALIZATION

No multinational broadcaster can disregard the issue of local relevance and very few can get away with broadcasting an all-English audio feed across Europe, as most news networks do. For the channels that want to keep a single video feed across Europe there exist several localization options. The first is to localize the soundtrack only, which can be achieved either through translation or multi-lingual services (Table 10.1). The choice of translation technique, which includes subtitling, dubbing (full lip synchronization), or lecturing, depends on a variety of factors including cost, the nature of programming, audience habits and tradition.

Table 10.1: Linguistic adaptation (multi-lingual or translation) of pan-European services, 2008

	Languages
ESPN Classic	Dutch, English, German, Polish, Portuguese
EuroNews	Arabic, English, French, German, Italian, Portuguese, Russian, Spanish
Eurosport	Bulgarian, Czech, Danish, Dutch, English, Finnish, French, German, Greek, Hungarian, Italian, Norwegian, Polish, Portuguese, Romanian, Russian, Serbian, Spanish, Swedish, Turkish
Extreme Sports	Czech, Dutch, English, German, Hungarian, Portuguese, Romanian, Russian, Swedish
France 24	Arabic, English, French
Motors TV	English, French, German, Greek
Travel Channel	Danish, Dutch, Greek, Norwegian, Portuguese, Romanian, Serbian, Slovenian, Swedish
TV 5Monde	Danish, Dutch, English, French, German, Portuguese, Russian, Spanish, Swedish
Zone Club	Bulgarian, Czech, Dutch, English, Norwegian, Portuguese, Romanian
Zone Reality	Bulgarian, Croatian, Czech, Danish, Dutch, English, Finnish, Hungarian, Icelandic, Norwegian, Polish, Portuguese, Romanian, Russian, Slovenian, Swedish

Source: company sources; *M&M Guide 2007*, pp.64–5.

Scandinavia is accustomed to subtitling, as are Holland, Belgium, Portugal and Romania. France, Germany, Italy and Spain (the large markets) and Hungary are traditionally dubbing countries. Lecturing consists of a voice-over that is recorded behind the original soundtrack. Viewers can hear the actors' voices and emotions and get the translation in the background. It is popular in Poland, Ukraine and Russia. It is an acquired taste and all attempts to change audience customs have failed so far. Considering that most of the imported programming comes from either the USA or the UK, a familiarity with the English language enters into the equation. Countries where English is a strong second language (the Netherlands, the Nordic region) prefer subtitles, while the French or the Spanish would rather have dubbing.

There are also commercial considerations and subtitling is the norm in small territories. The normal subtitling rate is around €12 a minute and dubbing can be 20 to 40 times more expensive. Dubbing costs start at around €200 a minute for cartoons and go up to €500 and above for more sophisticated products. And since small markets import most of their programming – not having many local programmes to go around – it makes it even less viable to spend money on dubbing.

The momentum has been with subtitles for several years. The cost of dubbing has prompted many channels to offer subtitles in traditional dubbing territory. For increasingly sophisticated audiences, Clint Eastwood in Swedish or Scarlett Johansson in Italian sound decidedly odd. Subtitles can be used for pedagogic purposes and help an audience to get acquainted with the broadcaster's language. TV5Monde has introduced subtitles in several languages in order to facilitate the understanding of French.

Channels that cross borders with live or near-live transmission such as sport or news use a *multi-lingual* signal. It means that a single video feed is covered by different languages and that there is no original language and translating process. Broadcasters who opt for this technique have journalists in booths commenting on the action in different languages simultaneously. Arte's news bulletin is bilingual and the images are voiced over in French and German. The other networks to use a multi-lingual technique include EuroNews, Eurosport and Motors TV.

Cross-border networks sometimes split their video feeds in order to insert local windows. This system is mostly used to place ad-hoc commercial breaks in certain markets (Table 5.4). Another possibility is when broadcasting a country-specific feed that is nearly identical to the regional network except for language, commercials and a few programme links and shows. As well as their pan-European feed, ESPN Classic and E! International Network have separate stations servicing France, Britain and Italy, Extreme Sports has local stations in France, Britain and Poland, VH1 in Russia, Britain and Poland, Eurosport in France and Britain, and both VH1 and Zone Reality do the same in the UK because of the strength of this advertising market.

Localization is particularly convenient for networks that wish to remain pan-regional and need an extra push in certain territories. Otherwise, it presents broadcasters with insurmountable problems without really addressing the difficulties inherent in dealing with a multinational audience. Arte's and Euronews's bulletins are faceless because the same images must be voiced over in different languages. It does not need to be an issue but many viewers prefer anchors. Transnational feeds are notoriously complex to schedule because lifestyles and viewing habits vary enormously across Europe. Prime time is at 7:00 pm in Scandinavia, 8:00 pm in France and 9:30 pm in Spain. School breaks and national holidays are never the same in any two countries, which is an issue for pan-European children's networks. Europeans speak different languages, live in different climates and have different tastes and interests.

As MTV discovered in the 1990s, Europeans' eclectic music tastes cannot be satisfied with a single European-wide station. They also realized that music markets do not evolve at the same pace: while Britain is particularly quick to adopt American acts, countries like France lag several months behind. Thus MTV European was showing international artists who were not equally relevant to all markets. Cartoon Network faced a similar problem: a character such as Bugs Bunny was a classic in one market and completely unknown in another.

Different market conditions prevail in each country, as determined by broadcasting legislation and policy, the shape of the distribution platforms and the weight of public service broadcasting. For instance, the French government has reinforced the quota requirements of the TVWF/AVMS Directive, requesting that television schedules contain at least 60 per cent of programming of European origin. Local regulatory regimes regarding decency, swearing and nudity remain different across Europe, requiring channels to be cautious about some of the material they broadcast.

These factors have brought many international broadcasters to conclude that their expansion goals will only be met by a responsive approach to local realities. For the stations without a strong international identity or that do not have specific reasons for keeping a pan-regional feed, it is particularly imperative that they blend as much as possible with local channels and become entirely relevant to local audiences. Cultural diversity and economic competition have thus forced international broadcasters to adopt a more radical localization strategy.

CHAPTER 11

WHEN THE LOCAL MEETS THE GLOBAL: TRANSNATIONAL TV NETWORKS

The limits of localization, that is a centralized approach to local adaptation, have prompted many broadcasters to review the way they operate across borders. Since the mid-1990s many have built *transnational TV networks*, which can be defined as *networks of local channels around a core broadcasting philosophy*. Local channels share a concept, brand, research and ideas, part of the programming and library titles, resources and infrastructures, but develop according to their respective environment. They employ local staff, register with local regulatory bodies and set up their own schedule, mixing shared network content with their own material. Table 11.1 lists most pan-European TV networks currently operating in Europe.

Multi-territory operations and transnational networks undoubtedly bear resemblances although differences remain. Networks have a larger reach than multi-territory TV operations. The AETN, Disney and Sony properties were set up on a multi-territory basis and progressively formed a network (Chapter 10). However, the other networks started with a European-wide feed that was gradually broken down into country-specific channels. The satellite feeds are run in parallel to the local channels either as a complement to existing ones (Bloomberg) or to fill the gaps – sometimes momentarily – between their country/region-specific channels (such as Cartoon Network, Discovery, MTV and Nickelodeon). The local channels of pan-European networks are more integrated with one another than those of a multi-territory operation, not least because the latter's stations can be managed under licence or established as joint ventures with local partners.

As mentioned in Chapter 2, WH Smith Television was Europe's first attempt at establishing a transnational TV network in the late 1980s. The European Sports Network was an ensemble of differently named channels available in local languages.[1] In the early 1990s, the TESN affiliates began to differentiate the international video feed by introducing local programming windows during prime time. The network was merged into Eurosport in 1993 but played a pioneering role in the history of transnational television.

Table 11.1: Pan-European TV networks, 2008

Country- and region-specific channels[a]

Animal Planet	Benelux, Germany, Italy, Nordic, Poland, UK/Ireland
AXN	Germany, Italy, Poland/Hungary/Czech Republic/Slovakia/Romania/Bulgaria, Portugal, Spain
Bloomberg	France, Germany, Italy, Spain, UK
Boomerang	France, Germany, Hungary, Italy, Nordic (Denmark, Norway, Sweden), Poland, Romania, Russia, Spain, Turkey, UK
Cartoon Network	France, Germany, Hungary, Italy, Nordic (Denmark, Norway, Sweden), Poland, Romania, Russia, Spain, Turkey, UK
Discovery	Benelux, Denmark, Finland, France, Germany, Hungary, Italy, Nordic, Poland, Romania, Russia, Spain/Portugal, Sweden, UK/Ireland
Disney	Belgium, Finland, France, Germany, Italy, Norway/Sweden/Denmark, Poland, Spain/Portugal, UK/Ireland
The History Channel	Czech Republic/Slovakia/Hungary/Slovenia/Romania/Poland, France, Germany, Greece, Italy, Scandinavia, Spain/Portugal, UK/Ireland
Jetix	Bulgaria, Central/Eastern Europe, Croatia, Czech Republic, France, Germany, Greece, Hungary, Italy, Netherlands, Poland, Russia, Scandinavia, Spain, UK/Ireland
MGM Channel	Central Europe, Germany, Greece, Ireland, Netherlands, Portugal, Russia, Spain
MTV	Adria (Bosnia/Croatia/Macedonia/Serbia & Montenegro, Slovenia), Baltic (Estonia/Latvia/Lithuania), Denmark, Finland, France, Germany, Hungary, Italy, Netherlands, Norway, Poland, Portugal, Romania, Sweden, Spain, UK/Ireland, Ukraine
National Geographic	Benelux, Central Europe, Eastern Europe, France, Germany, Italy, Ireland, Poland, Portugal, Romania, Scandinavia, Spain, UK
Nickelodeon	Austria, France, Germany, Italy, Netherlands, Nordic, Poland, Portugal, Spain, Turkey, UK
Turner Classic Movies	Central/Eastern Europe, France, Italy, Netherlands, Poland, Scandinavia, Spain, UK

Sources: company sources; *M&M Guide 2007.*
[a]Germany usually includes Austria and German-speaking Switzerland, and France includes French-speaking parts of Belgium and Switzerland.

The other networks began forming in the mid-1990s. Cartoon Network launched its first country-specific channel in the UK in 1994, Bloomberg, Disney and Nickelodeon started their continental operations in 1995 (in France, the UK and Germany respectively), Fox Kids (now Jetix) launched in Britain the following year, and AXN in Spain in 1998. But the most radical and ambitious regionalization programme was launched by MTV in 1996.

THE MTV STORY

From the start of its operations in Europe in 1987 until the mid-1990s, the MTV management did not feel the need to localize their pan-European feed (Chapter 2). The MTV business model was based on the expansion of distribution, which reached about 52 million homes before regionalization started. Most of the revenue came from cable operators who paid MTV to carry the prestigious brand on their network. MTV executives were also duped by the simplistic vision of globalization that prevailed in management circles. They could see different cultures coming together but had overlooked the strength of the local in the globalization mix. They imagined that the appeal of their product was universal and marketed it through the slogan of 'One World – One Music'. The playlist remained dominated by Anglo-American acts and most music videos shown on the European feed were of either British or American origin. For MTV language was not an issue because they believed that most Europeans, especially youngsters, would have some knowledge of English.

This model came to an end in the mid-1990s when the newly installed top executives of MTVNE, Brent Hansen and Simon Guild, realized the fallacy of these views. Guild, the chief operating officer, used the following metaphor to describe the changes that MTV went through during this period: the network was on board *Titanic* and as the steamer was approaching the iceberg they put everyone in lifeboats, only to discover that all went in different directions. Not everybody wanted to go to New York after all![2] They grasped that viewers were not connecting with the channel at an emotional level because it was not their music, their language and culture. It was at this stage that they began to see the differences above the commonalities among European cultures and to take local tastes into account.

The iceberg was the competition since MTV was haemorrhaging viewers to local stations. The strongest challenge came from VIVA, the German music channel launched in 1993, but other stations were launched in Scandinavia, the Netherlands (TMF), Italy (Video Music and TMC2) and France (M6 and MCM) (Chapters 7 and 8). They copied MTV's format but provided content in the local language and played music that was closer to local tastes than the American network's playlist. Their success prompted MTV to review its internationalization strategy and start its extensive regionalization programme.

MTV began splitting its pan-European feed in 1997. MTV Central (German-speaking territories) went live in March, followed by MTV UK & Ireland in July and MTV Italia in September. MTV Nordic, covering Scandinavia, was added in June the next year. The second wave of channels was launched in 2000, with MTVf in June (France), MTV Polska in July (Poland) and MTV España and MTV nl (the Netherlands) in September. MTVNE then turned its attention to the smaller markets. MTV Romania went on air in June 2002 and MTV Portugal in July 2003. In 2005 MTVNE divided its Nordic feed into separate channels for Denmark (May), Finland, Norway and Sweden (September). MTV Adria was launched in September of the same year and comprises five feeds covering Bosnia, Croatia, Macedonia, Serbia and Montenegro, and Slovenia. Each station has its own shows and presenters, and the imported programming is translated into five languages. MTV Baltic, launched in the summer of 2006, is based on the same principle and is a set of three channels covering Lithuania, Latvia and Estonia. MTV Turkey was launched in October 2006, and MTV Ukraine and MTV Hungary in September and October of the following year.

MTVNE has built Europe's most extensive TV network within a decade, and the company is digging deeper into each market by launching several MTV-branded stations. Some of these channels are country-specific, such as MTV Brand New in Italy, MTV Idol in France, MTV Entertainment in Germany or MTV Dance in the UK, while others have multi-territory coverage (MTV 2, MTV Base, MTV Flux and MTV Hits). Key countries can access about four MTV-branded channels, and even more in the case of the UK (Table 7.4). The company still runs a pan-European feed that is restyled each time the regionalization programme progresses.

Even at the early stages of the regionalization programme, researchers found significant differences between MTV UK, Nordic and Central in terms of programme type, music genre and origins of artists.[3] Today, MTV channels can be as distinct from each other as the local audience and local staff want them to be, as long as they remain true to the MTV brand.

GENRES, NETWORKS AND DIFFERENTIATION

The children's networks have followed the MTV model and today run highly differentiated channels. Jetix, for instance, which started with a pan-European signal, buys up to half of its programming locally. Localization is not merely pursued to comply with European legislation. Although European quotas initially acted as an incentive, every head of programming and acquisition knows that their channels must be relevant to local kids if they are to cut through the competition.

The most homogenous networks are in factual entertainment. Each Discovery feed in Europe is localized in a variety of ways. In addition to language, schedule and on-air promotional elements, some shows are reversioned for each territory. They can be introduced by a different host, be rescripted or have segments taken in or out so that, for instance, local experts can be brought in and statistics that are relevant to a certain audience can be inserted. However, Discovery's only local programming teams are in Germany and the UK, and for everywhere else the programming is done from London. Although some shows are bought locally, especially in these two countries, programmes remain largely the same throughout the network and shows are simply reshuffled across Europe. It is in the nature of the genre that shows which work well somewhere tend to do so across all territories. All the shows that Discovery co-produces with the BBC and other broadcasters are designed for an international audience. The network has had regional offices for many years but appointed local channel managers in 2005 only, when it started to decentralize activities such as on-air and off-air marketing.

The programming of the National Geographic network is even more centralized. All National Geographic's TV stations pool their resources to buy content which is acquired globally in Washington, DC. This enables the network to create economies of scale and gives it leverage during negotiations. The global head of content then creates a programming blueprint that is loosely applied worldwide. Each station determines its own schedule on the basis of this framework. National Geographic airs some local programmes but these tend to be the exception rather than the rule. In the past some stations would air shows introduced by local presenters, but like Discovery, Nat Geo found that reversioning, linguistic and scheduling localization can be enough to satisfy a local audience.

WHEN THE LOCAL MEETS THE GLOBAL

Networks constitute the most elaborate answer to the difficulties of operating TV channels across frontiers, allowing broadcasters to combine local adaptability with global scale. Within a network, channels have many ways of differentiating themselves. While sharing programming, they can set their own schedule in order to adapt to the local market. For instance, the Turner Classic Movies network is built around the MGM library that holds the worldwide rights of classics such as *Casablanca* and *Gone with the Wind*. These benchmark movies will be shown across the network but never at the same time, on the same day, or even in the same season. They can be aired with a focus on the director or an actor in the manner that *Casablanca* can be shown in the context of a Humphrey Bogart season in one market and an Ingrid Bergman season in another.

Networks can acquire material that is specific to a market. TCM schedules more local movies in countries where there is a strong cinema tradition such as Spain and France. All Disney channels have a budget and are free to acquire content from local European producers. At Jetix, out of 400 new half-hours acquired every year in Europe, around half are pan-European and the rest are bought locally. At Boomerang, Time Warner's classic cartoon network, the head of programming tries to buy any cartoon that is a classic in a particular market. It will be *Babar* and *Barbapapa* in France and *Danger Mouse* and the *Pink Panther* in Britain. Even though Sony takes advantage of its huge library of formats, series and movies for its AXN network, it prefers to acquire properties that are suited to the local market rather than acquire global rights and put them on every channel.

When networks began to be involved in local production they started with promos and interstitials. As advertising revenue and audiences grew they expanded into fully fledged programming. Today local content is produced both at national and regional levels. MTV stations have a long tradition of creating their own music and lifestyle shows, and all Disney channels have a budget for local programming. Both Disney and Time Warner set up development hubs in London with the purpose of creating and commissioning original content for their European channels (Chapter 8).

Networks can vary the positioning of their channels from one territory to another according to local variables ranging from audience tastes to the competition. TCM is a classic movies channel in the UK and Scandinavia and has a more contemporary feel in France and Spain. Discovery has positioned its channel very differently in France than in the rest of Europe. The numerous documentary channels in France (Odyssée, Thalassa, Planète) have prompted the network to shift its emphasis towards people and real-life stories. In the UK, the Jetix brand has a strong action/adventure component and is quite heavily skewed towards boys. In the Nordic region, where parents keep a close eye on what their children watch, Jetix brings a softer version of the channel. For instance, the Jackie Chan series, in which the cheeky hero is impudent with his parents, was never shown there. MTV remained closer to its initial remit of music television for longer in the UK than in Italy, where it transformed itself into a youth channel in the late 1990s.

While channels evolve according to their environment, they share attributes and resources at network level. They have in common a broadcasting philosophy. The foundation of all transnational TV networks – and pan-regional TV channels for that matter – is a well-defined television concept and the selling of a clear proposition to the audience. Network channels also share a brand that is often translated into a common visual identity. The five European Bloomberg TV channels are scheduled independently and broadcast in their own language but have a similar look and feel and share a common style and layout. They all display the signature multi-screen format simultaneously delivering market data, financial market updates and breaking news headlines.

Branding plays a significant role in a multi-channel television environment. Stations need to be quickly identified by viewers flicking through the categories of their EPG (Electronic Programming Guide). The consolidation of distribution platforms, which began in the early 2000s, has reinforced this trend. A pay-TV operator who has acquired a dominant position in a market can force broadcasters to accept lower carriage fees for their channels. The only strategic advantage these programmers have is a distinct content and a strong identity, and thus media executives spend an increasing amount of money and energy marketing their channels. Networks have the advantage over local competitors of being able to tap into the expertise, and sometimes the financial assets, of a large corporation. Having access to such resources, they usually have excellent brand equity and companies such as Disney, Discovery and MTV perform well in consumer surveys.

Another benefit of networks is their capacity to recycle content and share programming. For factual broadcasters, the cost of acquiring and producing content is such that the ability to exploit a property across a

European or worldwide network has become crucial. Networks also offer flexibility in terms of distribution since programmes do not have to be shown everywhere: they can be seen in one country, a handful of territories or across the network. If the rights for a show cannot be acquired for a particular territory, or if it is inappropriate for a certain audience, then more suitable material can be found for the territory in question.

Within a network, channels can come together for shared moments. Jetix invites local teams to its own children's European football cup every June and transmits the live final across the network. The Bloomberg channels simultaneously broadcast interviews with CEOs and international decision makers whose comments are likely to have an immediate impact on the stock market. It is MTV that has the most impressive line-up of pan-European live events: MTV Winterjam is a winter live music event that is staged in a ski resort; Isle of MTV is a pan-European club tour that culminates in an open-air event; MTV Shakedown is a pan-European summer dance competition and MTV Live/A Night With . . . is an artist's concert that is given pan-European airtime. The season's highlight is the MTV Europe Music Awards, Europe's biggest music awards ceremony, hosted in a different city every year. MTV Europe also links up to MTV's global events, the MTV Movie Awards and the MTV Video Music Awards. These events create a sense of occasion and help networks to generate a 'regional feel' for the audience.

Channels can share resources and infrastructures, allowing networks to generate economies of scale and leverage costs over more than one market. Several networks run pan-regional television studios and practise what is called 'gang shoots'. Disney shoots different versions of the same show for each Disney channel in Europe on the same set in the same studio. MTV offers visiting overseas artists doing promotional tours in Europe the opportunity to give interviews to as many MTV channels as they wish without ever leaving London. The company flies its presenters to studios in Camden Town, North London, and artists spend 15 minutes with each, covering the continent's key territories in a couple of hours.

Networks also centralize departments that deal with acquisitions, procurement, legal affairs and copyright agreements, distribution, research and IT. For instance, once a local channel decides to acquire a show, the legal aspect of the deal is supervised by the network's central corresponding department. Most networks have a European media centre from which they play out their local channels. Centralization brings several advantages beyond economies of scale, notably consistency and accrued leverage during negotiations with third parties, whether it is the acquisition of an IT network or a TV series.

London as Europe's media hub

Most networks direct their European operations from London, which has become Europe's hub of international television. The role that the British capital plays in PETV can be compared to that of Hollywood and the American motion picture industry. Like Hollywood, London offers many competitive advantages to the companies that locate in the city, most notably an attractive labour market and a tight network of service companies.[4]

London's diversified labour market is a rich reservoir of skills and provides international broadcasters with all their employment needs, from finance directors to part-time translators in the most exotic languages. The British capital houses many legal, financial and research companies that serve both the domestic and the international television industries. The headquarters of most global advertising and communication groups are located in London (Chapters 5 and 8). It is where pan-European advertising accounts are held and pan-European campaigns are planned. Even the few international broadcasters that are not based in the British capital, such as Eurosport or EuroNews, have advertising sales teams in the city.

The same is true of 'localization houses', the companies that offer language-versioning services through their own international networks of offices and studios. All Europe's leading players, including Broadcast Text, SDI Media, VSI and Chello Zone, are based in London (several clustered around Heathrow airport). Another benefit of the British capital is the English language, which is convenient for companies with a cosmopolitan workforce. Add to the equation a fairly attractive tax regime and it explains why most international broadcasters have chosen London as their European headquarters.

MANAGING THE TRANSNATIONAL

Running a transfrontier TV network requires an organizational capability that is able to deal with the scope and complexity of a multinational operation. Transnational companies have responded in a variety of ways to the challenge of crossing borders and the opportunities presented by overseas markets. In their classic study, *Managing Across Borders*, Christopher Bartlett and Sumantra Ghoshal have identified four types of strategic approaches to internationalization.

Multinational companies are characterized by a decentralized organizational structure that devolves assets and responsibilities to local subsidiaries. Such an approach is taken when adaptation to the local environment and responsiveness to local markets are decisive. A multinational company is run as a 'portfolio of national businesses' and it is a model that is often adopted in the FMCG sector, as exemplified by Unilever.[5] The *global organization* places the emphasis on global economies of scale and efficiency. It is run from a headquarters that keeps hold of assets, resources and responsibilities. Subsidiaries are tightly controlled and their role is limited to local operations such as the sale and distribution of standard products. This model suits the electronics industry and an illustration is provided by Japanese electronics firm Matsushita. *International companies* stand somewhere in between the multinational and global corporations. Local subsidiaries are allowed some leeway to adapt to the local environment and certain assets and functions are decentralized, but the overall organization remains controlled by the parent company. Subsidiaries are given some autonomy but knowledge, products and decisions flow for the most part from the core to the periphery. This model suits the 'managerial culture of US-based companies' and was adopted by Procter & Gamble, among others.[6]

According to Bartlett and Ghoshal, several firms have begun integrating the organizational characteristics of the fourth ideal type, the *transnational organization model*. This organizational structure is called the 'transnational solution' because it is supposed to enable companies to achieve simultaneous global efficiency, local responsiveness and worldwide knowledge transfer.[7] Essentially, the transnational model incites a corporation to move beyond a 'hub and spokes' organizational structure and adopt an *integrated network configuration*. Local subsidiaries break the pattern of dependence/independence towards the headquarters to become units in a web of 'relationships based on mutual interdependence'.[8]

The key organizational characteristics of the transnational company are *network integration* and *flexibility*. Some assets and decisions are centralized, while others are localized. Some subsidiaries are closely controlled from headquarters, others are given full autonomy. The headquarters is not the custodian of all centralized resources and responsibilities, which are dispersed throughout the network. The role of subsidiaries is differentiated and the most important among them can make a distinct contribution to the company's worldwide and integrated operations. Local units continuously collaborate and share knowledge, sometimes with one another, sometimes in a small group and sometimes at network level (Table 11.2).

Table 11.2: Characteristics of four organizational models

Organizational characteristics	Multinational	Global	International	Transnational
Configuration of assets and capabilities	Decentralized and nationally self-sufficient	Centralized and globally scaled	Sources of core competencies centralized, others decentralized	Dispersed, interdependent and specialized
Role of overseas operations	Sensing and exploiting local opportunities	Implementing parent company strategies	Adapting and leveraging parent company competencies	Differentiated contributions by national units to integrated worldwide operations
Development and diffusion of knowledge	Knowledge developed and retained within each unit	Knowledge developed and retained at the centre	Knowledge developed at the centre and transferred to overseas units	Knowledge developed jointly and shared worldwide

Source: Bartlett and Ghoshal, *Managing Across Borders*, p.75.

Where do transfrontier TV networks fit among these international strategies? They have all adopted some of the features of the transnational model. They have established multi-directional communication flows between the headquarters and local offices. Local teams are continuously encouraged to exchange their ideas and their expertise about their own market. These communication flows are extensive and are organized around emails (MTV claims to have been a pioneer user), videoconferences and get-togethers. In all these companies, teams and managers are engaged in a constant cross-border conversation and can meet as frequently as every other month.[9]

However, networks differ in their patterns of decision making, the amount of autonomy they grant to subsidiaries and the level of interdependence among these local units. The company that is closest to Bartlett's and Ghoshal's international model is Disney. Local subsidiaries are given a certain amount of autonomy and entrusted with local knowledge and operations but remain monitored by the headquarters in Burbank. The integrity of the brand and its consistency across borders is paramount to Disney and the company likes to make sure that its standards are always met. The factual entertainment networks, Discovery and Nat Geo, also operate closely to the international model. Despite their fully localized feeds, their organizational structure shows that global economies of scale remain a priority.

MTVNE and the transnational cockroach

It is MTVNE that most resembles a transnational company. The process started in 1997 when Hansen and Guild broke down the network's pan-European structure and shifted the company's centre of gravity to the local level. Today most of MTVNE's 1200 employees work in local stations, with large production centres in Berlin, Milan and London employing up to 300 staff.

MTVNE's organizational structure has been designed to encourage sharing. The company is organized into four regional groups (excluding emerging markets): UK and Nordic, Benelux, Germany and Central Europe, and Southern Europe, which takes in Italy, Spain, Portugal and France. Within these groups, channels share a fair amount of ideas and material because they naturally gravitate together. There is one large channel in every group (UK, Germany, the Netherlands and Italy) so that the smaller stations learn from them. Teams have a strong incentive to share material because there is no transfer pricing mechanism at MTVNE. Instead of spending money on a new on-air look, a team can just take it from any other channel.

Local teams are given autonomy to adapt and translate the MTV brand to the local market. There is no rule book that tells them how their channel should look. The MTVNE network is increasingly *integrated* and local teams collaborate with one another regularly. Certain channels have developed expertise and capabilities in specific areas and the other teams can go directly to them for advice and guidance. London-based executives are not interested in knowing who is borrowing what from whom. The Dutch are skilled at interactive applications, the Italians are good at on-air packaging and the British know how to position channels when competing with hundreds of other stations in a crowded EPG.

Local teams meet and communicate all the time. They may need to address a multi-territory client issue. For instance, if an advertiser wishes to run a pan-European campaign, MTVNE must ensure that the pricing is coherent across all territories. Staff get together for personal development purposes. MTVNE is a fairly small organization – by design – and the head of marketing, say in Germany, must be able to talk about his or her craft to counterparts across the network. Operational groups gather to share knowledge and ideas.

The production groups and on-air departments (intros, promos, trailers, title sequences, etc.) meet about twice a year, or when they reface the channels. The first purpose of their meetings is to use the same creative base across the network by sharing and repurposing the material. A piece that was produced by a local team can be revoiced, rescripted and aired by somebody else. For instance, MTV Central ran a campaign for ringtones that was centred around a cockroach. The idea originated in Argentina, was produced in Canada and adapted to the German market. Another aim is to challenge people to produce good creative work by generating emulation among local teams.

Editorial teams have a weekly videoconference call as channels are always on the lookout for new programming and material to share. There are weekly music conferences when music people talk about pan-European priorities, such as marketing campaigns around musicians or the local acts they wish to push on the network. The management (80 people in Europe) meet annually, senior executives every three months and heads of channel every six weeks. Europe also participates in MTV's global creative gatherings. A fortnightly conference call brings together heads of region, who also take part in the larger annual global creative conference. These global get-togethers give Europeans the opportunity to meet people from MTV USA, the network's largest channel. Everything travels across the network: short promos, marketing campaigns, interviews with musicians and full-length pieces such as specials on artists. Channels also exchange formats and produce their own versions of shows that were successful elsewhere – always a badge of honour for the originating channel.

The result is a network that is complex, flexible, responsive and efficient. It is complex because any local team is part of an intricate web of relationships and must be able to juggle four different layers of programming. Stations like MTV Lithuania or MTV Denmark air local shows, programmes from their region (e.g. the Baltic or Nordic Chart Show), while they will share pan-European programming (e.g. the Europe Music Awards) and will have access to MTV's global live shows and vast library of programmes (*Cribs, Dirty Sanchez, Home Wreckers, Jackass, Pimp My Ride*, etc.).

The MTV network is designed to transform continuously. It is based on relationships and incentives rather than rules. According to the management, the network draws its power from its ability to mix ideas from around the world. It helps MTV keep its finger on the pulse and be responsive to the needs and fads of millions of youth across Europe. Responsiveness is combined with global efficiency reached through economies of scale, the sharing of knowledge and programming and an extensive global library of shows.[10]

THE TRANSNATIONALIZATION OF RIGHTS

It is now apparent that transnational TV networks are more successful in certain genres than in others. They perform particularly well in international and business news – naturally enough – but also in music television and factual entertainment, and they dominate children's television. But they are much less pre-eminent in sports and movies. The main reason lies with rights acquisition.

The unavailability of pan-European rights for key properties such as TV series and movies counted among the many obstacles to the development of PETV in the 1980s and early 1990s. Rights holders were first concerned about signal theft and copyright infringement when the signal spilled over to third countries. Crucially, the Hollywood majors have long refused to sign deals with pan-European channels.[11] They all have well-established sales infrastructures across Europe and long-term commitments to customers in motion pictures distribution. It is far more profitable for content providers to slice the rights attached to their properties and sell them piecemeal. A distribution division will set high sales targets for any exciting title it has on its books and knows that it will make far more money selling it market by market than on a pan-European basis.

Where possible, independent production companies proceed in a similar way. They are advised by their trade association, the Independent Film & Television Alliance (IFTA), to sell territory by territory, not simply in order to monetize the property more efficiently but to avoid the practice of *cross-collateralization*. When an independent producer sells the multi-territory rights of its property to a distribution company, possibly owned by one of the majors, this distributor assumes overall risk for the property. Thus, if the property does well in a market and performs poorly in another, the distribution company offsets the losses made in one market with the gains made elsewhere. It then goes back to the producer and tells them that having yet to recoup the money it gave them as a global advance because of losses in one territory, it cannot give them any more cash. However, if the independent producer sells its property to different distributors in different territories, and that property performs well in Italy and bombs in the UK, the scenario is completely different: the producer makes great returns from the Italian market even though the UK distributor is very unhappy as it is unable to recover its advance.[12]

The fact that the majors and independents both insist on territory-linked deals partly explains why PETV networks have failed to make an impact in the movie genre. As seen in Chapter 7, many cross-border movie networks are based around library titles, and may even buy many properties separately for each market. For instance, Turner Classic Movies organizes the '28 days of Oscar' every February and shows two or three Oscar-winning or Oscar-nominated movies across the network each day. But every local channel gets its own titles and in the few cases where a multi-property deal is signed, it is very rare that the movie can be shown across the whole network.

Wherever the NBC UGN channels broadcast they acquire the individual rights for that territory. The channels communicate and exchange ideas on a regular basis but their acquisition departments scout trade fairs and festivals independently from each other. When the UGN channels in France and Italy ran an Alfred Hitchcock season they broadcast separate programme packages. Audiences in each market favour different movies and the rights holder avoids involvement in cost-cutting multi-territory deals knowing that there is enough demand for individual sales of these titles.[13]

The sports rights market bears similar characteristics. Eurosport has no problem acquiring the broadcasting rights for the championships of most federations but it is outgunned for the most popular sports. In football, the live rights for the top domestic leagues and the Champions League are naturally out of reach. The Union of European Football Associations (UEFA), Europe's governing body of football, created the Champions League for the chief purpose of getting hold of the competition's broadcasting rights, which were in the hands of the clubs with the previous competition, the Cup Winners' Cup. And demand is such for these rights that the UEFA sells them market by market. As a result, premium sports rights such as live football and Formula One are most often controlled by pay-TV providers or terrestrial broadcasters.

The situation used to be similar in the other genres but cross-border TV networks have progressively turned things around. When Cartoon Network started broadcasting in Europe, they realized that there were many historic cartoons that they could not show because long-term deals were in place with local parties in a number of countries. TBS has been busy buying back these rights ever since, and it has not always been an easy process, as Peter Flamman, vice president for business development, TBS Europe, acknowledges:

> One of the things that we've been doing since I last saw you [July 2002], we've been doing a lot of work, basically, it is like detective work, to unravel the rights. So if there is some market where we've not been able to use some of the older rights, we've been doing a lot of work to kind of track down where they were sold to, have they run out? Or, in some cases, to buy back the rights, to give us the ability to launch channels in markets where there might have been a problem, because two or three crucial cartoons have been sold to somebody and you know that they are the ones that everyone is familiar with in the market, so you really really want to have them for when you launch your own channel. So we have been doing a lot of work in that area.[14]

Such issues do not arise with new cartoons. All the entertainment conglomerates sell the rights (if at all) to properties they produce or co-produce with the full knowledge that they need some of these rights for their own TV channels. This is why they have established a coordination process between their broadcasting operations and programme sales division (e.g. between Warner Bros and TBS or between the Disney channels and Buena Vista International Television). Distribution arms are keen to serve a growing market of TV channels and do not easily turn down serious offers from third parties. However, they always discuss their relevant properties with the in-house channels and are cautious about the rights they sell. They tend to trade very specific rights (e.g. terrestrial, Hungary) and keep as many rights as possible attached to the property (e.g. Internet, mobile, merchandising). The licence period is usually fairly short (e.g. two years). As seen in Chapters 7 and 8, entertainment conglomerates increasingly give priority to their channel business if there is a tussle between the two divisions: *a programme sale is a transaction, a channel is an asset.*

Acquisitions for children's and factual entertainment networks

Acquisitions from third parties have also become much easier for transnational TV networks. Until recently the rights of most properties were fragmented across Europe and it was almost impossible for an international broadcaster to find a show with a clean slate of rights. Within a few years the very same networks that were at the margins of the distribution circuit have become the 'requisite route' for distributors and producers (with the enduring exception of the Hollywood majors).[15] Transnational children's networks are now the indispensable one-stop shop for sellers, to the point where it has become rare to see a co-production that does not include the sale of its pay-TV rights to an international broadcaster in its financial plan. Today cross-border TV networks have priority over local cable and satellite children's channels and distributors block the sale of their properties until they have settled the fate of their pan-European rights.

The most lucrative contracts remain those with large terrestrial stations but such transactions do not preclude deals with transnational networks. International broadcasters have the resources to make attractive offers to producers. In addition, since most of these broadcasters operate fully localized networks, they do not have to buy the pan-European rights: they can exclude territories if these rights are not available everywhere or if a local team deems the property unsuitable for its market.

For small to medium-sized production companies, pan-European deals present several advantages despite them not being the most financially attractive option. Such companies rarely have the sales infrastructure to sell efficiently at international level. BKN, for instance, is engaged in the production and distribution of children's animated television programmes with a worldwide catalogue of about 55 titles and 1,625 episodes. Nicola Andrews, a BKN sales executive, principally deals with agents because she is responsible for Europe, the Middle East, Africa, Australia, New Zealand and North America. Pan-European deals enable her to concentrate on a few big transactions in the USA and get Europe's smaller markets out of the way.[16]

There is also the issue of licensing and merchandising, an ever-growing chunk of the revenue derived from children's programming. Shows do not last forever and a multi-territory deal enables a producer to get its programming out in several markets rapidly. For the content provider, it is a case of weighing up the income it might get from licensing and merchandising against the more certain and immediate return from programming sales. It can be worth sacrificing programming sales revenue for the sake of accrued visibility in the hope of racking up income from licensing and merchandising. Children's TV networks can offer European-wide exposure and have greatly benefited from the need for rapid distribution that comes with the licensing and merchandising income stream.

A similar evolution can be observed with factual entertainment channels. With any show or TV series that Discovery or Nat Geo produce, co-produce or commission, they ensure that they keep the rights they need for their own global TV network. In fact, as both networks try to control their programme supply and not let the market dictate it, they have moved away from straight acquisitions to co-productions and commissions. When their acquisitions team see something they like, they take it off the market as early as possible through pre-sales agreements. All the shows and series that come through this supply line have the necessary rights for global distribution.

For the smaller channels that remain acquisitions-led, signing multi-territory deals with suppliers is becoming easier. As Steve Cole, vice president at Zone Reality, testifies, suppliers are increasingly aware of international channels:

> A good example, and I will not name names, [is] a medium-sized UK-based distributor I approached right at the very beginning, at the end of 1999, about buying some of their programmes. And they did not respond. I wrote to them two or three times, nobody came back to me. A year later, a new person arrived at that company and introduced himself to me by email immediately. 'I started a few days ago, I would love to be able to do some business with you, can we meet, blah blah blah.' We did a deal within a month of that person arriving.[17]

These adjustments in the rights market are taking place because of the advantages that pan-European deals present to many suppliers. As producers and distributors develop relationships with PETV networks they get accustomed to their needs and requirements. Not only do they propose properties with the appropriate set of rights but also programming with international appeal that is suitable to a multi-territory environment.

From an international perspective, the TV rights market has developed into a two-tier system. Properties that are exceptionally attractive such as Hollywood blockbusters and key sports events are still sold territory by territory and media by media (terrestrial, cable and satellite, Internet, etc.). This strategy enables the holders of strong rights to maximize revenue. Most other properties in sports, fiction and factual entertainment can be acquired at multi-territory or even pan-European level.

Cross-border TV networks do particularly well in the genres in which rights are available on a transnational basis, but today they are challenging local stations for a growing range of rights. They produce, co-produce and commission an increasing proportion of the material they broadcast, which enables them to bypass the constraints of the rights market. As strong rights owners such as Disney, TBS or the BBC focus on building their own assets, their TV networks have access to key properties. Further, international broadcasters are flexible about where they buy rights and do not have to show a property on their entire network.

MARRYING THE LOCAL AND THE GLOBAL

Pan-European TV networks constitute today's most sophisticated answer to the dilemmas faced by international broadcasters. Networks enable management teams to articulate the local and the global in a unique way by combining global efficiency and local flexibility. Local channels can adapt to a specific environment and develop their own schedule, positioning and programming. At the same time, they benefit from the network, sharing with other stations a broadcasting philosophy, style, brand, programming, resources and infrastructure. Networks are interactive systems where the flow of communication is not only vertical – from head office to local teams and vice versa – but also horizontal among channels exchanging ideas and experience. While local teams benefit from the network's global expertise, the latter takes advantage of their local knowledge.

Thus transnational TV networks have the ability of moving anywhere within the local/global matrix: they can be local/local when stations take independent decisions that affect their particular territory, they can be global/global when they leverage their scale to press an advantage, and they can be local/global when they mix local and cosmopolitan elements in a team, a channel or a strategy.

Networks break down the opposition between the local and the global to make each term an extension of the other. They have the ability to generate knowledge in both dimensions and in combinations of these dimensions. This transnational generation of knowledge and interaction between the two terms becomes a driver for growth and creativity. In the process, networks acquire their unique transnational quality that makes them far more than the sum of their parts.

CHAPTER 12

RECONFIGURING COMMUNICATIONS NETWORKS: TELEVISION FOR A GLOBAL ORDER

GLOBALIZATION AND TELEVISION

The relationship between television and globalization is complex. Transnational television does not merely participate in the globalizing process: it also reflects our globalized world. Without a growing and increasingly integrated world economy, BBC World News or CNBC would be irrelevant. These channels would not exist if investors, corporate executives, politicians and civil servants did not need to keep abreast of international developments in finance, industry and politics. They would not be able to keep afloat if multinationals did not book airtime to hone their corporate image and advertise their global brands. At the same time, these networks add to the communication flow that helps the same executives and companies to build their businesses across frontiers. This chapter examines these complex relationships by analysing the involvement of transnational TV networks in four globalizing processes: deterritorialization, mobility, world-system integration and the cosmopolitan mode of production.

TRANSNATIONAL TELEVISION AS DETERRITORIALIZED COMMUNICATION

Transfrontier television networks have a relationship to place and time that is entirely different from that of terrestrial television channels. Traditionally, television has been circumscribed by a national territory and at times played an active role in the construction of national identities. Transnational television channels and networks challenge the bond between television and the nation-state in a way that is best comprehended by the concept of deterritorialization. The most commonly used definition of the notion is that of Néstor García Canclini, who explains it as 'the loss of the "natural" relation of culture to geographical and social territories'.[1] Culture becomes disembedded from territory and loses its connection to place. John Tomlinson has described this disjuncture as 'the weakening or dissolution of the connection between everyday lived culture and territorial location'.[2]

Ever since the advent of the telegraph, the media has been recognized as a deterritorializing force. It is the theme underpinning all the McLuhanesque theories about the globalizing influence of communications.[3] Through the media people become familiar with places they have never visited, come to like or dislike people they have never met and get to know fictional characters better than their neighbours. They learn about the performances of stock exchanges around the world and worry about events that take place thousands of miles away from their homes. Anthony Giddens calls this phenomenon 'displacement', which he defines as 'our insertion into globalised cultural and information settings, which means that familiarity and place are much less consistently connected than hitherto'.[4] Deterritorialization is also evoked in the context of transnational migrants, where the disconnection between place and culture is most apparent.[5]

International TV channels are not simply deterritorializing but deterritorialized cultural artifacts. By definition, their reach expands beyond the boundaries of nations, and in a minority of cases their distribution spans the world. Global channels like BBC World News, CNN, Deutsche Welle-TV or RTP Internacional can ensure their worldwide *primary distribution* with approximately seven satellites whose footprints are large enough to cover entire continents. The signal is then taken over by cable and satellite operators for the second stage of the distribution before it finally reaches the consumer. TV5Monde, for instance, has carriage deals with about 25 satellite bouquet operators and more than 6,000 cable networks worldwide, Trace is distributed through a network of 22 satellites and Fashion TV is aired through 32 satellites and is on over 1,200 cable systems.

Schedules are less time-specific on satellite than terrestrial television. The programming of national stations is based around the viewing cycle of a specific territory with clearly defined moments, breakfast television for example. Transnational TV networks adapt feeds to local times but their programming remains more homogenous over a 24-hour period. Discovery broadcasts documentaries, CNN news and MTV music videos whether it is 3:00 pm or 3:00 am. Global TV networks are produced in more than one place: AJE and CNN have newsrooms in different countries and CNBC produces a transcontinental morning show. Disney, Time Warner, MTV and SPTI have production facilities in Europe as well as in America and acquire, produce and commission programming from almost anywhere in the world.

No TV channel is entirely free from geographical and cultural boundaries. Markets have local characteristics that must be respected and all broadcasters must abide by national and regional regulations. But cross-border TV channels are not defined by place. They are not contained by boundary but rather they bundle together, divide and target territories according to resources and commercial objectives.

Like many globalizing forces, transnational TV networks redefine the relation between place, space and time. These channels tear apart the relation between place and television through their reach, schedule, programming and organizational structure. They reflect – and help sustain – a global economic order in which the connection between national territory and patterns of production and distribution has broken down. They belong to the age of cosmopolitan capitalism that Karl Marx forecasted more than 150 years ago:

> The bourgeoisie has through its exploitation of the world market given a cosmopolitan character to production and consumption in every country. To the great chagrin of [reactionaries], it has drawn from under the feet of industry the national ground on which it stood.[6]

CONTENT EVERYWHERE: TELEVISION FOR A MOBILE WORLD

In a world of interconnected economies the flows of capital, commodities and people intensify. Mobility of the individual takes different forms and encompasses business travellers, tourists, migrants and the ever-growing number of individuals who lead a transnational lifestyle and have family or business connections in two or more countries. It is a social and economic order in which PETV channels fit completely since they are at the forefront of the anywhere/anytime/any platform type of delivery. Non-residential distribution is one of the industry's strengths and PETV stations can be seen at airports, bars, restaurants, retail outlets, hospital wards, overseas military bases, embassies and banks' trading floors. The core of the non-residential business remains hotels. In Europe, the Middle East and Africa, the leading channels are in more than 60 per cent of the entire hotel industry, and the percentage increases with the number of hotel stars. In Europe alone, BBC World News, CNN, EuroNews, Eurosport, Fashion TV, Sky News and TV5Monde can be watched in between one and two million hotel rooms.[7]

PETV channels can also be seen on cruise ships and planes.[8] Many international stations have in-flight licensing agreements with companies that handle airlines' outsourced content acquisitions. A few airlines still receive a master tape that the cabin crew load onto the in-flight entertainment system but live TV is possible through high-speed broadband connection. It is more difficult for an aeroplane than a cruise ship to receive a satellite signal since an aircraft crosses through a number of time zones and satellite footprints over a short time span. Etihad Airways, Lufthansa and Singapore Airlines were among the first airlines to offer in-flight Internet and on certain routes passengers are able to watch live TV via this connection.

In recent years the most rapid growth in distribution has come from the Internet and mobile television. All news networks stream video on their own website and have agreements with online distribution platforms such as Joost or YouTube. Most networks, including those in entertainment, have signed mobile licensing agreements with carriers and distributors. Out-of-home and mobile TV is obviously not the preserve of cross-border channels but they are ideally suited to this type of distribution. It is easy to dip in and out of EuroNews, Fashion TV or MTV, which privilege short-format programming and address audiences ready and willing to shift to new platforms. All children's networks have also secured multi-territory mobile distribution deals for content and derived products such as games and ringtones. Disney, for instance, has distributed its own-branded mobile content across Europe since 2006 and has launched its own mobile phone service.

WORLD-SYSTEM INTEGRATION AND COSMOPOLITAN MODE OF PRODUCTION

Many fields of activity are integrating on a world scale. The globalization of these domains involves a multiplicity of processes including the emergence of networks, systems of exchange and webs of relations.[9] It also entails the emergence of multinational and/or global organizations, the enmeshing of players with one another and the development of networks of communication. Transnational TV networks are very much part of the globalizing processes that affect these fields. They add to the global flow of data and information, networks of communication and systems of exchange that drive the integration of these fields on a world scale. Transfrontier TV channels participate in the worldwide integration of domains of activity as diverse as media, finance and politics.

These networks also feed into what may be called the 'cosmopolitan' mode of production that is typical of industries such as fashion and music. These two fields of activities do not operate as integrated systems, but in fashion as in music local centres of production are nonetheless connected to each other. More than ever, musicians and designers are aware of and influenced by what is being done in the rest of the world. Global trends hybridize local creations as styles and genres are circulated worldwide. In recent years, international television has become an integral part of this process in helping artists to operate in a cosmopolitanized environment.

Media

Multinational media corporations are among the few companies that have the scope, expertise, financial resources and organizational structure to operate television channels on a global scale. At the same time, these TV networks have acquired a great importance for these companies. As seen in Chapter 8, they constitute assets, drive international revenue, offer conglomerates more control over the distribution process, help them to build franchises and add opportunities for diversification and content integration across media platforms. Cross-border TV networks contribute to the worldwide integration of the media industry because they help diversified entertainment conglomerates achieve many strategic objectives.

Some scholars estimate that this trend poses a risk to media pluralism and cultural diversity.[10] These views rest on a neo-Marxist interpretation of the local and the global which are seen in necessary opposition to one other. This observation transposes the Marxist interpretation of social classes in perpetual conflict to the relation between place and culture. These academics terrify their audience depicting globalization as a tsunami-like phenomenon that eradicates everything in its path. The truth is much more subtle as it is erroneous to think of the relation between the local and the global as necessarily conflicting. Conglomerates have long realized that in order to run a successful international business they must adapt to local differences and integrate diversity at all levels from management to programming. Global media also constitute a business opportunity for local companies with arrangements such as joint ventures and output deals. There is no basis for belief that it is a zero sum game between the local and international cultural fare. Products designed for the world market have an appeal that is distinct from those intended for a local audience. Viewers decide independently to consume either of these products – they do not cancel each other out.[11]

Media globalization is sometimes criticized because local elites feel they are losing control – and rightly so – over people who choose to consume cultural products from beyond national borders. But global media is simply another layer added to the existing local, national and regional communications systems. Sometimes these layers are entwined and sometimes they work independently from each other. This added complexity can be misconstrued as a threat, but the global is simply rebalancing the relation between these layers and curbing the influence of the national dimension, which has been overwhelming in the recent past.

Music

The popular belief is that MTV contributes to homogenize music taste and production worldwide. Although the network began its international expansion under the banner 'One World – One Music' and used to broadcast one playlist across Europe, it would no longer exist today had it not changed strategy. As detailed in Chapter 11, MTV has become Europe's most localized network, planting local channels all over the continent. Playlists are established according to local tastes, as measured by audience feedback to the channel (e.g. requests, text messages), and also the music played by local radio stations, music sales, the local press and local music scene.

However, it remains true that MTV, alongside the Internet and MP3 players, facilitates young people's access to global music. MTV playlists do tend to carry more international acts than the local competition simply because the latter channels may choose to adopt a 'localist' agenda and position themselves thus. MTV's strategy is entirely focused on ratings and the network's stations air the videos that the local audience want to see. The result is a higher proportion of international acts than local bands on European playlists (Table 12.1). These percentages reflect audience choice and the fact that European youth do not mind where their music comes from. As there cannot be enough local talent to satisfy their taste – especially for those living in small countries – it must be expected that they turn to international acts. Table 12.2 shows that MTV has no predilection for global music as the proportion of local acts can rise up to 90 per cent outside Europe.

Table 12.1: Origin of music on MTV stations' playlists in Europe, 2006

	Local (%)	International (%)
MTV Adria	20	80
MTV Poland	20	80
MTV Germany	20	80
MTV Italy	30	70
MTV Romania	50	50
MTV France	30	70
MTV Netherlands	25	75
MTV Russia	50	50
MTV Spain	40	60
MTV Sweden	25	75
MTV Denmark	30	70
MTV Norway	20	80
MTV Finland	15	85

Source: MTV.

Table 12.2: Origin of music on MTV stations' playlists outside Europe, 2006

	Local (%)	International (%)
MTV Base Africa	30	70
MTV Australia	40	60
MTV China	70	30
MTV India	90	10
MTV Japan	70	30
MTV Mandarin	70	30
MTV Philippines	70	30
MTV SAM (South East Asia)	20	80
MTV Thailand	50	50
MTV Brasil	40	60
MTV Latin America – North	30	70
MTV Latin America – South	40	60

Source: MTV.

The fact that MTV European playlists carry a lot of international music does not imply that these channels are in any way similar or that everybody is listening to the same bands. Local audiences select their favourite music genres and artists from the international repertoire, and their preferences vary markedly from one culture to another.

MTV takes pride in treating all labels, independent or otherwise, on an equal footing. The network's label managers devote a lot of time and energy to making everyone feel special. Nonetheless, MTV's global reach makes it a particularly enticing proposition for the big labels with international acts to promote. Each week representatives from MTV's European regions view newly submitted videos for playlist consideration. Those selected may not end up across the network but will be shown in several countries at least. Labels receive a list of territories of where each video will be shown. When a key market does not show up, say because the artist is not played on the local radio, a label's international sales manager may decide to pursue the matter. She or he will have her/his local person contact the local MTV channel in order to push the video.[12]

MTV also selects three or four priority videos per month for a minimum of a hundred plays over five weeks on all MTV Europe channels. With a rotation commencing two weeks before the record's release date, an artist selected for network priority receives blanket pan-regional support at a key moment of the sales cycle. MTV also organizes several international music events, such as the MTV Europe Music Awards, which are beamed around the world. Labels, mindful of these shows' exceptional coverage, encourage their artists to attend, present an award or possibly perform, when invited by MTV.

MTV's international influence is probably most marked in the youth fashion and music genres that are strongly visual such as Hip-Hop and R'N'B. The network has unparalleled access to international music stars such as American Hip-Hop artists, whose lifestyle and fashion feature regularly on MTV shows. MTV is also influential because of its professional audience. Artists, label executives, stylists and video producers, frequently flick through MTV to pick up ideas and check the latest trends.

It is undeniable that MTV facilitates young people's access to international music and contributes to the cosmopolitization of the music scene. The network is at the heart of global music flows and plays a part in the worldwide circulation of mainstream music genres. It must be emphasized that this role is distinct from cultural homogenization. When local artists or label executives adopt international trends they reinterpret them and blend them with the local music scene. MTV is a locally driven network and it is the local audiences who decide what they like among the genres and artists on offer. Music might be a universal language but it is spoken in many different dialects.

Fashion

The status of Fashion TV has been rising steadily in the select world of fashion. Today a fair share of its viewers is made up of professionals working in the industry, as well as the fashion-savvy public. As seen in Chapter 7, Fashion TV is globally distributed and reports from catwalks around the world. Its international outlook suits an industry with production centres scattered across the globe that are connected to each other. Fashion TV is becoming a tool of the trade for a whole range of fashion professionals. The network can introduce young designers to a worldwide audience and help the more established ones to maintain a global presence. Industry figures such as buyers for labels and department stores are constantly on the move and Fashion TV can help them get an overview of the various fashion weeks in the international calendar. Models like to watch friends, rivals – and themselves – and aspiring ones can learn about the profession. A model agency can follow a model's career through his or her appearances, and for those who need to book a model, Fashion TV has agencies' contact details on its website. The network airs a range of shows about the people and the professions (designers, photographers, models, hairdressers, etc.) that resonate with fashion's insiders.

In just a few years Fashion TV has become a valuable source of information for the fashion industry, even though it has yet to acquire the prestige and influence of *Vogue* or Style.com. The network accentuates the cosmopolitan character of the fashion trade by adding to the international visibility of brands and facilitating the multicultural exchange of trends and ideas.[13]

Finance

The growing integration of financial markets, the expansion of international capital flows and the internationalization of financial institutions such as banks and stock exchanges are among the many facets of financial globalization.[14] International finance has always required global information systems that were traditionally provided by specialists such as Reuters, but today business television is adding to the flow of financial information.

Both Bloomberg Television and CNBC Europe are widely distributed in the financial sector. They are available via the Internet at traders' desks, on TV screens on trading floors and even in the cafeterias of financial institutions. Today these channels count among the trade's key information platforms. A survey conducted in 2006 found that 100 per cent of financial professionals regularly use news or business TV channels, 93 per cent read newspapers, 91 per cent consult real-time data terminals and 82 per cent turn to online sources. The most-watched station is CNBC Europe (63 per cent of financial professionals watch it on a regular basis while at work), followed by Bloomberg TV (52 per cent), CNN (21 per cent), N-TV (16 per cent), Sky News (11 per cent), BBC World News (5 per cent) and Reuters TV (5 per cent).[15] There are several reasons for the popularity of television.

Business channels continuously break news stories. In a trade where delays of a few seconds can cost millions, newspapers are irrelevant because they lack freshness.[16] Bloomberg Television and CNBC Europe have excellent access to CEOs and other senior business figures. Such interviews give the financial community an opportunity to hear the news from the horse's mouth and can move share prices within minutes. Traders, analysts and fund managers also appreciate business and financial analysis delivered *in real time*, as share prices scroll past on their data screens. Commentators and experts help to contextualize and clarify data by pointing to the day's key trends. They analyse the factors that move the market and try to predict where it is heading. These views make financial markets more intelligible for those involved. Markets and exchanges previews are also deemed extremely useful. They take place early in the morning for the European exchanges and at midday for the US markets.

The financial community sees global coverage as an essential tool. There is a clear consensus among professionals that all the major global markets are completely interconnected, with the lead provided by the USA.[17] CNBC Europe makes extensive use of its global newsgathering resources to provide 24-hour coverage of the world's leading stock exchanges. It helps that the station is part of a worldwide network of channels and franchises covering the USA, Asia (CNBC Asia), the Middle East (CNBC Arabiya) and Africa.[18] Similarly, the European Bloomberg channels are part of an international network encompassing Europe, Asia-Pacific, the USA and Latin America. Both networks have adapted their programming to the international nature of financial markets, offering continuous insights from the USA and programmes with global insights, such as CNBC's intercontinental signature show *Worldwide Exchange* (Chapter 9). The programme is watched by about 900,000 people every week. Viewers appreciate how the format of the show acknowledges the existence of a global financial system and reflects that decisions taken in the USA, Japan or China can influence trading in Europe.[19]

Politics

Since the Second World War politics has become globalized in several ways. Political and economic relations have intensified among nation-states, which have become further connected by a web of treaties and agreements. A global political system has emerged, dominated by the United Nations and international governmental organizations (IGOs) like the World Trade Organization and the International Monetary Fund. These institutions help to establish international regimes (or sets of rules) in fields ranging from human rights to telecommunications. Global governance, involving national, international, governmental and non-governmental players alike, is increasingly used by governments seeking solutions to transnational issues on drugs, migration or global warming.[20]

Among the international news stations surveyed in Chapter 9, the 'Big Three' (AJE, BBC World News and CNN International) are in the best position to deal with the complexity of global politics. Their newsgathering facilities give them the ability to break international news and give real-time and round-the-clock coverage of international events. They can use their worldwide resources and network of affiliates to adopt a global perspective on key events and rise above the national angle that characterizes the treatment of international news by terrestrial broadcasters. Coverage routinely includes news reports and viewpoints from different parts of the globe, allowing journalists and analysts to explore the worldwide ramifications of those events. These networks have designed a range of programmes that deal with international issues and which are tailored to a multinational audience (Chapter 9).

Viewers turn to international news channels for diverse reasons. They may dislike the sensationalism of their local news TV channels or need to improve their English, but predominantly because they have a cosmopolitan outlook. Thirty-five per cent of BBC World News viewers take at least six international flights a year, 52 per cent stay outside their home country for at least one month a year and 36 per cent work for an organization that has operations overseas.[21] The global news networks are watched by the business and political elites, as shown by the EMS and EOLS data (Chapters 5 and 9).

Government officials, high-ranking civil servants, diplomats and business leaders can usually access the news networks at their workplace, since they are available on the cable systems of parliaments and governmental offices across Europe. In the USA, these channels are available at the White House, the Pentagon and the UN headquarters. Global news channels are particularly relied upon at times of crisis. For instance, during the war in Afghanistan in 2002 the US Secretary of State Colin Powell advised his president and vice president to 'stay away from CNN' because of the added pressure brought by continuous war coverage.[22] All the networks provide substantial coverage of the global get-togethers, when international power brokers meet, ranging from the G8 summit to the Davos World Economic Forum.

WORLD TRADE, MULTINATIONALS AND TRANSNATIONAL TV NETWORKS

The relation between transnational TV networks and globalization is reinforced by the role these channels play in world trade. Cross-border television facilitates international commerce through its ability to answer the communications needs of a growing number of multinationals. Global news and business channels do not merely convey crucial information to corporate executives across Europe, they constitute *elite-to-elite communication platforms* at international level. The stakeholders (clients, shareholders, employees, etc.) of most multinationals are bound to be spread across many countries and transnational television facilitates communication among them. For instance, the overwhelming majority of shareholders of a company like Nokia are based outside Finland, so when its CEO is interviewed by a business news network he can reach them across Europe in one stroke. Global news and business channels also figure prominently in multinationals' business-to-business communication plans. The flexible solutions they offer, such as ad-funded programming, sponsorship or multi-platform deals, enable transnational companies to communicate a corporate message effectively to a targeted international audience.

As seen in Chapter 5, cross-border channels are well suited to help multinationals promote their brands. PETV channels are often the first port of call for non-European companies and multinationals from emerging economies. These stations' wide geographical coverage enables them to build up multi-territory brand recognition without having to navigate the complexities of the European media market. PETV is the first pathway to Europe of many Asian brands.

In the second half of the twentieth century, international trade grew much faster than national economies to constitute an ever-growing proportion of the global economy. In 1955 the volume of world trade stood at US$95 billion, rising to US$10,472 billion in 2005.[23] It is in this context that transnational television gains significance whereby cross-border TV networks play an active role in world trade and globalization, and resonate with people living and working in a world of interdependent cultures and economies.

CONCLUSION

NEW WORLD, NEW NETWORKS

The evidence presented in this book clearly points to a transnational paradigm shift in television. Cross-border TV channels struggled in the 1980s when they were in the grip of a range of problems that included poor satellite transmission, governments reluctant to grant access to their markets and a reception universe that was too small to attract advertisers. As I have described, the constellations came into alignment for transnational television in the late 1990s. The expansion of the reception universe enabled cross-border channels to increase their coverage and spread costs, direct-to-home broadcasting facilitated reception, digitization increased network capacity and viewers' choice, and the growth of supply on communication satellites lowered the price of transmission. European integration, the implementation of a fairly liberal audiovisual legislative framework and a viable international copyright regime legalized and facilitated transfrontier television. The restructuring of the advertising industry, and the growing number of companies with cross-border activities and multi-territory brands were also favourable developments. Diversified entertainment conglomerates entered the PETV industry with the scope and resources to develop a successful international TV business. Broadcasters understood how to deal with the complexities of a multinational operation: they not only adapted to local audiences but many created network-centric TV operations that enabled them to break down the opposition between the local and the global and make each term an extension of the other.

It is striking to note that similar shifts have occurred in other sectors of the economy over *the same period of time*. International logistics, 'which can be defined as the process of [. . .] managing the movement and storage of [. . .] goods [. . .] from the point of origin to the point of consumption',[1] underwent a period of comparable change:

> But beginning slowly in the 1980s, and picking up steam in the 1990s, the world of logistics began to undergo significant change. US deregulation of trucking and railroads in the early 1980s brought freight rates down

substantially, giving companies a taste of what was possible by way of profitability and operational enhancements emanating from the gritty and overlooked loading dock. The ocean shipping container, invented in the 1950s but by the 1980s ubiquitous in seaports around the world, enabled international shipments to move from inland point to inland point without having to be unpacked and reloaded into trucks near the dock.[2]

Other phenomena that have transformed logistics include the growth of global trade, the emergence of global brands and retailers, the move of manufacturing to low-cost economies, consolidation across industry sectors and the availability of information and communications technology.[3]

Similar observations have been made in the world of computing and the Internet. Thomas Friedman argues that a 'flat-world platform' emerged 'around the year 2000', which allegedly began a new era of globalization. This platform is:

> the product of a convergence of the personal computer (which allowed every individual suddenly to become the author of his or her own content in digital form) with fiber-optic cable (which suddenly allowed all those individuals to access more and more digital content around the world for next to nothing) with the rise of work flow software (which enabled individuals all over the world to collaborate on that same digital content from anywhere, regardless of the distances between them).[4]

Transnational television, international logistics and the Internet can be described as networks because all three are involved in cross-border flows of communication, commodities and data. Proper comparative research is needed but the shifts in all three networks point to a single force – globalization – that is reconfiguring them. As a result, these networks share some features. They have expanded rapidly over recent years and have acquired transnational capabilities and global scope. They are adaptable and highly responsive to risks and opportunities. In communications as in logistics, networks have adopted the same configuration – the tree shape – and make a distinction between primary and secondary distribution. As seen in Chapter 4, programme contribution applications consist of bringing a signal from point A to point B, the trunk, then point to multi-point programme distribution is the network's branches as the signal is dispatched separately to its final customers. Logistics also differentiates between primary transport (e.g. the giant container ships that navigate between, say, Shanghai and Southampton) and local delivery transport. The regional is often an intermediary level between the local and the global: for instance, multinational companies that provide services in all three fields frequently create regional operational hubs. Finally, all networks have localizing capabilities: international broadcasters adapt their products to local wants and needs, as do many Internet and software companies. And it is the logistics process that enables many electronics companies to customize products built from a common platform.

It was not long ago that television was the preserve of the nation-state. Many governments kept control of broadcasting to preserve national culture and engineer national identity. Any breach of their prerogatives was considered an infringement of the sacrosanct principle of 'cultural sovereignty'. The new paradigm does not make the national dimension disappear – national markets and audiences still have irreducible specificities – but it is curbing the influence of national governments over communications systems.

The transnational paradigm opens up communications systems and makes them evolve on four levels: local, national, regional and global. Sometimes these layers are intertwined and sometimes they work independently of each other. The new era is simply rebalancing the relationship between these dimensions and it is erroneous to misconstrue the global as a threat to the other levels. However, it remains true that the global is an important dimension of the new paradigm. The future of television – as is that of all networks – and globalization are bound up with one another. A powerful dialogic relationship is being built around networks and globalizing processes: globalization feeds off networks which in turn are transformed by it. Transnational networks are a globalizing force and at the same time are reconfigured by globalization.

Transnational television belongs to and brings about a world where globalization changes nations, cultures and life experiences 'from within'.[5] Nations are interconnected, cultures are hybridized and borders ambivalent. The transnational media challenge boundaries, question the principle of territoriality and open up 'from within' the national media. New communication flows and practices are shaping media spaces with built-in transnational connectivity, both reflecting and creating contemporary cultures pregnant with new meanings and experiences.

NOTES

Job titles and company names at time of interview. Details may have since changed.

Introduction

1   Kaarle Nordenstreng and Herbert I. Schiller, *National Sovereignty and International Communication* (Norwood, NJ: Ablex, 1979), passim; Ralph Negrine, 'Introduction', in Ralph Negrine (ed.), *Satellite Broadcasting: The Politics and Implications of the New Media* (London: Routledge, 1988), p.1.

2   See, for example, Marie Gillespie, *Television, Ethnicity and Cultural Change* (London: Routledge, 1995); Kevin Robins and Asu Aksoy, 'Whoever Looks Always Finds: Transnational Viewing and Knowledge-Experience', in J. Chalaby (ed.), *Transnational Television Worldwide: Towards a New Media Order* (London: I.B.Tauris, 2005), pp.14–42; Daya K. Thussu (ed.), *Media on the Move: Global flow and contra-flow* (London: Routledge, 2007).

3   Ulrich Beck, 'The Cosmopolitan Society and Its Enemies', *Theory, Culture and Society* 19(1–2) (2002), p.18; Ulrich Beck, 'The Cosmopolitan Perspective: Sociology of the Second Age of Modernity', *British Journal of Sociology* 51(1) (2000), p.87.

4   Ulrich Beck, *Cosmopolitan Vision* (Cambridge: Polity Press, 2006), p.18.

5   See Joseph D. Straubhaar, *World Television: From Global to Local* (Los Angeles: Sage, 2007), pp.1–29.

Chapter 1

1   Tim Westcott, 'Bloc Downconversion', *C&SE* June 1990, p.17.

2   'Watching the West', *C&SE* February 1987, p.15.

3   Toby Syfret, 'Pax Teutonica', *C&SE* August 1992, p.16.

4   Stephanie Billen, 'An equitable share-out?', *C&SE* November 1984, p.51.

5   Christian Brochand, *Histoire générale de la radio et de la télévision en France – Tome II 1944–1974* (Paris: La Documentation française, 1994), p.286.

6   François Godard, 'Monte Carlo or Bust', *C&SE* November 1993, pp.36–7.

7   Brochand, *Histoire générale*, pp.288–91; Andrea Esser, 'The Transnationalization of European Television', *Journal of European Area Studies* 10(1) (2002), pp.18–20.

8   Mack Palomaki, 'The TVRO: 20 years on', *C&SE* October 1988, p.31.

9   Steve Birkill, former technical director, *C&SE*, interview, 30 November 2004; Boris Chirkov, 'Beaming to eleven time zones', *C&SE* December 1984, pp.13–15; Steve Birkill, 'From 30 metre to 30 centimetre', *C&SE* January 1990, p.28.

10 Richard Setlowe, 'Many strands grew together to build cable', *Variety* 3–9

November 1997, p.66; Chris Woodman, '15 years of intelligence', *C&SE* May 1999, p.30; Mark C. Rogers, Michael Epstein and Jimmie L. Reeves (2002), '*The Sopranos* as HBO Brand Equity: The Art of Commerce in the Age of Digital Reproduction', in Daniel Lavery (ed.), *This Thing of Ours: Investigating* The Sopranos (New York: Columbia University Press, 2002), p.49.

11 Jeff Kupsky, head of network development, Turner Broadcasting System Europe, interview, 3 September 2003; Ken Auletta, *Media Man: Ted Turner's Improbable Empire* (New York: Norton, 2004), pp.29–35.

12 Auletta, *Media Man*, p.40.

13 Brian Haynes in *C&SE* January 1990, pp.20–1.

14 Brian Haynes, managing director (MD), Satellite Television, 1981–3, interview, 2 December 2004.

15 Haynes, interview; Brian Haynes, *Chronology of Satellite Television Plc*, undated/unpublished document; 'Europe's first satellite link promotes "Eurocable" idea', *Cable Age* 14 June 1982, p.13.

16 Malcolm Tallantire, former network director, Sky Channel, interview, 21 October 2004; Patrick Cox, former MD, Sky Channel and NBC Europe, interview, 11 October 2004; Haynes, *Chronology of Satellite Television Plc*.

17 Sophie Bachmann, *L'Eclatement de l'ORTF*: La Réforme de la délivrance (Paris: L'Harmattan, 1997).

18 Alain Peyrefitte, *C'était de Gaulle, vol. 1* (Paris: de Fallois/Fayard, 1994), p.98.

19 Jean-Luc Cronel, directeur du marketing, TV5, interview, 12 June 2002.

20 Cronel, interview; Simon Baker, 'In charge of the Eurobeams', *C&SE* March 1984, pp.16–17.

21 'TV-5: The free French footprint', *C&SE* January 1984, pp.68–9.

22 Cronel, interview; 'TV Cinq plus one', *C&SE* December 1985, p.25.

23 '3SAT makes its bid', *C&SE,* December 1984, pp.45–6; 'High German', *C&SE* March 1987, p.26.

24 In Nick Snow, 'Abonnee Televisie', *C&SE* October 1984, p.51; 'FilmNet-ATN: the useful combination', *C&SE* April 1985, pp.30–1.

25 'Euroview – premium channels', *C&SE* December 1987, p.16.

26 Lisa O'Carroll, 'Esselte's box office sell out', *C&SE* April 1990, pp.60–2; Piero Muscarà and Eleonora Zamparutti, 'The Other Rupert', *C&SE* January 1996, p.18; Göran Sellgren, 'Reshuffle at Nethold Nordic', *C&SE* April 1997, p.6.

27 'World Channel from Norway', *C&SE* December 1984, p.6.

28 'WPN: David among Goliaths', *C&SE* December 1985, p.xxv.

29 Richard Wolfe, chief executive officer (CEO), The Travel Channel, and MD, The Children's Channel, 1984–93, interview, 11 October 2004; 'Thorn EMI: The quiet giant prepares', *C&SE* January 1984, pp.70–1; Nick Snow, 'Farewell to Thorn EMI', *C&SE* May 1986, p.29.

30 Charles Levison, former MD, Music Box, and former joint MD, Super Channel, interview, 4 November 2004; 'Music Box: A way in?', *C&SE* September 1984, p.51; 'Music Box: Breaking records', *C&SE* April 1985, pp.26–7; 'MTV for Music Box?', *C&SE* August 1985, p.35.

31 Wolfe, interview; 'The Children's Channel: Growing Up?' *C&SE* November 1985, p.ii; 'Dutch debut for Children's', *C&SE* January 1988, p.6; 'Children's goes to foster parents', *C&SE* August 1991, p.6; Julian Clover, 'Flexible', *C&SE* December 1991, pp.19–20.

32   'Screensport's Anglo-American power', *C&SE* January 1984, p.73; 'Principal international cable programme providers', *C&SE* October 1984, p.52; Vanessa O'Connor, 'Screen Sport makes its play for Europe', *C&SE* March 1985, p.60; 'WH Smith takes over Screen Sport', *C&SE* August 1986, p.5.

33   'On the ball', *C&SE* June 1987, pp.22–7.

34   'Art Attack', *C&SE* June 1987, p.27.

35   'Arts cable culture club', *C&SE* January 1984, p.72; 'Arts Channel launched', *C&SE* November 1985, p.37; Glyndwr Matthias, 'Art and artifice', *C&SE* October 1987, pp.36–8.

Chapter 2

1   Alvin A. Snyder, *Warriors of Disinformation: American Propaganda, Soviet Lies, and the Winning of the Cold War – An Insider's Account* (New York: Arcade, 1995), pp.105– 20.

2   Ibid., pp.7–11.

3   Ibid., pp.43–72.

4   Ibid., pp.39–40.

5   Simon Baker, 'The World network', *C&SE* February 1986, pp.11–13.

6   Snyder, *Warriors of Disinformation*, pp.73–92; Ronald Reagan (Douglas Brinkley, ed.), *The Reagan Diaries* (New York: HarperCollins, 2007), pp.518 and 580.

7   Alan Simpson, former chief technician, Worldnet, interview, 21 April 2005.

8   Simpson, interview; 'Casting the Net', *C&SE* July 1987, p.29.

9   Snyder, *Warriors of Disinformation*, pp.120–5.

10   Neville Clarke, 'Pan-European TV?', *Irish Broadcasting Review*, 14 (Summer 1982), p.44.

11   Charles Barrand, 'Europa Television – The Transponder's Eye View', *EBU Review. Programmes, Administration, Law* 37/2 (1986), p.11.

12   Neville Clarke, 'Eurikon promises a new programme concept', *Intermedia* 11/3 (1983), p.29.

13   Neville Clarke, 'The Birth of the Infant Eurikon', *Intermedia* 12/2 (1984), p.50.

14   Stylianos Papathanassopoulos, 'Towards European Television: The Case of Europa-TV', *Media Information Australia* 56 (May 1990), p.60.

15   Vanessa O'Connor, 'Climbing a Euro-mountain', *C&SE* July 1986, p.54; Richard Collins, *From Satellite to Single Market: New Communication Technology and European Public Service Television* (London: Routledge, 1998), pp.143–9.

16   Richard Hooper, MD, Super Channel, 1987–8, interview, 20 October 2004.

17   Among ITV companies the shares were split as follows: Granada, 23.2 per cent; Central Television, 17.5 per cent; London Weekend Television, 11.7 per cent; Television South, 11.7 per cent; Yorkshire Television, 6.9 per cent; Anglia Television, 5.8 per cent; Tyne Tees Television, 2.0 per cent; Scottish Television, 2.0 per cent; Harlech Television, 2.0 per cent; Television South West, 0.7 per cent; Grampian Television, 0.5 per cent; Ulster Television, 0.5 per cent; Border Television, 0.3 per cent and Channel Television, 0.1 per cent. *C&SE* 1 January 1987, p.15.

18   Hooper, interview; Nick Snow, 'Super Channel reaches for Sky', *C&SE* January 1987, pp.14–16; Vanessa O'Connor, 'Super on the market', *C&SE* May 1988, pp.33–4.

19   Claire Burnett, 'Once bitten, twice shy', *C&SE* January 1990, p.53.

20   'ITN keeping Europe informed', *C&SE* July 1987, p.24.

21   Hooper, interview; Snow, 'Super Channel reaches for Sky', pp.15–16; 'ITN keeping Europe informed', p.24.

22   O'Connor, 'Super on the market', pp.33–4; Claire Burnett, 'Pan-European mirage', *C&SE* January 1990, pp.16–17.

23   Burnett, 'Once bitten, twice shy', p.56; Julian Clover, 'Super's *Ruud* awakening', *C&SE* April 1994, p.40.

24   Colin McGhee, 'The World from Atlanta', *C&SE* October 1984, p.16; 'Live from America', *C&SE* October 1985, p.26.

25   Auletta, *Media Man*, p.39; Colin McGhee, 'Turner: The crusader by satellite', *C&SE* March 1985, p.9.

26   'Live from America', p.26; 'CNN: Hitting the ground running!', *C&SE* November 1985, p.v.

27   Simpson, interview; 'Better than a newspaper?', *C&SE* July 1987, p.15; 'CNN for Soviet Union?', *C&SE* June 1989, p.14.

28   'Bob Ross's year', *C&SE* November 1988, p.69.

29   N-TV was among the first and was launched with the help of CNN in Germany in November 1992. Other examples include BBC News, France's LCI and RAI News 24.

30   Background information from Chris Cramer, president, CNN International, interview, 9 July 2002.

31   Wolfe, interview; 'MTV picks up the beat', *C&SE* January 1987, p.18.

32   Sumner Redstone, *A Passion to Win* (New York: Simon & Schuster, 2001), pp.107–42.

33   Glyndwr Matthias, 'Face the music', *C&SE* September 1987, p.25.

34   Claire Burnett, 'Flip-side', *C&SE* August 1988, pp.33–6; Paul Barker, 'Paying to party', *C&SE* March 1991, pp.19–21.

35   Burnett, 'Flip-side', p.35. Only at a later stage did MTV notice that individual cultural tastes varied among Europeans, Chapter 11.

36   Lisa O'Carroll, 'Putting the Booth in', *C&SE* September 1988, pp.66–7; 'BT Vision pulls out of programming', *C&SE* May 1989, p.12; 'Maxwell bows out of MTV', *C&SE* October 1991, p.8; Redstone, *A Passion to Win*, pp.166–7.

37   Claire Burnett, 'New World', *C&SE* April 1989, p.28; John Flinn, 'America's cable giant', *C&SE* April 1992, p.50.

38   Carriage fees are paid to broadcasters by content aggregators or channel packagers, such as pay-TV platforms, for the right to carry their channels on their systems.

39   Burnett, 'New World', pp.28–33.

40   Tim Westcott, 'A foot in both camps', *C&SE* January 1991, pp.25–6; Paul Barker, 'Narrow minded', *C&SE* September 1992, pp.22–7; 'US Discovery brand set for global expansion', *C&SE* February 1993, p.14.

41   Burnett, 'New World', p.32; 'Discovery studies Scandinavian version', *C&SE*, November 1992, p.10.

42   'No clear picture for Screen Sport', *C&SE* June 1986, p.8; 'WH Smith takes over Screen Sport', *C&SE* August 1986, p.5; 'Jeux, set et match', *C&SE* February 1988, pp.25–6.

43   'TV Sport looks into French "window"', *C&SE* January 1991, p.10; 'TV Sport to launch French strand', *C&SE* March 1991, p.8.

44   'WHSTV channels on a surer footing', *C&SE* July 1991, p.6; Paul Barker, 'Beggar's banquet', *C&SE* January 1992, pp.17–20.

45 'Screensport tries Eurosport merger', *C&SE* November 1992, p.8; 'ETN channels shut down following merger', *C&SE* February 1993, p.6.

46 Richard Collins, 'Supper with the devil – a case study in private/public collaboration in broadcasting: the genesis of Eurosport', *Media, Culture & Society* 20/4 (1998), pp.655–6; 'A sporting chance', *C&SE* February 1988, p.37.

47 Agnès Pierret, sport news producer, EBU, interview with author, Eric Darras and Dominique Marchetti, 16 June 2000; Collins, 'Supper with the devil', p.656.

48 'A sporting chance', p.37; 'Love all', *C&SE* February 1989, pp.47–8; 'DSF Renews Court War With Eurosport', *C&SE* October 1995, p.8.

49 Collins, 'Supper with the devil', p.659.

50 'Eurosport to replace Sky', *C&SE* November 1988, p.6.

51 Mathew Horsman, *Sky High* (London: Orion Business, 1998), pp.25–117; 'The end of BSB', *C&SE* December 1990, pp.16–20.

52 'EC calls time on Eurosport', *C&SE* March 1991, p.6; 'WHSTV writ stifles Eurosport rescue', *C&SE* June 1991, p.6; 'Games Without Frontiers', *C&SE* September 1993, p.52; Collins, 'Supper with the devil', p.659.

53 France's Bouygues joins Eurosport', *C&SE* September 1991, p.6; 'Games Without Frontiers', p.52.

54 'Eurosport claims lion's share of revenue', *C&SE* April 1993, p.8.

55 Background information from Arjan Hoekstra, deputy MD, British Eurosport, interview, 6 June 2000; Jacques Raynaud, general manager, Eurosport, interview, 25 April 2005.

56 'Sky takes on Arts', *C&SE* January 1988, p.5; 'Culture Vulture', *C&SE* August 1988, pp.19–20.

57 'Artful move', *C&SE* February 1989, pp.46–7; 'Art and life', *C&SE* April 1989, pp.33–4; 'The Arts Channel goes off air', *C&SE* May 1989, p.6.

58 'EBC extends service', *C&SE* September 1989, p.10.

59 In Glyndwr Matthias, 'Risky business', *C&SE* November 1988, p.61.

60 Wolfgang Koschnick, 'Gnome go?', *C&SE* May 1990, p.27; 'EBC forced to close', *C&SE* August 1990, p.8.

61 'SAT 1: a serious contender', *C&SE* April 1985, p.29; Vanessa O'Connor, 'SAT1 one year on', *C&SE* February 1986, pp.19–21; Vanessa O'Connor and Nick Snow, 'On your Marks . . .', *C&SE* November 1987, pp.14–18.

62 'Kirch bid for Sat1 fails', *C&SE* October 1989, p.8; Wolfgang Koschnick, 'Sat1 at the brink', *C&SE* November 1990, pp.16–23; 'New Alpine window for Sat1', *C&SE* March 1992, p.9; Toby Syfret, 'Pax Teutonica', *C&SE* August 1992, p.16; 'European Satellite Television Ownership', *C&SE* February 1995, pp.20–1.

63 'RTL-Plus, the "refreshingly different" channel', *C&SE* February 1986, pp.21–2; Paul Barker and Lisa O'Carroll, 'Taking flight', *C&SE* April 1991, p.32; Julian Clover, 'Vorsprung durch Thoma', *C&SE* April 1993, p.20.

64 'Pro 7 – the new Eureka', *C&SE* February 1989, p.8; 'Fifth column', *C&SE* September 1988, pp.25–6.

65 Glyndwr Matthias, 'The New Face of Scandinavian TV', *C&SE* July 1989, pp.14–15; Madeleine Hurd, Tom Olsson and Patrik Åker (eds), *Storylines: Media, Power and Identity in Modern Europe* (Stockholm: Hjalmarson & Högberg, 2002).

66 Lena Ewertsson, *The Triumph of Technology Over Politics? Reconstructing Television Systems: The Example of Sweden* (Sweden: Linöpink Universitet, 2001), pp.87–8 and 288–94.

67   'Scanning new horizons', *C&SE* February 1988, p.34; 'TV3 ahead of target', *C&SE*
      March 1989, p.8; Lisa O'Carroll, 'Charging ahead', *C&SE* November 1989, p.42.
68   Ewertsson, *The Triumph of Technology*, pp.340–2; O'Carroll, 'Charging ahead',
      pp.42–4; Julian Clover, 'Bonus Points', *C&SE* July 1993, pp.22–3.
69   Ewertsson, *The Triumph of Technology* pp.89 and 343–4; company source.
70   Glyndwr Matthias, 'Swedish Crackers', *C&SE* July 1989, pp.17–18; Paul Barker,
      'Beggar's banquet', *C&SE* January 1992, p.18.
71   *C&SE* June 1996, p.56.

Chapter 3

1   Paul Barker and Tim Westcott, 'More red than black', *C&SE* February 1991, p.16.
2   Toby Syfret, 'Petar the fifth', *C&SE* July 1992, pp.19–22.
3   Paul Barker, 'From pariah to paragon', *C&SE* June 1992, p.16.
4   Lisa O'Carroll, 'The remake of Napoleon', *C&SE* April 1991, pp.20–30.
5   See, for example, Paul Barker, 'Nouvelles cuisine', *C&SE* February 1993, p.32;
      Tania Alonzi, 'Growing up is hard to do', *M&M Guide 1998*, pp.18–19.
6   Chris Woodman, '15 years of intelligence', *C&SE* May 1999, p.32.
7   Richard Wolfe, 'A Thorn On Cable's Side', *C&SE* January 1994, p.44.
8   Cynthia Ritchie, 'Crunch time for cable', *C&SE* May 1994, p.18.
9   Tallantire, interview; Wolfe, interview.
10   See, for example, H. van den Bulck, 'Public Service Television and National
      Identity as a Project of Modernity: The Example of Flemish Television', *Media,
      Culture & Society* 23/1 (2001), pp.53–69.
11   See Herbert Schiller, 'Electronic Information Flows: New Basis for Global
      Domination?', in P. Drumond and R. Paterson (eds), *Television in Transition*
      (London: BFI, 1986), pp.11–20; R. Hughes, 'Satellite Broadcasting: The Regulatory
      Issues in Europe', in R. Negrine (ed.), *Satellite Broadcasting: The Politics and
      Implications of the New Media* (London: Routledge, 1988), pp.49–74.
12   Tallantire, interview.
13   Cox, interview.
14   Paul Barker and Julian Clover, 'Flags of convenience', *C&SE* March 1992, pp.16–17.
15   Glyndwr Matthias, 'Many happy connections', *C&SE* November 1987, p.27.
16   Nick Snow, 'Ten Years in the 21st Century', *C&SE* January 1994, p.21.
17   Helmut Koszuszeck, legal and business manager, AGICOA, interview, 7 December
      2005. AGICOA: the acronym translates into Association of International Collective
      Management of Audiovisual Works.
18   Cox, interview; 'Amsterdam row could stop TV-5', *C&SE* January 1984, p.6.
19   The SABEM acronym has since changed to SABAM.
20   Stephanie Billen, 'An equitable share-out?', *C&SE* November 1984, pp.51–2.
21   Levison, interview.
22   Paul Kempton in Julian Clover, 'Negative Equity', *C&SE* January 1993, p.18;
      Tallantire, interview.
23   Patrick Cox in 'Sky: still leading the pack', *C&SE* April 1985, p.22.
24   Cox, interview.
25   Nick Snow, former editor, *C&SE*, interview, 12 January 2005; Tallantire, interview.
26   'European TV channels by country', *C&SE* January 1984, p.19; Toby Syfret,
      'Commercial breaks – II', *C&SE* February 1987, pp.34–7.

27   Lisa O'Carroll, 'United we stand', *C&SE* July 1988, pp.16–18; Paul Barker, 'Paying to party', *C&SE* March 1991, p.19.
28   Toby Syfret, interview, 6 August 2004.
29   Toby Syfret, 'A Recall for the Euro-ad?', *C&SE* April 1989, p.56.
30   Syfret, interview.
31   There was a way round everything: dwarfs were used to advertise cereals in Austria!
32   Syfret, 'A Recall for the Euro-ad?', p.56.
33   In Noel Meyer, 'In Units We Trust', *C&SE* April 1996, p.76.
34   It programmed *Sky Trax* at 15:00 each day (a pop video and live music show produced in the Netherlands), followed by comedy shows at 17:30 (e.g. *The Brady Bunch*, *The Lucy Show*), followed by an action movie at 19:00 and sport at 21:50.
35   'Porn in a tea cup?', *C&SE* November 1988, p.17.
36   Ibid., p.16.

Chapter 4

1   Mario Hirsch, 'Toeing the European line', *C&SE* June 1988, pp.36–8.
2   Nicholas Hellen, 'Breaking with convention', *C&SE* January 1989, pp.45–7.
3   Cox, interview; Claire Burnett, 'Mixed blessings', *C&SE* November 1989, pp.17–25.
4   Richard Collins, *Broadcasting and Audio-Visual Policy in the European Single Market* (London: John Libbey, 1994), pp.53–80; Alison Harcourt, *The European Union and the regulation of media markets* (Manchester: Manchester University Press, 2005), pp.62–6.
5   Susanne Nikolchev and André Lange, *Transfrontier Television in the European Union: Market Impact and Selected Legal Aspects* (Strasbourg: EAO, 2004), p.18. See also Daniel Krebber, *Europeanisation of Regulatory Television Policy: The Decision-making Process of the Television without Frontiers Directives from 1989 & 1997* (Baden Baden: Nomos Verlagsgesellschaft, 2002).
6   Ibid., p.28.
7   Solon Management Consulting, *Economic Impact of Copyright for Cable Operators in Europe* (2006), pp.14–16.
8   Ibid., pp.15–16.
9   Koszuszeck, interview.
10   Berne Convention, Article 11bis.
11   For instance, it is Brian Haynes, founder of Satellite Television plc, who first enunciated the principle of the country of origin, back in 1982: 'We are totally unregulated but decided to impose the British standard on ourselves because this is the country of origin. Each country has its own regulations, and we felt that, because we could not meet them all, it would be best if we followed the practice of Britain's Independent Television, which seems to be well respected in Europe.' Cited in 'Europe's first satellite link promotes "Eurocable" idea', *Cable Age* 14 June 1982, p.14.
12   Annabelle Littoz-Monnet, 'Copyright in the EU: *droit d'auteur* or right to copy?', *Journal of European Public Policy*, 13/3 (2006), pp.438–55.
13   *EAO Yearbook Vol. 2 2000*, pp.56–7; Eutelsat proprietary data.
14   Birkill, interview; Vanessa O'Connor, head of communication, Eutelsat, interview, 21 January 2005; Steve Birkill, *STTI's International Satellite Television Reception*

Guidebook (Arcadia, OK: Satellite Television Technology International, 1982), pp.11–20; Simon Baker, 'In charge of the Eurobeams', *C&SE* March 1984, pp.16–20; Steve Birkill, 'Eutelsat I: Surprise markets', *C&SE* March 1987, pp.32–8; Péricles Gasparini Alves, 'Access to Outer Space Technologies: Implications for International Security', *Research Paper* (Geneva: UNIDIR, 1992), pp.46–9.

15   Burkhard Nowotny, 'Co-ordinate to accumulate', *C&SE* April 1993, pp.108–9.

16   Ibid., p.108.

17   O'Connor, interview.

18   Pierre Meyrat, CEO, SES, 1986–94, interview, 7 December 2005.

19   Julian Clover, 'Turning The Heat Up', *C&SE* October 1994, pp.20–5.

20   Kevin Livesey, head of product, BT Media & Broadcast, interview, 20 April 2005.

21   [Television Without Frontiers]; Wilfried Ahrens, *Astra: Fernsehen ohne Grenzen* (Düsseldorf: ECON, 1993).

22   George A. Codding, Jr, *The Future of Satellite Communications* (Boulder, CO: Westview, 1990), pp.100–4.

23   Virgil S. Labrador and Peter I. Galace, *Heavens Fill with Commerce* (Sonoma, CA: SatNews, 2005), p.63; Codding, *The Future of Satellite Communications*, pp.72–3.

24   Candace Johnson, former board member, SES, interview, 5 November 2005.

25   'Coronet: bloodied but unbowed', *C&SE* September 1984, p.6.

26   Meyrat, interview.

27   Johnson, interview; Simon Baker, 'Eutelsat in the 90s', *C&SE* July 1985, pp.9–12; Ahrens, *Astra: Fernsehen ohne Grenzen*, pp.70–9.

28   In Glyndwr Matthias, 'The Monopoly strikes back', *C&SE* March 1987, p.40.

29   Meyrat, interview.

30   Steve Maine, director, Visual & Broadcast Services, BT, 1990–4, interview, 17 November 2005.

31   Livesey, interview; 'Special focus: DBS', *C&SE* August 1987, pp.14–25.

32   Birkill, interview; Meyrat, interview; Johnson, interview.

33   Tallantire, interview.

34   Stuart Thompson, 'Berretta's way', *C&SE*, p.20.

35   <http://www.ses-astra.com/business/en/satellite-fleet/astra-fusion/dth-hotspot/index.php>, consulted December 2007.

36   'Eutelsat 2007 survey of satellite and cable homes', www.eutelsat.fr, consulted December 2007; Markus Payer, vice president (VP) media relations, SES ASTRA, interview, 30 November 2007.

37   O'Connor, interview; Livesey, interview; Ian Moir, VP operations & engineering, MTV Technology, interview, 15 July 2005.

38   Anne-Laure Vandamme, Permanent Services Market Manager EMEA, GlobeCast, interview, 24 March 2005; www.globecast.com.

39   Livesey, interview; Vandamme, interview.

40   Nicola Brittain, 'Space for more', *C&SE* July/August 2006, pp.10–16.

41   Company source.

42   Company source.

43   Austria, Belgium, Czech Republic, Hungary, Ireland, Netherlands, Poland, Romania, Slovak Republic and Slovenia. Liberty Global operates as Cablecom in Switzerland.

44   Naturally, these international TV distributors run their own multi-territory channels: the Sky platforms air Sky- and Fox-branded stations (Chapter 7), Chello

Zone, a Liberty Global division alongside UPC, manages a portfolio of nine transnational channels (Chapter 7), Canal Digital owns the Canal Plus brand in the Nordic territories and Viasat broadcasts several TV1000 and Viasat-branded stations on its DTH platforms (Chapter 2).

45   Julian Clover, editor, *C&SE* 1991–2, interview, 28 February 2005.

46   François Godard, 'Clash Of The Titans', *C&SE* February 1997, pp.38–40.

Chapter 5

1   An earlier and shorter version of this chapter was published in *Global Media and Communication* 4(2) (2008), pp.139–56.

2   'Europe's nascent merger boom', *The Economist* 3 September 2005, p.66.

3   Malcom Hanlon, media group director, Zenith Media, interview, 20 September 2002; Johan Boserup, global director of trading and accountability, Omnicom, interview, 30 January 2008.

4   *M&M Guide 2002–07.*

5   Richard Collins, *Satellite Television in Western Europe*, rev. edn (London: John Libbey, 1992), p.44.

6   Adrian Smith, account director, MediaCom, interview, 3 November 2004; Ian Clarke, global account director, OMD, interview, 17 July 2007; Sonia Marguin, EuroNews, head of research, interviews, 23 October 2003, 29 September 2004, 21 September 2006, 29 July 2007.

7   Huw Jones, account director, Mediaedge:cia, interview, 6 October 2004; Ian Bell, research manager, ZenithOptimedia, interview, 5 November 2004; Phil Teeman, account director, MindShare, interview, 28 January 2005; Géraud Benoit, client service director, Universal McCann, interview, 13 April 2005; Clarke, interview; Boserup, interview.

8   Melanie Smith, account director, Carat, interview, 18 October 2004.

9   In Barry Flynn, 'German ad-mission', *C&SE* October 1992, p.48.

10   Company source.

11   *EMS Guide 2007*, pp.190–7.

12   *EMS Guide 2007*, p.26.

13   Georgina Hickey, international business director, Carat, interview, 20 September 2005.

14   Based on research conducted by BSB Media and the European Opinion Leaders Survey (below and Chapter 9).

15   Adrian Smith, interview; Benoit, interview; Clarke, interview; Boserup, interview.

16   Tony Robinson, VP, Viacom Brand Solutions, Europe, interview, 15 March 2006; Marguin, interviews; Sylvie Burger, directrice de publicité, Fashion TV, interview, 30 October 2007; *M&M Guide 2007.*

17   Toby Syfret, 'Petar the fifth', *C&SE* July 1992, pp.19–20.

18   Toby Syfret, 'The Big picture', *C&SE* November 1994, p.46.

19   BARB: Broadcasters' Audience Research Board; GfK: Gesellschaft für Konsumforschung; SKO: Schulten Kantoorinstallaties B.V. te Oldenzaal; TNS: Taylor Nelson Sofres.

20   Interview merged with NSS to form Interview-NSS in the late 1990s, and it became part of Synovate, the market research arm of Aegis, in January 2007.

21   *EMS Guide 2007*, pp.190–2.

22 *European Opinion Leaders Survey – presentation* (London: Icd research, 2007), p.2.
23 Matthew Hotten, Active Research, Jetix, interview, 11 November 2004; Marguin, interviews.
24 Belinda Barker, BSB Media, interview, 19 October 2004.
25 Nick Mawditt, head of research, CNBC Europe, interview, 23 March 2005.
26 Pip Brooking, 'How to reach business leaders', *M&M Europe* October 2005, pp.23–4.

Chapter 6

1   Michael Hedges, 'Ministers "save" TV5 Monde', followthemedia.com, 10 November 2007, <http://www.followthemedia.com/pubserve/TV5Monde10112007.htm>, consulted January 2008; Michael Hedges, 'Grand plan for France Monde reduced, replaced, redacted', followthemedia.com, 3 May 2008, <http://www.followthemedia.com/pubserve/TV5Monde03052008.htm>, consulted May 2008.
2   Jean-Luc Cronel, directeur du réseau commercial, TV5, interview, 25 January 2008.
3   Daniel Fiedler, coordinator, 3Sat, interview, 11 February 2008.
4   In partnership with ARD and ZDF, DW launched German TV in 2002, a channel specifically aimed at expatriates, but it was discontinued in 2006.
5   Martin Ziegele, editor assigned to the editor-in-chief, Deutsche Welle-TV, interview, 22 July 2005; Angelika Newel, head of distribution, Deutsche Welle-TV, interview, 3 April 2008.
6   Jean-Michel Utard, *Arte: Information télévisée et construction d'un point de vue transnational – étude d'un corpus franco-allemand* (PhD thesis, Strasbourg III, 1997), pp.16–17.
7   In *Le Monde* 26 September 1992; cited in Utard, 1997, p.39. Author's translation.
8   <http://arte-tv.com/fr/Impression/4982,CmC=890532,CmStyle=900344.html>, consulted March 2006.
9   For many years, a third of the station's income was provided by various European institutions.
10 François Godard and Paul Barker, 'Nouvelles cuisine', *C&SE* February 1993, p.32; 'EuroNews Receives First Private Backing', *C&SE* March 1995, p.12.
11 Stewart Purvis, CEO, 1995–2003, ITN, and president, SOCEMIE, interview, 4 August 2004. EuroNews has adopted a dual structure in order to guarantee editorial independence: the SOCEMIE (Société Opératrice de la Chaîne Européenne Multilingue d'Information EuroNews) is the company that operates the station and the SECEMIE (Société Éditrice la Chaîne Européenne Multilingue d'Information EuroNews) controls its editorial side.
12 Purvis, interview; Olivier de Monchenu, sales and distribution director, EuroNews, interview, 9 March 2005; Marguin, interviews.
13 Sir John Tusa, MD, BBC World Service, 1986–92, interview, 25 March 2005; see also Julian Clover, 'London calling the world', *C&SE* May 1991, p.20.
14 In the same year BBC Enterprises got involved with another project. The corporation was offered a free transponder on Olympus, a DBS satellite launched by the European Space Agency. The BBC took up the offer and drew plans for BBC Enterprise, a channel with factual and educational programming that would have doubled up as a mechanism of programme delivery to broadcasters. A test period

unveiled several difficulties, not least that Olympus was one of the few satellites transmitting in MAC (Multiplexed Analogue Components), the abortive European transmission standard (Chapter 8). The BBC soon gave up to concentrate on BBC TV Europe. Wayne Dunsford, director of channels, BBC Worldwide, interview, 13 December 2004; Tim Westcott, 'London calling', *C&SE* September 1990, pp.28–32; Tim Westcott, 'Step by step', *C&SE* September 1990, pp.33–6.

15   Clover, 'London calling the world', p.20.

16   Tusa, interview; Rachel Attwell, deputy head of television news, BBC, interview, 15 June 2005; Daniel Dodd, head of strategy for journalism, BBC, interview, 1 May 2007.

17   Attwell, interview; Richard Sambrook, director, BBC World Service and Global News, BBC, interview, 12 June 2007.

18   Anne Barnard, chief operating officer, BBC World, interview, 5 April 2005; Dodd, interview; Sambrook, interview.

19   Marc Young, MD, BBC Prime, interview, 11 July 2002; Dunsford, interview; Dean Possenniskie, senior VP, Global Channels – EMEA, BBC Worldwide, interview, 11 February 2008.

Chapter 7

1   See David Page and William Crawley, *Satellites over South Asia: Broadcasting, Culture and the Public Interest* (New Delhi: Sage, 2001); Naomi Sakr, *Arab Television Today* (London: I.B.Tauris, 2007).

2   For the UK see <http://www.barb.co.uk/viewingsummary/ weekreports.cfm?report=multichannel&requesttimeout=500>; for France see <http://www.mediametrie.fr/ resultats.php?rubrique=tv&resultat_id=425>, consulted March 2008.

3   Nikolchev's and Lange's study of transfrontier television (Chapter 4) estimated that the audience share of 'foreign' channels in Luxembourg was as high as 84 per cent and above 60 per cent in Switzerland. Nikolchev and Lange, *Transfrontier Television*, p.18

4   Wolfe, interview; Paul Barker, 'King of the castle', *C&SE* March 1992, pp.34–8; Julian Clover, 'Big Boys' Games', *C&SE* October 1994, pp.42–5; Clover, 'Flextech finally kills off TCC', *C&SE* April 1998, p.8.

5   Peter Flamman, VP, business development, TBS Europe, interviews, 16 March 2002, 10 July 2002, 18 March 2005 and 27 June 2007; Finn Arnesen, senior VP, original animation and acquisitions, TBS Europe, interview, 23 March 2005.

6   Tim Westcott, 'New kids on the box', *C&SE* December 2000, p.26.

7   *TBI*, December 2004/January 2005 p.12; *M&M Guide* 2007, p.41.

8   Company source.

9   'Hi-ho, hi-ho, it's off to Sky we go', *C&SE* February 1989, p.43; Lisa O'Carroll, 'Murdoch's poisoned apple', *C&SE* June 1989, p.16.

10   Nick Bell, 'Getting Animated', *C&SE* December 1994, p.22.

11   Andy Fry, 'Atlantic crossing', *C&SE* April 2000, p.12.

12   John Hardie, MD, Walt Disney Television, EMEA, interview, 5 April 2005.

13   Steve Aranguren, VP of global original programming, Disney Channels Worldwide, in Anna Carugati, 'Disney Channel Worldwide Invests in UK Original Production', WorldScreen.com, 28 November 2007, <http://www.worldscreen.com/ newscurrent.php?filename=disney112107.htm>, consulted February 2008.

14   Mansha Daswani, 'Disney Channel Unveils New Original Movies', WorldScreen.com, 10 April 2008, <http://www.worldscreen.com/newscurrent.php?filename=disneychannel041008.htm>, consulted May 2008.

15   Rick Plata, director of advertising sales, Fox Kids, interview, 19 April 2002.

16   Paul Taylor, CEO, Jetix, interview, 18 May 2005; *Annual Review and Financial Statements*, Jetix Europe, 2004, pp.8–9.

17   Company source; WorldScreen.com – TV Kids Weekly, 22 April 2008, 'Focus On Wayne Dunsford', <http://www.worldscreen.com/propertycurrent.php?filename=dunsford042208.htm>, consulted May 2008.

18   François Thiellet, président-directeur général, Thema, interviews, 15 June 2006 and 10 March 2008.

19   'BabyFirst TV Celebrates First Anniversary', WorldScreen.com, 11 May 2007, <http://www.worldscreen.com/newscurrent.php?filename=babyfirst051107.htm>, consulted October 2007.

20   The contribution of entertainment conglomerates to the PETV industry is fully examined in Chapter 8.

21   Taylor, interview.

22   Tanja Flintoff, head of programming and production, MTV European, interviews, 2 July 2002 and 15 March 2006.

23   Richard Godfrey, senior VP, MTV Productions Europe, interviews, 17 April 2001 and 26 February 2004; Simon Guild, chief operating officer, MTVNE, interview, 20 July 2004.

24   Thiellet, interview.

25   Philippe Rouxel, VP, sales and marketing, Lagardère Networks International interviews, 13 September 2002 and 6 April 2005.

26   Thiellet, interview.

27   Marian Williams, VP programming, EMEA, Discovery Networks Europe, interviews, 23 March 2005 and 25 February 2008.

28   Jay Leno quipped in a promotional video for the new channel: 'First we ruined our own culture, now we're going to ruin yours'. In Julian Clover, 'Super's *Ruud* Awakening', *C&SE* April 1994, p.41.

29   Sarah Callard, 'Nat Geo replaces NBC Europe', *C&SE* May 1998, p.8; Gilles Storme, head of research, National Geographic and Sky News, interview, 18 November 2004; company source.

30   Simon Pollock, VP and MD, Europe and Asia, AETN International, interviews, 23 November 2004 and 9 July 2007.

31   Chris Wronski, chairman, Zonevision, interview, 11 March 2004; Steve Cole, VP, Reality TV, interview, 25 January 2007.

32   Sylvie Burger, directrice de publicité, Fashion TV, interviews, 29 August 2006 and 30 October 2007.

33   John Trumpbour, *Selling Hollywood to the World: US and European Struggles for Mastery of the Global Film Industry, 1920–1950* (Cambridge: CUP, 2002); Jean Chalaby, 'American Cultural Primacy in a New Media Order', *The International Communication Gazette* 68(1) (2006), pp.33–51.

34   Kevin McLellan, senior VP, international, E! International Network, interview, 27 June 2006.

35   Wolfe, interview; in June 1996 Landmark launched a second station in Europe, the Weather Channel. Four localized services were established in the UK, the

Netherlands, Germany and Italy. The station never broke even and was closed down in early 1998. Julian Clover, 'Financial storm closes Weather Channel', *C&SE* March 1998, p.3.

36   Company source.

37   Christina Foley, commercial director, EMEA, Hallmark, interview, 8 October 2006; *Broadcast*, 11 March 2005, p.18; *M&M Guide 2007*, p.28.

38   Wronski, interview; company source.

39   Jason Thorp, head of programming, Universal Television Networks, interview, 2 May 2002; Dan Winter, head of press, Sci Fi Channel, interviews, 24 February 2005 and 22 May 2007; Julian Clover, 'Cash Crop', *C&SE* October 1995, pp.22–4.

40   Marin Kariz, area sales manager, HBO Adria, email communication, 11 July 2007; Monika Wirth-Schreiber, junior regional marketing manager, HBO Central Europe, email communication, 13 August 2007.

41   Ross Hair, senior VP of international networks, Sony Pictures Television International, interview, 22 August 2007.

42   Flamman, interviews; Auletta, *Media Man*, pp.49–50.

43   Company source.

44   Company source.

45   Ben Money, head of research, British Eurosport, interview, 16 February 2005; Gregory d'Assche, acquisition department, Jacques Raynaud, general manager, David Orman, sales director, all at Eurosport, interviews, 24 March and 25 April 2005.

46   Phil Jones, MD – Europe, Extreme Sports Channel, interview, 11 August 2004; company source.

47   Philippe Deleplace, directeur général adjoint, Motors TV, interview, 26 January 2005.

48   Dominique Sauvêtre, pan-European sponsorship manager, Motors TV, interview, 29 February 2008.

49   Tony Stimpson, director of programming, Europe, ESPN Classic, interviews, 17 November 2006 and 10 March 2008.

50   Stimpson, interview.

51   Company source (Playboy); Belinda Dillon and Ed Ryan, 'Porn to be wild', *C&SE* November 1998, pp.18–24; Anna Tobin, 'Playboy plans to localize across the globe', *C&SE* February 1999, p.8; Andy Fry, 'Selling Sex', *C&SE* June 2001, pp.32–6.

Chapter 8

1   'Premiere's premiere', *C&SE* April 1991, pp.28–9; 'Nethold/Canal+ Deal Keeps Hughes Out', *C&SE* October 1996, pp.6–7; François Godard, 'Analysis Canal+: Under surveillance', *C&SE* April 1998, pp.39–43.

2   Alessandra Zane, chargée de mission, Multithématiques, interview, 11 June 2002.

3   English is by far the most widely spoken second language in every single country of the European Union and the proportion of people who can speak English has increased in most Member States since 1990; 'Languages of Europe', <http://ec.europa.eu/education/policies/lang/languages/index_en.html>, consulted July 2007.

4   Graham Mytton, Ruth Teer-Tomaselli and André-Jean Tudesq, 'Transnational Television in Sub-Saharan Africa', in J. Chalaby (ed.), *Transnational Television Worldwide*, pp.96–127.

5   Simon Baker, 'Go-go for the dodo', *C&SE* November 1988, pp.34–6.

6   Barry Flynn, 'Joined at the hip', *C&SE* November 1992, pp.18–20.

7   Meyrat, interview; Snow, interview; Jean-Luc Renaud, 'Mac is dead, long live European HDTV', *C&SE* December 1990, pp.68–72.

8   Tim Westcott, 'Bouncing baby', *C&SE* March 1991, pp.22–3.

9   See, for example, Edward Herman and Robert McChesney, *The Global Media: The New Missionaries of Corporate Capitalism*, (London: Cassell, 1997); Willam M. Kunz, *Culture Conglomerates: Consolidation in the Motion Picture and Television Industries* (Lanham: Rowman & Littlefield, 2007). A few activist investors, who can take their case more forcefully to the conglomerates than academics can, claim that they are ill-adapted to the digital age. It is difficult to predict what the technological future holds but on the evidence of media groups' performance in transnational television, they seem to be in a position to meet the challenges of the digital world. They have the scope and resources to deal with the increased level of technological complexity and explore tomorrow's business models. Their brands and franchises are certainly spreading seamlessly through the new distribution channels opened up by digital media. If anything, the Internet gives conglomerates more opportunities to develop synergies across media platforms.

10   Teeman, interview; Boserup, interview.

11   The Walt Disney Company, *Annual Report 2007*, p.79; Viacom, *Annual Report 2007*, p.84.

12   Sumner Redstone, with Peter Knobler, *A Passion to Win* (New York: Simon & Schuster, 2001).

13   Company source; The Walt Disney Company, *Annual Report 2006*, pp.2–9, *Annual Report 2007*, p.53.

14   Company source.

15   News Corporation, *Annual Report 2005*, p.5; *Annual Report 2006*, pp.4–9; Bruce Dover, *Rupert's Adventures in China: How Murdoch Lost a Fortune and Found a Wife* (Edinburgh: Mainstream, 2008), p.46.

16   News Corporation, *Annual Report 2007*, p.5.

17   Company source.

18   Liberty Global, *Annual Report 2007*, p.2.

19   Chris Dziadul, 'Chellomedia snaps up doc channel', Broadband TV News, 8 September 2008, <http://www.broadbandtvnews.com/?p=7906>, consulted September 2008.

20   Pollock, interview.

21   The exception is Bertelsmann, which controls RTL, Europe's largest terrestrial broadcaster, but has stayed away from cross-border cable and satellite TV channels.

22   Anna Carugati, 'Sony Pictures Entertainment's Michael Lynton', WorldScreen.com, May 2007. <http://worldscreen.com/print.php?filename=lynton0507.htm>, consulted August 2007.

23   Hair, interview; see also 'SPTI's Ross Hair', Anna Carugati, WorldScreen.com, October 2006, <http://worldscreen.com/print.php?filename=hair1006.htm>, consulted August 2007.

Chapter 9

1   Company source; Cramer, interview.
2   Richard Sambrook, BBC World Service and Global News, BBC, interview, 12 June 2007.
3   Richard Porter, head of news, BBC World, interview, 5 July 2007.
4   Based on independently conducted research commissioned by BBC World, 2007. The rapid growth of BBC World and the World Service in Muslim countries in Asia, Africa and the Middle East in 2007 attests to the trust that Muslim audiences have placed in the corporation's international services. Sally Hillier, 'Good figures at global', *Ariel* 22 May 2007.
5   Interview, 26 April 2007.
6   Ibid.
7   See Martyn Bond (ed.), *Europe, Parliament and the Media* (London: The Federal Trust, 2003).
8   James Anderson (ed.), *Transnational Democracy* (London: Routledge, 2002).
9   See *European Journal of Communication*'s special issue on the European public sphere and the media, 22(4) (2007).
10 Stella Tooth, senior publicist, Sky News, interview, 25 February 2007.
11 Sky News was voted the Royal Television Society News Channel of the Year six times between 2001 and 2007.
12 John Ryley, head of Sky News, interview, 15 March 2007.
13 Ibid.
14 Ziegele, interview; Newel, interview.
15 Marina Dzhashi, TV presenter, Russia Today, 15 June 2007, presentation at the European Journalism Training Association's annual conference, Paris.
16 'Audition du Ministre des Affaires Etrangères, M. Dominique de Villepin, par la mission d'information commune de l'Assemblée Nationale sur la création d'une télévision française d'information à vocation internationale', Paris, 30 April 2003, <http://www.diplomatie.gouv.fr/actu/bulletin.asp?liste=20030516.html&submit.x =7&submit.y=6>, consulted March 2007.
17 Nobuhiro Habuto, deputy MD, JSTV, email communication, 11 March 2008.
18 A particular drawback of news, from a commercial perspective, is that networks do not dare run commercials when reporting the world's greatest disasters, at the time when everybody is watching them.
19 *Le Canard Enchaîné*, 10 January 2007, p.7.
20 Dover, *Rupert's Adventures in China*, p.46.
21 See Ben Dowell, 'Disillusioned of Doha', *MediaGuardian* 31 March 2008, pp.1–2.
22 Ibid., p.1.
23 Cox, interview; Chris Graves, MD, business development, Dow Jones, interview, 29 April 2002; Paul Barker and Julian Clover, 'Something in The City', *C&SE* February 1996, pp.26–30; Miranda Watson, 'Taking Stocks', *C&SE* February 1997, pp.22–9.
24 In Paul Barker, 'City Slicker', *C&SE* October 1994, p.34.
25 Barker and Clover, 'Something in the City', p.28.
26 Graves, interview; Jeremy Pink, VP of news and programming, CNBC Europe, interview, 9 May 2002; Mike Aarons, satellite manager, interview, 15 November 2004; Mawditt, interview.
27 Bronwyn Curtis, editor-in-chief, Bloomberg Television, interview, 25 April 2002;

Amanda Booker, programme and channel relations, Bloomberg Television, interview, 3 April 2008; Miranda Watson, 'Taking Stocks', *C&SE* February 1997, pp.26–9.

Chapter 10

1   A few channels that include a specific linguistic community in their target audience are also designed to reach viewers outside this constituency and thus are not migrants' stations in the strictest sense of the term: TV5Monde provides subtitles in several languages and Deutsche Welle-TV broadcasts in English every other hour.
2   Monica Pizzoli, area manager, Europe, RAI, interview, 17 March 2008.
3   Lopes de Araújo, head of international broadcasting, interview, 25 July 2006.
4   Tan Ishikawa, deputy MD, Japan Satellite TV (Europe), interview, 29 April 2002; Habuto, email communication.
5   Shaney Burney, head of programming, Zee Network Europe, interview, 11 March 2008.
6   Naomi Sakr, *Satellite Realms: Transnational Television, Globalization and the Middle East* (London: I.B.Tauris, 2001), pp.30–9.
7   Monroe Price, 'The market for loyalties: Electronic media and the global competition for allegiances', *Yale Law Journal* 104/3 (1994), pp.667–705.
8   Dr Wengung Shao, chief operating officer, Phoenix Chinese News & Entertainment, interview, 12 September 2002.
9   Kevin Robins and Asu Aksoy, 'From spaces of identity to mental spaces: Lessons from Turkish-Cypriot cultural experience in Britain', *Journal of Ethnic and Migration Studies* 27/4 (2001), pp.702–3.
10 See, for instance, Hugh Miles, *Al-Jazeera: How Arab TV News Challenged the World* (London: Abacus, 2005).
11 Andy Fry, 'Minority report', *C&SE* September 2004, p.44.
12 Luc-Emmanuel Bertolelli, head of European distribution, ADD, in Fry, 'Minority report', p.44.
13 Vandamme, interview; www.globecast.com.
14 Robins and Aksoy, 'Whoever Looks Always Finds'; see also Karim H. Karim (ed.), *The Media of Diaspora* (London: Routledge, 2003), Olga G. Bailey, Myria Georgiou and R. Harindranath (eds), *Transnational Lives and the Media* (Basingstoke: Palgrave Macmillan, 2007).
15 Alexandre Michelin, senior VP, programs and services, Canal Plus, interview, 11 June 2002.
16 Thiellet, interview.

Chapter 11

1   Screensport in the UK, TV Sport in France, SportNet in the Netherlands and SportKanal in Germany.
2   Guild, interview.
3   Keith Roe and Gust De Meyer, 'Music Television: MTV-Europe', in Jan Wieten, Graham Murdock and Peter Dahlgren (eds), *Television Across Europe* (London: Sage, 2000), p.153.

4   Allen J. Scott, *On Hollywood: The Place, The Industry* (Princeton: Princeton University Press, 2005).

5   Christopher A. Bartlett and Sumantra Ghoshal, *Managing Across Borders: The Transnational Solution – 2nd Edition* (Boston, MA: Harvard Business School Press, 1998), p.56.

6   Ibid., p.57.

7   Ibid., p.65.

8   Ibid., p.148; Geoffrey Jones, *Multinationals and Global Capitalism From the Nineteenth to the Twenty-first Century* (Oxford: Oxford University Press, 2005), p.167.

9   Insisting on the importance of sharing information, Finn Arnesen, the senior VP of original animation and acquisitions at TBS Europe, remarked that 'If anyone's got anything to hide, they probably shouldn't be working at a transnational company like us', interview.

10   Godfrey, interviews; Guild, interview.

11   The Hollywood majors currently are: Metro-Goldwyn-Mayer, Paramount Pictures (Viacom), Sony Pictures Entertainment (incorporating Columbia Pictures and TriStar Pictures), Twentieth Century Fox (News Corporation), Universal Studios (NBC Universal), Walt Disney and Warner Brothers (Time Warner).

12   Lawrence Safir, VP for European affairs, IFTA, interview, 12 May 2006.

13   Dirk Boehm, head of communication, NBC Universal Germany, interview, 2 March 2005; Francesca Ginocchi, head of marketing, NBC Universal Italy, interview, 1 April 2005.

14   Interview, 18 March 2005.

15   Benoit Runel, senior VP, programming & acquisitions, Jetix, interview, 7 December 2004.

16   Nicola Andrews, VP sales & marketing, BKN, interview, 30 March 2005.

17   Interview, 25 January 2007. On Zone Reality's programme acquisitions see also Timothy Havens, *Global Television Marketplace* (London: BFI, 2006), pp.139–46.

Chapter 12

1   Néstor García Canclini, *Hybrid Cultures: Strategies for Entering and Leaving Modernity* (Minneapolis: University of Minnesota Press, 1995), p.229.

2   John Tomlinson, *Globalization and Culture* (Cambridge: Polity Press, 1999), p.128.

3   See, for example, Martin Albrow, *The Global Age: State and Society Beyond Modernity* (Cambridge: Polity Press, 1996), p.115.

4   Anthony Giddens, *The Consequences of Modernity* (Cambridge: Polity Press, 1990), p.141.

5   Arjun Appadurai, 'Disjuncture and difference in the global cultural economy', in Mike Featherstone (ed.), *Global Culture: Nationalism, Globalization and Modernity* (London: Sage, 1990), pp.295–310.

6   Karl Marx and Friedrich Engels, *The Communist Manifesto* (Harmondsworth: Penguin, 1967), p.83.

7   There are companies that specialize in distributing TV channels in the hotel industry. When taking on a new business, Otrum Asa, a Norwegian concern, analyses the guest mix in terms of nationality and profile (leisure, business or conference) and installs a system which enables the hotel management to know

which stations are being watched. The channels package is then tailored according to these statistics and set independently from the local cable and satellite offering. A French establishment, for instance, would add Japanese or Russian channels according to demand. If a lot of Scandinavians book into the same hotel, the French version of Eurosport would be replaced by the Nordic one, and Bloomberg's French feed would give way to the pan-European one. Fredd Causevic, president & CEO, Otrum Asa, interview, 15 April 2005.

8   Cruise ships protect their satellite dishes against rough weather inside globes and fit them with satellite-tracking devices.

9   David Held, Anthony McGrew, David Goldblatt and Jonathan Perraton, *Global Transformations: Politics, Economics and Culture* (Cambridge: Polity Press, 1999), p.27.

10 See n.9, Chapter 8.

11 In the news segment evidence shows that viewers of global news channels are also avid consumers of local news. Proprietary research, BBC World, 2007.

12 Donna Vergier, director of international, Mute International, interview, 29 September 2006.

13 Evidence collected by telephone at various fashion labels in London.

14 See Held et al., *Global Transformations*, pp.189–235.

15 *Positioning of Business News Channels*, CNBC proprietary research, 2006.

16 'If you walk around Coutts and ask if anyone has a copy of the FT you'd struggle because it's old news', says a securities dealer at the bank. *Talking Heads – Senior Financial Professionals*, CNBC proprietary research, 2004.

17 *Financial Traders Focus Group*, CNBC proprietary research, November 2005.

18 Johannesburg-based CNBC Africa launched in June 2007.

19 *Worldwide Exchange Research – CNBC* Europe Viewertrack, CNBC proprietary research, March 2006.

20 Held et al., *Global Transformations*, pp.49–86.

21 <http://www.bbcworldinternationalist.com>, consulted March 2008.

22 Bob Woodward, *Bush at War* (New York: Simon and Schuster, 2002), p.87.

23 <http://stat.wto.org/StatisticalProgram/WSDBViewData.aspx?Language=E>, consulted February 2008.

Conclusion

1   Alan Rushton and Steve Walker, *International Logistics and Supply Chain Outsourcing* (London: Kogan Page, 2007), p.4.

2   Peter M. Tirschwell, 'Foreword', in Douglas Long, *International Logistics: Global Supply Chain Management* (Norwell, MA: Kluwer, 2003), p.xvi.

3   Rushton and Walker, *International Logistics*, p.19.

4   Thomas L. Friedman, *The World Is Flat: The Globalized World in the Twenty-First Century* (London: Penguin, 2006), pp.10–11.

5   Ulrich Beck, 'The Cosmopolitan Society and its Enemies', *Theory, Culture & Society* 19(1–2) (2002), p.17.

INDEX

Film titles, newspapers and TV programmes in italics; with a few exceptions, companies and organizations listed under full name unless in list of Abbreviations